POVERTY AND PROGRESS IN THE U.S. SOUTH SINCE 1920

Previously published in this series:

* These volumes have been produced for the European Association for American Studies (E.A.A.S.).

** This title is not a volume in the series, but closely connected with it.

*** This volume is produced with assistance of the Historical Documentation Center for Dutch Protestantism, Vrije Universiteit Amsterdam.

POVERTY AND PROGRESS IN
THE U.S. SOUTH SINCE 1920

edited by

Suzanne W. Jones and Mark Newman

VU UNIVERSITY PRESS
AMSTERDAM 2006

EUROPEAN CONTRIBUTIONS TO AMERICAN STUDIES

This series is published for the Netherlands American Studies Association (N.A.S.A.) and the European Association for American Studies (E.A.A.S.)

Founding editor:
Rob Kroes

General editor:
Ruud Janssens
Amerika Instituut
Spuistraat 134
1012 VB Amsterdam

VU University Press is an imprint of
VU Boekhandel/Uitgeverij bv
De Boelelaan 1105
1081 HV Amsterdam
The Netherlands
E-mail: info@vu-uitgeverij.nl

ISBN 90 8659 048 9 (ECAS no. 65)
NUR 686

Design cover: De Ontwerperij (Marcel Bakker), Amsterdam
Cover illustration: Carroll Cloar, *Where the Southern Cross the Yellow Dog*, casein tempera on masonite, 1964, Memphis Brooks Museum of Art, Memphis, Tennessee

In memory of Stuart Kidd

CONTENTS

PREFACE

Poverty, disease, and illiteracy had long bedeviled the U.S. South, even before the agricultural depression of the 1920s became subsumed within the Great Depression of the 1930s. The essays collected in this volume examine a variety of responses to economic depression and poverty; they recount specific battles for civil, educational, and labor rights; and they explore the challenges and alternatives to the corporate South in the post World War II agribusiness era. Scholars from both the U.S. and Europe assess how far the South has come both socially and economically in the last century, what forces (from the Sears Roebuck Catalog to the Civil Rights Movement) have been at work in its transformation, and whether the region's reincarnation as the Sunbelt has lifted the burdens of southern history. Their research reveals that globalization brought progressive ideas to the South early in the twentieth century but that unfair labor practices have lingered through century's end. Contributors assess labor strikes and demonstrations that have not always found a place in histories of the region and revisit and reassess key southern figures from Erskine Caldwell and James Agee to Albert Gore and Lyndon Johnson. They draw our attention to neglected writers whose representations of poverty deserve more critical attention and provide literary-critical readings of contemporary authors and filmmakers. The essays examine history and folklore, letters and memoirs, fiction and journalism, documentary film and public celebrations, in order to convey some of the political and cultural implications of poverty in southern places.

In the first of the collection's essays, Waldemar Zacharasiewicz considers the response of interwar southern fiction writers to rural poverty. The writers that he examines did more than simply depict the deprivation and inequities of life for the southern white rural poor; they recognized their humanity, worth, and diversity of thought, which encompassed not only aspirations for educational opportunity and economic advancement, but social and political conservatism.

By examining the responses of rural southerners to the Sears Roebuck catalog which had achieved a wide southern circulation by the 1920s, Marcel Arbeit uncovers another aspect of southern storytelling and aspiration for personal development beyond simply material acquisition. Arbeit draws on autobiography and fiction centered on the experiences of the lower and lower-middle classes to reveal a world in which the Sears catalog served as both a wish book and a dream book that enabled impoverished young readers to fantasize about lifestyles and opportunities far removed from the drudgery of their own lives. The catalog, Arbeit finds, also functioned for some adults as an aspirational guide.

In his writings for serious magazines and newspapers in the 1930s and early 1940s, novelist Erskine Caldwell focused on the underside of southern life by condemning lynching, portraying the depths of poverty, and describing the deleterious effects of the New Deal on tenants and sharecroppers. Edwin Arnold's essay explains that while Caldwell created some unsympathetic characters in his fiction, he regarded himself primarily as a social reformer and was unafraid to expose the South's ills at a time when others defended their region against its external critics. Despite Caldwell's later disavowals, he espoused support for Communism during the Depression.

James Agee also endorsed Communism during the 1930s, impressed by its avowed humanitarian concern. Robert Brinkmeyer's essay focuses on the narrative strategy that Agee employed in *Let Us Now Praise Famous Men* as he sought to enable his readers to understand the poverty, dignity, and individuality of southern tenant farmers, and to comprehend the rootedness of tenants' problems in a prevailing social and economic system, which Agee believed could be changed by an enlightened majority. Brinkmeyer argues that Agee sought to move beyond stereotypes of the poor and to inspire his readers to work for change by detailing the lives of the impoverished without sentimentality, preachiness, or condescension.

Although the fate of dispossessed agricultural workers understandably dominates studies of southern rural poverty in the 1930s, the decade also saw the great textile strike of 1934. However, the workforce of the Dutch-owned American Enka rayon plant in Hominy Valley, North Carolina, did not participate in the strike. In her study of the mill, Anneke Leenhouts argues that American Enka successfully cultivated good labor relations by drawing on its Dutch experience of benevolent paternalism. The company built good quality mill houses and fostered company spirit by offering its workers sports, social, and cultural activities.

American Enka, like other southern textile mills, excluded African Americans from its workforce in the 1930s. The black struggle against oppression features in several of the collection's essays. Elizabeth Hayes Turner explores the evolution of Juneteenth from an African American celebration of the announcement of emancipation in Texas in June 1865 to today's national and multiracial celebration of black history and culture. After the retreat of Juneteenth into the private sphere during the 1940s, the successes of the civil rights movement made possible its reemergence as a public celebration, one with which some politicians have been eager to associate themselves in the not always fulfilled hope of political gain.

While historians have quite correctly noted the endurance and fortitude of African Americans, Sharon Monteith's study of Sarah E. Wright's *This Child's Gonna Live* is a reminder that oppression, poverty, and the harsh struggle for survival brought casualties, but anger and resistance as well. Monteith places this 1969 novel about Depression-era poverty in the rural South in the context of the Moynihan Report of 1965, the War on Poverty's failure, and the emergence of the Black Power movement. In a detailed reading, she situates Sarah E. Wright's novel between Zora Neale Hurston and Richard Wright and Alice Walker and Ernest Gaines, and she emphasizes the abject poverty at the heart of the novel's concerns.

Although President Lyndon Johnson's Great Society did not live up to its initiator's grandiose promises, Johnson deserves recognition for his contribution to civil rights legislation and other measures that helped create a biracial democracy in the South and an increasingly, if selectively, prosperous region. Tony Badger's essay examines the relationship between Texan Johnson and Tennessean Albert Gore, two politicians whose Washington careers began in the late 1930s and ended with the 1960s. Sharing much in their backgrounds and in their aspirations for regional uplift, the two men became political allies who helped to advance the South's economy and overturn legal racial discrimination. Yet, as Badger explains, their relationship was soured by a bitter personal rivalry for political influence and the nation's highest office that was subsequently augmented by disagreement over American intervention in Vietnam.

Johnson and Gore occupied the uncomfortable position of being racial moderates at the height of southern massive resistance to public school desegregation in the 1950s. Paul Mertz's essay turns to the local level by exploring the role of Arlington's white moderates as Virginia adopted a range of massive resistance laws. Arlington schools were subject to a federal court desegregation order that, when implemented, would have triggered the closure of its public schools under new state legislation. White moderates formed the 3,400 strong Arlington Committee for Public Schools that argued for the continuation of public education, with or without desegregation, and that was prepared to challenge massive resistance through the courts. A suit became unnecessary when enforced school closures in some other Virginia locations brought successful court action that overturned massive resistance and restored public education. Massive resistance in the South began to retreat as many whites prioritized public education over segregation.

With de jure discrimination overturned, the African American struggle for equality focused increasingly on seeking to remedy the results of discrimination. Mark Newman's essay discusses the efforts of black plantation workers in Mississippi to raise their wages and limit working hours by forming the Mississippi Freedom Labor Union (MFLU) and taking strike action in 1965. The strike failed because it accelerated an ongoing pattern of worker displacement by machines and herbicides, but also because of divisions within the civil rights movement and among its supporters.

Kieran Quinlan's essay takes a different approach to southern progress by reexamining the religious beliefs of William Alexander Percy and his younger cousin Walker Percy. Quinlan argues for a reconsideration of the older Percy whose apparent homosexuality and loss of religious faith make him in some ways more modern that his orthodox Catholic and clearly heterosexual cousin. Quinlan contends that Will Percy's religious thoughts had much in common with those of Catholic Modernists, while the Catholic convert Walker Percy roundly rejected the Modernists.

The collection's remaining four essays consider challenges to agribusiness and alternatives to welfare in the second half of the twentieth century. Nahem Yousaf discusses Stephanie Black's 1990 documentary *H-2 Worker*. Black secretly filmed the peonage experienced by Jamaican sugar cane workers in Palm Beach County, Florida, in the 1980s, allowing the workers to speak for themselves, with a minimum of narrative overview, and cross-cutting between the system's defenders and its critics and victims. The workers were part of a global plantation economy easily disposed of and replaced when they went on strike, much like the MFLU strikers in 1965.

Sarah Robertson's essay also discusses an effort to give voice to the impoverished and marginalized, while offering a wider criticism of the impact of corporations. Robertson analyzes Janisse Ray's *Ecology of a Cracker Childhood* (1999) and finds within it tensions between Ray's eco-criticism and her wish to impart the humanity and individuality of her impoverished Georgia family. For Ray, her father was less a junk dealer than someone with the skills to recycle old products into new forms of his own inventive design. Just as Ray seeks to rescue her father from redneck stereotypes, so she also wishes to rescue the poor from simplistic representation and belittling. At the same time she advocates protecting the land from the ravages of agribusiness, an effort that she believes would also serve to unite southerners, regardless of race or class. Robertson provides insightful but measured criticism of Ray's depiction of her family past and vision for a southern future.

Suzanne Jones's essay examines Barbara Kingsolver's 2000 novel, *Prodigal Summer*, set in southern Appalachia. Like Ray, Kingsolver also develops an environmentalist theme and similarly demonstrates commitment to community and family. Jones explains that Kingsolver avoids romanticizing indigenous farmers, while recognizing their knowledge and worth. Whereas Ray suggests that environmental concern can unite southerners of diverse backgrounds, Kingsolver intimates that a combination of local and newcomer knowledge and cooperation can help solve southern Appalachia's ecological and economic difficulties. Jones concludes that the novel largely succeeds by revealing the interdependencies of humans and the natural world.

Dan Carter explores the attitude of southern conservatives toward the issue of poverty over the past half century. For much of southern history, notes Carter, white southerners—particularly upper class white southerners—have viewed poverty through the prism of race. With the brief rise of Lyndon Johnson's Great Society during the 1960s, that connection became a critical building block for the political transformation of the region. But a new generation of white southern Republicans built their political success upon a philosophy that linked blackness, increasing welfare costs, and higher taxes to a once dominant Democratic Party. Carter concludes that although overt racist rhetoric has declined over the last twenty years, white southern conservatives continue to oppose any significant governmental support for the poor, often justifying their position on the basis of fundamentalist religion as well as traditional laissez-faire economics.

Threaded throughout the collection is evidence that positive change has come from within the South as often as from without—and not just from the region's progressive activists, educators, novelists, and politicians but from those who aspired to educational opportunity and economic advancement. This collection suggests that the study of the U.S. South's history, literature, and culture will continue to reveal new insights and directions that will sustain the vibrancy of southern studies and that will bring concerns of economic class more to the center of American studies.

Suzanne W. Jones and Mark Newman

Part I Confronting Economic Depression

PROGRESS FROM POVERTY:
EDUCATION AND SELF-IMPROVEMENT IN RURAL REGIONS

Waldemar Zacharasiewicz

When Lyle Lanier expressed his scepticism concerning the advantages of the general advocacy of progress in "A Critique of the Philosophy of Progress," many members of the diverse group who supported the manifesto *I'll Take My Stand* were, no doubt, in agreement with his conservative creed.[1] They shared the view of the psychologist among the Agrarians that progress meant merely an increase in production and the ideology of industrialism, and his diagnosis of the "incompatibility of the doctrine of progress with the conditions necessary to the stability and integrity of family life in the South."[2] In particular, Andrew Lytle's "The Hind Tit" graphically juxtaposed the virtues of the yeoman farmer and the "bric-à-brac culture of progress."[3] The changes in the South due to the promotion of the "New South" had alerted spokesmen both of the patriarchal and the popular traditions among them to the questionable consequences of the intrusion of "Liberal Capitalism" in the South, and they feared that the identity of southern culture was increasingly under threat.

Yet, none of these conservative thinkers could ignore the fact that the economic depression of rural areas affected the daily lives of millions of tenant farmers and their families.[4] Even before the photo documentaries of the near destitution of both white and black sharecroppers were produced,[5] there was already in the 1920s a keen awareness of the extreme poverty in rural areas, which prompted a growing number of writers to present it graphically and argue passionately for reforms. What could not be overlooked was the interconnection between the paucity of educational opportunities and the inability of tenants and their families to raise themselves from the vicious circle of poverty and of total dependence on their landlords.

---

[1] See Richard J. Gray, *Writing the South: Ideas of an American Region* (Cambridge: Cambridge University Press, 1986), 151. See also Gray, *Southern Aberrations: Writers of the American South and the Problems of Regionalism* (Baton Rouge: Louisiana State University Press, 2000).

[2] *I'll Take My Stand: The South and the Agrarian Tradition, by Twelve Southerners* [1930], new introduction by Louis D. Rubin, Jr. (Baton Rouge: Louisiana State University Press, 1962), 147.

[3] *I'll Take My Stand*, 205. On the exponents of diverse positions in the manifesto see Gray, *Southern Aberrations*, 109-154. In the manifesto John Gould Fletcher provided a problematical defense of the institution of the academy and expressed his scepticism concerning public education (see *I'll Take My Stand*, 92-121).

[4] The number of tenants had significantly increased so that by the late 1930s more than 40 percent of the farmers in the South were tenants (see also note 11).

[5] On Erskine Caldwell and Margaret Bourke-White, *You Have Seen Their Faces* (New York: Modern Age Books, 1937) and James Agee and Walker Evans, *Let Us Now Praise Famous Men: Three Tenant Families* (Boston: Houghton Mifflin, 1941), see William Stott, *Documentary Expression and Thirties America* (New York: Oxford University Press, 1973).

Already at the turn of the century enlightened observers had identified this central problem in Dixie: the lack of financial means and poor regulations concerning education. Middle-class professionals from the South and northern philanthropists alike all pointed to the fact that in the states of the former Confederacy the provisions made for education were painfully inadequate as the resources from taxes in the impoverished South were too limited. Moreover the duplication of the racially segregated school system made a bad situation even worse.[6] Better school buildings, better teachers, the adoption of laws on compulsory school attendance to fight wide-spread illiteracy were urgently needed. (About 4 million people over the age of 10, both black and white were illiterate.)[7] Equally new legislation seemed essential to curb child labor, which was common in the mill towns, where children as young as 10 made up a significant proportion of the work force toiling 12 hours and more per day; of even greater importance was the monitoring of these regulations. The practice of employing young children in the cotton culture sub-regions, where there was the highest percentage of illiterates, deprived them of any chances of amelioration. The annual reports of the Commissioner of Education documented the striking deficiencies of the system and suggested improvements, which private and public initiatives such as the "Conference for Southern Education" (from 1898 onwards) and the "Southern Education Board" and later the "General Education Board" supported.[8]

Just before their reunion in the South after their Grand Tour, Charles W. Dabney, 1855-1945, the prominent educator and future college president of the University of Tennessee and of the University of Cincinnati, had conceded in a letter to his beloved, Mary Brent, that their home country lacked the picture galleries and the opera they had enjoyed in Berlin, Germany, but he had still taken consolation in the fact that they would return "to a land the most fertile and a people the most honest that God governs."[9] Yet, a quarter of a century later, Dabney was among the advocates of far-reaching reforms and gave full support to this cause. He collected documentation in the various states of Dixie and integrated statistical evidence on general education in his subsequent comprehensive publication *Universal Education in the South*, 1936.[10]

The introduction of agricultural experiment stations and the demonstration techniques prompted by the severe damage caused by the boll weevil in the cotton

---

[6] See C. Vann Woodward, *Origins of the New South: 1877 – 1913* (Baton Rouge: Louisiana State University Press, 1971), 398-412.

[7] See Woodward, 400, who gives this figure for 1900. See also under "Illiteracy" in Charles Reagan Wilson and William Ferris, eds., *Encyclopedia of Southern Culture* (Chapel Hill: University of North Carolina Press, 1989), 251-253.

[8] Charles William Dabney, *Universal Education in the South*. 2 vols. (Chapel Hill: The University of North Carolina Press, 1936), vol. 2, on the Conference for Education in the South (3-53) and on the Southern Education Board (54-73). See also Woodward, *Origins of the New South*, 398-406.

[9] Charles William Dabney, Letter of Nov. 30, 1879 (Ms. 1412, series 2.1, Dabney Papers, UNC Southern Historical Collection, Chapel Hill, NC).

[10] The two volumes offer a historical survey of the problems with education in the South in the nineteenth century (first volume), and of the efforts of reforming education in the twentieth century, and the situation in the different states.

belt, first in Texas, marked a significant step forward in the field of vocational-agricultural education. Still, in spite of increased public spending and improvements in agricultural practices, such as diversification and rotation of crops with the consequent growth in production, the situation remained grave. While some political initiatives such as the founding of Farmers' Unions and of cooperatives marked a step forward, the problems in the rural South continued though the increased need of cotton during the Great War led to some improvement in the second decade of the twentieth century. Yet with the ensuing slump in the market, the insolvency of many small farmers caused a further growth in the number of sharecroppers and a worsening of rural poverty.[11] With the economic problems came a decline in conditions in the field of education and in schools, with sharp salary cuts for the teachers and the reduction of school terms especially in rural areas affecting the lives of a generation of pupils, developments which federal programs such as the Work Progress Administration (WPA) tried to counteract.

Fiction writers in the various sub-regions of the South could not ignore these facts. Two novels by Dorothy Scarborough highlight the urgency of the need to offer better education in Texas. Her fiction combines a fairly straightforward and detailed demonstration of the inadequacy of the economic and social system with a sense of a potential bridge of the gap between the social classes of planters (and affluent farmers) and sharecroppers. A complementary situation occurs in a "reformist" novel by Harry Harrison Kroll set in the Mississippi Delta, which similarly deserves analysis. Another sub-region, the backwoods of north central Florida, provides the setting for two fictional texts by Marjorie Kinnan Rawlings, in which rural people are shown stoically enduring a harsh fate. The land with its richly varied fauna and lush vegetation offers periods of idyllic joy to Rawlings' protagonists, who feel the supreme joy of "working with the earth," of overseeing and even initiating growth, a pleasure which may be increased through training and education. The "pastoral" vision is, however, qualified by the rendition of being pitted against unpredictable, overwhelming natural forces and broadened by the inclusion of the perspective of outsiders who witness the backwardness of the poor whites but also become involved in their learning process in the seemingly edenic land. The struggle for survival and a good life on the land, and the tensions about the role of education in the fight against poverty are also apparent in some of Eudora Welty's texts, which exhibit the whole gamut of possible responses to the complex social reality of the Deep South in yet another sub-region, the hills of Mississippi.

Scarborough's novels encapsulate several of these concerns in the form of a hybrid between a romance and a social chronicle, and render in traditional narratives in omniscient narration, the problems of the deprivation of southern tenant farmers and their children. Her fiction is particularly illustrative of the disadvantages

---

[11] According to J. Wayne Flynt, *Dixie's Forgotten People: The South's Poor Whites* (Bloomington: Indiana University Press, 1979), 66-67, a 1937 report from President Franklin D. Roosevelt to Congress pointed out that 55 percent of all southern farms were operated by tenants in 1930, and 39 percent of the landless farmers were sharecroppers in 1937 ("Farm Tenancy: Message from the President of the United States Transmitting the Report of the Special Committee on Farm Tenancy," February 6, 1937, House Document No. 149, 75th Congress, 1937).

suffered by the children of "renters," a situation which evokes compassion and even anger in both narrators and readers. The withholding of basic rights, such as that of primary education, necessarily keeps them locked into a vicious circle. Their growth and their imagination are stunted by the heavy burden of agricultural work they are forced to undertake in the cotton fields and elsewhere.

The opening chapters of *Can't Get a Red Bird*[12] dramatize the burden of peonage and the desperate battle of young Johnny Carr to cling to some hope for the future. The economic system exploits him and turns eleven-year-old Johnny into a robot, forcing him to toil 12 hours a day. Necessity takes him out of school and burdens him with the tasks of an adult, in particular that of ploughing the fields in place of his invalid father. The severe disappointment of the boy is emphatically conveyed to the reader. He had looked forward to continuing going to school and to listening to an enthusiastic young teacher, but now is compelled to support his ageing and sickly parents after the departure of his siblings.

> Johnny's breast burned as if he had swallowed concentrated lye. His muscles tensed and stiffened, feeling already the struggle of toil beyond their strength. His shoulders sagged as if a cotton bale had fallen on them. The gaping furrows opened up to swallow all his school, his Professor, his dreams, his boyhood. He felt the wrenching agony of passing in an hour from childhood to maturity, his spirit racked and tortured. His dreams would all be narrowed to a cotton field. Instead of the glad adventurer, he was to be a prisoner between the furrows, chained to a plough, a slave to a cotton sack! He would rather die![13]

A similar constellation of characters and a comparable situation occur in Scarborough's first novel, *In the Land of Cotton*.[14] Here the reader's attention is first caught by a heavy sack of cotton being dragged between the rows of cotton plants by a twelve-year-old boy, Ben Wilson, barefoot, in old brown patched overalls, who like his father Jeff has to labor the whole day to make ends meet for his large family. Ben has, however, benevolent and powerful friends who are ready to help him to raise himself from the vicious circle of poverty. The friendship of the eight-year-old Serena Llewellyn, is important for Ben as she is the youngest daughter of the neighboring planter, the upright and very humane owner of "Green Acres."

A moving and somewhat romantic episode when young Ben passionately protects Rena against a furious prison guard hunting a pathetic, escaped black convict in their fields strengthens the link between the son of the poor sharecropper and the daughter of the plantation owner. This allows him as he grows older to aspire to marry the girl, who naturally has many suitors though she has always liked Ben. His seriousness is rewarded and his eager desire to study at Baylor is fulfilled,[15]

---

[12] Dorothy Scarborough, *Can't Get a Red Bird* (New York: Harper and Brothers, 1929).

[13] Ibid., 46-47.

[14] Scarborough, *In the Land of Cotton* (New York: Macmillan Company, 1923). Her novel opens in September 1908 and takes us through years of drought and floods, which destroy the harvest but also the homes of the tenants, and the war years until the late 1920s.

[15] See *In the Land of Cotton*: "'Lord knows I hope my boy won't ever have to be a renter!' cried Mrs. Wilson passionately, with a look at the tall lad who sat silent on the porch steps.

though there is no happy ending in his private life. Ben is killed trying to protect his benefactor's cotton gin against "nightriders" threatening destruction unless the cotton harvest is abandoned during a slump in the price of cotton. Ben's self-imposed task of reforming the system which has ruined so many tenants and of organizing the farmers' cooperatives is eventually undertaken by a young lawyer, Mr. Bob, who as a kind of substitute carries on Ben's project, a crusade for a reform of the system, with Rena's support, which includes the promotion of a better education for the children of the tenants.

A comparison of the two novels by Scarborough reveals a definite pattern in the plots of her fiction: to rise from the lower level of white society is only possible through proper education or at least a keen desire for education, and this virtue enables her deserving male protagonists to contemplate or even attain a personal goal—to win a well-educated female partner from a higher social class. *Can't Get a Red Bird* illustrates the point. For John Carr's future rise to the respected position of a free farmer who raises cattle and grows a cash crop, and his role as a spokesman of farmers it is crucially important that he wins Ellen/Honey, Rufe Barrett's stepdaughter, against wealthier rivals from both the city and the country.[16] He had felt trapped, and had also keenly sensed the lot of other small children toiling in the fields, similarly deprived of their childhood. Eventually John is able to initiate improvements in the rural region by collaborating with government agents in the fight against the boll weevil and promoting a diversification of crops.

The book includes another factor which prevents Johnny's complete resignation in all the years of hopeless drudgery before he wins Honey: There seems to be a strain in his make-up which raises him above the level of dumb acceptance of his fate, and that is evoked in the numerous references to his Celtic traits, as the narrator stresses the Irish heritage of the hero:[17]

> His spirits lifted with Celtic illogicality – his dreams enlarged and filled with light like the gay paper lanterns in the live oaks. . . ."Are you Honey?" he asked with a dash of his Irish audacity in his disarming smile (132-133).

> But what would they [these young fellows] know of romance. Was it because he was Irish that he felt different? Was it because his mother had told him of fairies, of leprechauns, and such, that he knew there was something to life besides ploughing and picking cotton? (149).

'That's partly what I came to ask you about,' said Jeff Wilson. 'Ben, here, wants to go to college. I want him to do something better'n I've been able to do,—but I can't help him any. He was bound I should ask you if you know of any way it might be managed.' . . . Mr. Llewellyn deliberated a moment, before he spoke. 'We'll see if you can get into Baylor University—even if you have to be conditioned. You can work your way and nobody will think any the less of you for it" (168-169).

[16] It is not insignificant that Honey is a college girl ready to teach school, a skill she uses after their marriage. When they have to struggle to make ends meet, John eagerly tries to make up for decades lost and learns geography and history under her tutelage.

[17] See also Honey's upbraiding of him, "You're very Irish, aren't you? And where have you been keeping yourself all this time, Irishman?" (178).

This character trait supports his struggle to save enough money to acquire a farm for his elderly parents and eventually also to secure for himself a place for his own family. This ethnic factor in his gene pool, which in reality could not be sufficient to account for his eventual success since a major part of the other settlers in the South, its white tenant farmers included, shared his Celtic background, represents an important myth. To the authorial narrator this collective autostereotype helps to account for John's ability to raise himself from extreme poverty and to escape the *cul-de-sac* of penury.

Johnny's mind is filled with the melodies and songs that are sung at social gatherings and tunes produced by a local fiddler accompanying their dances. Johnny's personal success is bound up with this redeeming feature in a life of drudgery, thus providing relief for the reader, thereby moving the otherwise naturalistic novel of rural life towards a pastoral romance.[18] Numerous folk songs and ditties, even musical scores, are integrated in the text. While this practice reflects the author's personal interests and her own published collections of music,[19] justice is done to an important aspect of popular culture in the South. Scarborough's readers are thus made aware of the folk songs, hymns, and country music as an integral part of white folk culture, which some of the documentaries exposing the deprivation in the 1930s omitted. In this manner she depicts significant aspects of rural life, which tend to humanize poor white folk, who, by way of contrast, are presented as mere grotesques driven by their inner urges in Erskine Caldwell's sensationalist books of fiction from those decades.[20] In spite of these positive traits it cannot be denied that Scarborough's novels have numerous shortcomings. Her books have been dismissed by critics such as S. J. Cook for their dubious political stance – the avoidance of attacks on the class system and the easy acceptance of traditional values and the somewhat mechanical sequence of set "conversations" on the evils of the single-crop system.[21] The condescending way in which African

---

[18] One of them encapsulates the challenge to Johnny referred to in the title of the book, *Can't Get a Red Bird*.

[19] See her publication first of *On the Trail of Negro Folk-Songs* (Cambridge: Harvard University Press, 1925), and then her *A Song Catcher in Southern Mountains. American Folk Songs of British Ancestry* (New York: Columbia University Press, 1937) collected in Appalachia.

[20] The reductive presentation of the life style of impoverished rednecks which omitted this part of their cherished heritage elicited critical comments by experts. See Richard H. King, *A Southern Renaissance: The Cultural Awakening of the American South, 1930-1955* (New York: Oxford University Press, 1980), on Agee's patronizing attitude towards the three families in the "Education" section and on his omission of their religious life as reflected in songs, etc. (220-225). This redeeming feature in the lives of poor folk in the mountains is mirrored in the musical talent of Strowbrod, Ruby's irresponsible father, in Charles Frazier's popular historical romance *Cold Mountain* (1997).

[21] See Sylvia J. Cook, *From Tobacco Road to Route 66: The Southern Poor White in Fiction* (Chapel Hill: University of North Carolina Press, 1976). Gray (*Southern Aberrations*, 164-172) regards her novels as curious and often potent hybrids, mixing social realism with the romantic and legendary, and sees the redeeming qualities in these manifestations of "reformist pastoral" (166).

Americans are presented as thoughtless children just living for the moment is another obvious flaw in her novels. Her choice of epithets for them, such as jocund and carefree,[22] illustrates Scarborough's reliance on racial stereotypes and reveals further limitations of her insights. But what her novels demonstrate is that an improvement of the social and economic situation in the cotton belt is dependent on the basic training of children and adults and on far-reaching reforms of the educational system and of the existing obsolete farming methods.

A similar situation occurs in Harry Harrison Kroll's 1931 novel *The Cabin in the Cotton*, which focuses on the dilemma in which a young son of a deceased tenant farmer, Dan Morgan, finds himself in the Delta.[23] His education has been sponsored by the plantation owner, Mr. Wilson Lord. The ambitious and competent Dan works as his store manager and accountant. He would like to go to college and is eager to rise up the social ladder, but he is torn between a sense of loyalty to the other sharecroppers, who cannot achieve solvency due to the excessive interest rates on all goods they have to borrow from their landlord before the harvest, and his own debt of gratitude to Mr. Lord. He is also torn between his love for Juny Stovall, a young woman of his own social class, and his love-making with Nordie Lord, his employer's sexually emancipated daughter. An even greater dilemma for Dan in the book is the pressure put on him by Mr. Lord's tenants who want him to profitably sell in Memphis the cotton they have stolen from their landlord's share. Mr. Lord, for his part, needs Dan as the chief witness in cases of arson and burglary, which should send the ringleaders to the penitentiary for many years. Dan finds a role model to solve these dilemmas in Robert Bruce, an attorney all too well aware of the injustices of the system. Dan has been upbraided and derided for his 'iddication' to which he looks back from the turmoil of the present conflict with nostalgia:

He reached the dark hulk of [the high-school] building, stopped, traced its pattern against the night. It was beautiful, and his remembrance of those years within its walls were days and seasons of joy. . . . Dan had loved his studies, had found an abiding pleasure in the process of learning (243).

But eventually he throws in his lot with the underdogs when evidence of his own father's abuse by the landlord is revealed, thus cancelling his own debt to the latter.[24]

---

[22] See the description of the "gay negroes" in the "cotton patch" (Foreword ix-x), and, for instance, 206-207.

[23] Harry Harrison Kroll, *The Cabin in the Cotton* (New York: Ray Long & Richard R. Smith Inc., 1931).

[24] "what the planter said about white trash sending their children to school was true. The new seventy-five thousand dollar school plant over on the Clarksdale and Memphis highway could testify to that. Though it was a plant built and paid for by Lord and other planters more or less avowedly for the purpose of educating planter children, it was nevertheless open to all who might take advantage of what it had to offer; . . . So long as there was cotton to be picked in the fields, wood to be hauled in the winter, chores to be done about the cabins, tenant young ones had poor attendance records at school. Lord swore about this failure to take advantage of opportunity, of course; but he, and all the planters, tacitly concurred to the arrangement. A tenant brat picking cotton was doing something worth doing. A tenant brat reciting a grammar lesson – well, that was something different" (241-242).

Scarborough and Kroll thus dramatize the plight of young male tenants and suggest that the only hope of individuals such as Ben Wilson, Johnny Carr, or Dan Morgan, lies in receiving a better education.

Marjorie Kinnan Rawlings in her fiction set in Florida engages the reader's interest especially in the lives of girls and young women from the lower social class. As Richard Gray has shown in his analysis of her first novel *South Moon Under*,[25] and as her novella *Jacob's Ladder* demonstrates, her fiction depicts most persuasively the "fight for survival" of the children of poor whites, who, however, evince a certain strength and resilience in both their struggle with nature, and with the inequities and the unfair regulations of the social system, which seemingly ignores the needs of the poor whites.

Never having had any schooling, very little food, and no home to speak of, Florry, for instance, the puny daughter of Old Jo Leddy in *Jacob's Ladder*, follows the young Mart from her father's cabin while the latter is in a drunken stupor, and over the following years enjoys a precarious existence with him.[26] They are severely tested in their various attempts to make a living by trapping skunks, possums, foxes, even mink and otters and hunting game, by fishing, from swampy "hammocks," in inland lakes and canals, and even in the Gulf, and by moonshining. They encounter the destructive forces of nature and suffer from the treachery or avarice of collaborators or employers, such as Eph, for whom Mart spends a month in prison, or a store owner who robs Mart of his only remaining possessions, his traps. They need all the courage and stoicism they can muster to cope with such ordeals. There are, however, some moments of hope and of (semi)-idyllic experiences in this rural region especially for Florry, when she feels close to and enjoys natural objects and pets. It is not insignificant that eventually it is Florry who takes the lead when Mart is at the end of his tether and takes them back to the piney woods of her childhood where Mart subdues Florry's father, Old Jo, while a hurricane again, as at the beginning, pounds the forest. There they will have a home after the failure of Mart's various attempts at making a living, including a short, unsuccessful period as a farmhand for a Yankee grower of oranges.

This element in the plot reminds the reader of Rawlings's own reminiscence reprinted in *The Marjorie Rawlings Reader*, where she describes her encounter with her tenant Tim, and with his tawny, puny, illiterate wife and their baby child.[27] It also mirrors her own farming experience, cultivating orange groves in northern Florida.[28] This phase in her life is also reflected in her later novel *Golden Apples*, published in 1935.[29] There one of the two tenant children, Luke Brindley, becomes

---

[25] See Gray, *Southern Aberrations*, 185-188.

[26] References are to the reprint of a revised version of the story in Marjorie Kinnan Rawlings, *The Marjorie Rawlings Reader*. Selected and edited by Julia Scribner Bigham (New York: Charles Scribner's Sons, 1956), 436-504.

[27] See "Antses in Tim's Breakfast," *The Marjorie Rawlings Reader*, 288-291.

[28] See Rawlings' reports on these efforts in her correspondence. See *Selected Letters of Marjorie Kinnan Rawlings*. Eds. Gordon E. Bigelow and Laura V. Monti (Gainesville: University Presses of Florida, 1983), and Rawlings, *Max and Marjorie: The Correspondence Between Maxwell Perkins and Marjorie Kinnan Rawlings*. Ed. Rodger L. Tarr (Gainesville: University of Florida Press, 1999).

[29] Rawlings, *Golden Apples* (New York: Scribner, 1935).

fascinated by the project of grafting the sour oranges that grow in the "hammock," the malaria-infested, thickly-wooded area, on the neglected virgin forest-like estate owned by a foreigner. As squatters, young Luke and his sister Allie have lived there for a number of years after being driven from the rented farm of their deceased parents three years after their deaths. Using traditional omniscient or authorial narration with an occasional narrowing and focusing on the perspective of her characters, Rawlings captures the idiom of the poor whites, transcribes it with all its irregularities and deviations from various standards of educated language, underlining the complete absence of schooling and any training suitable to ameliorate the lives of the "poor trash" characters.[30]

In the second half of the novel admittedly the focus shifts from the lower class to members of the upper class, especially to Richard Tordell, a young man banished—after wrongful accusations—from England to the almost forgotten estate of an uncle, the very spot where the poor whites are squatting. Tordell overcomes his despair and survives a close shave with death through malaria only through the exertions of Luke and the dedicated care of the shy Allie, with whom he becomes involved in an idyllic episode (chapter 17). The tragic end of this relationship between the upper-class foreigner and the illiterate girl is, however, balanced for the reader by Tordell's recognition of a goal and worthwhile task to which Luke's vision and newly learned skills contribute: cultivating a grove of oranges. This desire Luke developed under the tutelage of a strong woman, Camilla Van Dyne, who persists in her stoic dedication to her dream in spite of the destruction of many years of horticultural work through frost. Stoicism is a virtue generally lauded in Rawlings' fiction, in which men and women regularly appear as puny things at the mercy of the elements.[31]

The individual progress of both the poor white and the young "remittance man" exiled from England through shared painful experience and training in horticulture leads to Tordell's acceptance of the swampy Florida countryside as his home. In a sense the scion of a family from the Home Counties in the heart of England thus reverses the direction of the transatlantic movement, in which intellectuals from the South, such as J. C. Ransom and other Fugitives and members of the Agrarian circle, were involved in those decades. Though there is no reference to Florida alligators in Rawlings' text, it seems as if Richard Tordell eventually sheds the habits and clothes of his Hampshire past like the hero at the end of Ransom's witty poem "Crocodile." The macrocephalous Robert Crocodile abandoned the scenes of social life in Oxford in favor of his native habitat in the southern bayous.

> His dear friends cannot find him. The ladies write
> As usual but their lavender notes are returned
> By the U.S. Postmaster and secretively burned.
> He has mysteriously got out of sight.

---

[30] Luke, aged fourteen, and Allie, a child of ten, cannot continue going to school, though they are eager to do so: "But the corn and cane and potatoes and butchering had been absorbing, and the business of schooling seemed trivial, with a living to be made," (*Golden Apples*, 15).

[31] See Gray, *Southern Aberrations*, 184-188.

Crocodile hangs his pretty clothes on a limb
And lies with his fathers, and with his mothers too,
And his brothers and sisters as it seems right to do;
The family religion is good enough for him.

Full length he lies and goes as water goes,
He weeps for joy and welters in the flood,
Floating he lies extended nearly a rood,
And quite invisible but for the end of his nose.[32]

That Rawlings inserted in the penultimate chapter a description of Tordell's foxhunt with his affluent friends from Sawgrass Landing, which signals the extent of Tordell's acculturation to his new home, may, however, suggest a willingness on the part of the writer to hint at some Atlantic continuity among the better classes.[33] One may wonder whether this unexpected episode in the novel was included as an indirect response to Ransom's tributes to British rural culture in his lead essay to *I'll Take My Stand* and in his correspondence. Ransom regarded rural Britain as a model for the traditional lifestyle of the South, which he saw as currently in jeopardy through the activities of the advocates of the New South. John Peale Bishop, John Crowe Ransom, and Allen Tate had at various points expressed a sense of elective affinity between the South and Europe, and had variously described the South as "the last stronghold of European civilization in the western hemisphere."[34]

That there were various conservative forces not only among the upholders of the patrician tradition but also among the common people—the yeoman and tenant farmers—impeding progress is also reflected in southern fiction, both from the cotton belt and from other subregions of the South, for example the hills of

---

[32] See John Crowe Ransom, *Selected Poems* (New York: Alfred A. Knopf, 1974), 65-67. An earlier version of the text appeared in *The Fugitive* 4, Dec. 1925.

[33] See Ransom's statement in "Reconstructed but Unregenerate" in *I'll Take My Stand*, 3-6, "England was actually the model employed by the South. . . . I have in mind here the core of unaltered Europeanism, with its self-sufficient, backward-looking, intensely provincial communities. The human life of English provinces long ago came to terms with nature. . . . it is the character of a seasoned provincial life that it is realistic, or successfully adapted to its natural environment, and that as a consequence it is stable, or hereditable." See also Ransom's later Guggenheim year in the South of England prompted by his sympathy for the culture of rural Britain.

[34] Letter by Allen Tate to Donald Davidson, in *The Literary Correspondence of Donald Davidson and Allen Tate*. Eds. J. T. Fine and T. D. Young (Athens, Georgia: University of Georgia Press, 1974), 230. See the expression of similar sentiments by John Peale Bishop, who, in 1931 in a letter to Allen Tate, claimed that "with us Western civilization ends." *The Republic of Letters in America: The Correspondence of John Peale Bishop and Allen Tate*. Eds. T. D. Young and J. J. Hindle (Lexington: University Press of Kentucky, 1981), 47-48. See Mark G. Malvasi, *The Unregenerate South: The Agrarian Thought of John Crowe Ransom, Allen Tate, and Donald Davidson* (Baton Rouge: Louisiana State University Press, 1997), passim. See also my essay on "A Separate Identity Asserted: Agrarian Affinities With European Culture," in Klaus Rieser and Walter Hölbling, eds., *What is American? New Identities in U.S. Culture (Festschrift für Arno Heller)* (Wien: LIT-Verlag, 2004), 191-210.

Mississippi. Decades after the years of the Great Depression Eudora Welty lauded the inspirational efforts of teachers, such as Ms. Lorena Duling of Jackson, Mississippi,[35] and depicted the moderate success of her rural counterparts in instilling in the children of hill farmers the desire to learn and adopt new ways of action. The hill people in *Losing Battles*, which is set in the 1930s, in which the farmers had to wrestle with drought and poverty, showed their conservatism in their opposition to the new-fangled ideas advocated by various teacher figures. Not only had the rich land-owning class opposed any attempt "to educate a fellow above the station he moves in" (a patrician nineteenth century comment), but also representative poor whites themselves had offered such notorious (late nineteenth century) comments as "My grandfather—he raised me—figured going to school wouldn't help me pick cotton any better."[36]

Yet the painful experience of defeat of some dedicated educators, whom Welty paid tribute to in several interviews, is also balanced by the success apparent in the careers of former pupils who made it outside their immediate narrow circle: Judge Oscar Moody, one of the graduates from Julia Mortimer's Banner school, owes his success and social rise to the encouragement received from this teacher, who all her life had to struggle with reactionary attitudes among the rural folk. The desire of clans to control and neutralize new ideas brought into the family by young women trained as teachers, such as Gloria, Jack Renfro's wife, in Welty's novel *Losing Battles*, does not undermine the impetus towards reforms and modernization. But it seems at times as if strategies strengthening the cohesion of such clans and their rituals (as in their songs and narratives) told at family reunions were set against the struggle of individuals to change mindsets and abandon traditional modes of behavior in the interest of fighting and overcoming poverty.

Welty, who had come to know the whole range of social classes when she traveled through many counties of Mississippi taking photographs for the WPA, was ready to juxtapose the lives of impoverished hill farmers as potentially more fulfilled (bucolic and fruitful) to the potential emptiness and rootlessness of townspeople in "Death of a Traveling Salesman." Yet this text also reflected her awareness of the plight and extreme poverty of tenants, who are completely dependent on their landlords. In the revised version,[37] in which the perspective is narrowed to that of the

---

[35] See her tributes in Peggy W. Prenshaw, ed., *Conversations with Eudora Welty* (Jackson: University Press of Mississippi, 1984), and in Prenshaw, ed., *More Conversations with Eudora Welty* (Jackson: University Press of Mississippi, 1996). See the 1979 interview with Louis D. Rubin in *More Conversations*, 35-38, about the importance of teachers.

[36] See the entries on "Rural and Agricultural Education" and "Illiteracy" in Wilson and Ferris's *Encyclopedia of Southern Culture*, 264 and 252.

[37] In the course of her revision of her first published story Welty, who in 1979 offered instructive comments on this revision, enhanced the effect by renaming the husband of the woman "'in a formless garment' "Sonny", thus providing an additional reason for the fact that the traveling salesman, Mr. Bowman, mistakes him for the son of the pregnant woman. Their extreme poverty does not, however, undermine their pride. In the revised version we thus more intimately share Bowman's amazement at his discovery of his mistake and his becoming painfully aware of his exclusion from this poor but idyllic existence. For a comparison of the two versions published in 1936 and in 1941 respectively, see Lawrence J. Dessner, "Vision and Revision in Eudora Welty's 'Death of a Traveling Salesman'," *Studies in American*

feverish salesman Bowman, Welty dramatizes his surprise at the fact that Sonny has to "borry" even their fire. These sharecroppers do not have matches, nor do they even miss such conveniences. In the revised story Sonny also wears a uniform coat from the nineteenth century, which is indicative of their indigence, but also of the proud sense of tradition among these tenant farmers in the hills of Mississippi: "He wore muddy blue pants and an old military coat stained and patched. World War? Bowman wondered. Great God, it was a Confederate coat."[38]

Poverty is also dramatically depicted in Welty's story "The Whistle," which through the hyperbolic account of the extremes to which tenants are driven by the need to protect their crop reveals the destitution of weary, poor tomato farmers: Jason and Sara Morton are prematurely old.[39] At a whistled signal from their landlord they have to protect their plants against the freezing cold with their own quilts and even clothes. This leaves them shivering in the night, so that they are finally forced to burn their furniture. Sara's memories and dreams about the celebration of a rich harvest and visions of fertile land and warmth[40] contrasted with the intense discomfort and nightmarish reality are vividly mediated to the readers through the use of free indirect discourse reflecting Sara's despair and involving the readers in imaginatively sharing the lot of the rural couple.[41]

In contrast to Scarborough's or Kroll's fiction and the bulk of Rawlings' texts, where dialogues predominate, Welty's stories employ modernist techniques, and certainly in the revision of her first published story "Death of a Travelling Salesman" use a "figural perspective," to use Franz Stanzel's narratological term.[42] It conveys the perspective of the outsider, the traveling salesman, who gradually discovers the truth, which originally eluded him, about the fruitfulness of the pastoral couple (they are expecting a baby) and enjoy happiness in spite of their

---

Fiction 15.2 (1987): 146-159, and Waldemar Zacharasiewicz, "Eudora Welty's 'Death of a Traveling Salesman' und Flannery O'Connor's 'The Displaced Person'. Ein Vergleich," in Klaus Lubbers, ed., *Die englische und amerikanische Kurzgeschichte* (Darmstadt: Wissenschaftliche Buchgesellschaft, 1990), 349-368.

[38] Eudora Welty, *The Collected Stories of Eudora Welty* (New York: Harcourt, 1980), 124.

[39] "Every night they lay trembling with cold, but no more communicative in their misery than a pair of window shutters beaten by a storm. Sometimes many days, weeks went by without words. They were not really old—they were only fifty; still, ..." ("The Whistle", 57-58).

[40] See "she began to imagine and remember the town of Dexter in the shipping season. . . . Jason and Sara themselves are standing there, standing under the burning sun near the first shed, giving over their own load, watching their own tomatoes shoved into the process, swallowed away – sorted, wrapped, loaded, dispatched in a freight car" ("The Whistle," 58-59).

[41] See "She was so tired of the cold! That was all it could do any more – make her tired. Year after year, she felt sure that she would die before the cold was over. Now, according to the Almanac, it was spring. . . . But year after year it was always the same. The plants would be set out in their frames, transplanted always too soon, and there was a freeze. . . . When was the last time they had grown tall and full, that the cold had held off and there was a crop?" ("The Whistle", 58).

[42] See Franz-Karl Stanzel's concept in *A Theory of Narrative* (Cambridge: Cambridge University Press, 1984).

extreme poverty. Welty's adoption of a quasi-dramatic technique in *Losing Battles*, a tour de force, presents a special case, of course.

Welty, alerted to the deficiencies of the social system in her WPA-tour through the counties of Mississippi, but not an advocate of "crusading,"[43] also helps us to recognize the effect of advances in narrative technique: the advantages of allowing the reader to involve himself or herself in the feelings and emotions of the characters more intimately, the full potential of narrative strategies associated with modernism. The use of narrated monologue and of quoted monologue, in addition to consonant psycho-narration, open to the reader the worlds of the characters, also from the lower classes of society, and move the focus of sympathy closer to them.[44] As Richard Gray has shown,[45] such an effect is already anticipated in Elizabeth Madox Roberts' remarkable achievement in *The Time of Man* (1926),[46] in which the reader is invited to step into the skin of a poor white woman, Ellen Chesser. The reader witnesses what happens from the beginning of the book when the wagon Ellen and her parents have traveled on has broken down somewhere in the tobacco belt, through her painful existence as a tenant farmer in which her opportunities are severely limited. Ellen, however, is not easily subdued, and the reader cannot help admiring her resilience, strength, vitality, and stubbornness, as one can share with her her dreams and her yearning for beauty and joy.

For all the various flaws in the narratives of Dorothy Scarborough, Harry Harrison Kroll and Marjorie Kinnan Rawlings, who somewhat mechanically demonstrate the ills of the social system and surrender to the appeal of stereotypes, theirs is by no means an insignificant contribution. They have opened their readers' eyes to the often unrealized human potential of semi-literate poor whites. As Faulkner's contemporaries, they made their reading public aware of the yearning of these poor folk for education and self-improvement in the face of a total lack of any opportunities, of their striving for beauty and "the good life" close to the earth, and of their sense of dignity.

---

[43] See her essay "Must a Novelist Crusade?" (1965), in Eudora Welty, *Stories, Essays, & Memoir* (New York: Library of America, 1998), 803-814.

[44] These terms were introduced by Dorrit Cohn, whose concept of narrated monologue corresponds largely to the more traditional term of free indirect discourse. See *Transparent Minds: Narrative Modes for Presenting Consciousness in Fiction* (Princeton: Princeton University Press, 1978).

[45] See *Southern Aberrations*, 178-181.

[46] Elizabeth Madox Roberts, *The Time of Man*. Rpt. with wood engravings by Clare Leighton (New York: Viking Press, 1945).

SEARS, ROEBUCK CATALOG GAMES:
THE PORTABLE SHOP WINDOW AND SOUTHERN LITERATURE

Marcel Arbeit

Every community with a strong storytelling tradition needs individuals endowed with imagination. In the farming communities of the South, the prospective storytellers were aided by a textbook of imagination distributed on a regular basis. It was a textbook almost every family received, rich and poor, but while the former usually got rid of it, the latter spent many an hour over it, full of emotions ranging from joy through envy to anger. This textbook was the Sears, Roebuck catalog.

Since 1893, when this catalog appeared for the first time as a 64-page booklet offering, cash on delivery, miscellaneous products from clothing, silverware, and weapons to sewing machines, farm wagons, and household equipment, it became a part of the life of several generations of Americans. Richard W. Sears, who became a railway station agent at North Redwood at the age of nineteen, started his own business in coal and wood, and built up his successful career as a merchant by selling watches, joined forces with Alvah Curtis Roebuck (for the first time in 1888) and after some peripeteia became a president of A. C. Roebuck, Inc., which changed its name to Sears, Roebuck & Company in 1893. The name was kept even after Roebuck withdrew from the firm because of health problems in 1895.[1]

From December 1893, the seat of the company was in Chicago and although the very first branch opened in Dallas, Texas (in 1906), the South hosted only a few of the factories manufacturing the products advertised in the catalog. From the 1906 catalog list of suppliers providing Sears, Roebuck with various lines of goods, only one was located in the South—a manufacturer producing organs in Louisville, Kentucky. On the other hand, among the best customers were southern farmers who gradually learned to buy most of their farming equipment this way, as it saved them a substantial amount of money—comparable products were much more expensive at local retail stores which obtained the goods from the producers only in small quantities and therefore were not able to provide their customers with massive discounts.

Frederick Asher, the son of Sears' one-time general manager Louis Asher, whose family came from Vicksburg, Mississippi, points out that Sears "was one of the first industrialists to realize the possibilities of the South where the cost of living was lower and where great reservoirs of cheap labor cut the costs of manufacturing."[2] Sears, Roebuck had a share in many factories, including those in the South. Although the firms stayed under the management of their previous owners, they were controlled by the selling company which in turn pledged to buy all they produced. That was a system profitable to both parties. When this business strategy was developed, the first advertisement ran in April 1902 in a dozen of the leading southern newspapers, offering "to buy the entire output or part of the output

---

[1] See Frederick Asher, *Richard Warren Sears: Icon of Inspiration—Fable and Fact About the Founder and Spiritual Genius of Sears, Roebuck* (New York: Vantage Press, 1997), 2-5.
[2] Ibid., 9.

of southern factories manufacturing furniture, woodenware, agricultural implements, machinery, blacksmiths' tools, vehicles, wagons, team harness, stoves and other heavy goods."[3]

These pragmatic reasons may have contributed to the fact that in the South, especially in poor rural areas, the influence of the company was much more evident than in the North, even though sales were approximately equal. In 1928 and 1929 two new mail-order plants were established in the South: in Atlanta and in Memphis. In 1937, even the cover of the catalog advertised the higher living standard of America which "doesn't need any rear-view mirror—our eyes are on the road ahead"[4] through a photograph of a happy and beautiful young couple who are pictured as though they are to walk together hand in hand for the rest of their lives.

While standard of living is definitely a major cultural element, the company did not influence only the economic situation of southerners, but its catalog, much more than the catalogs of other mail-order companies including those of their eternal rival, Montgomery Ward's, had a substantial impact on the southern cultural life in the narrower sense of the word as well. The evidence can be found in the works of leading southern writers of fiction and non-fiction. Without any claim to completeness, I chose examples from autobiographies, novels, short stories, poems, and essays by William A. Owens, Tim McLaurin, Olive Ann Burns, Fred Chappell, Randall Jarrell, Harry Crews, Lewis Nordan, and Elizabeth Spencer.

Although these authors come from different backgrounds, their use of the Sears, Roebuck catalog as a motif or a theme is connected with their illustration of class differences in the South. Most of the writers have a low or lower-middle class origin and rely on their childhood or adolescent memories, and even those whose roots are different created lower-class characters for whom the catalog meant progress, "good news" about the modern world. Only rarely is the catalog seen as a symbol of the collective hysteria for mass-marketed products or a marker of consumer society in the South, the role that fiction writers and, after them, literary critics in the late 1970s thrust upon large retail stores, such as K Mart, whose name was used to designate a specific type of realism.[5]

When southern authors deal with progress, it implies the progress of personal development as well. That is why the Sears, Roebuck catalog is frequently seen as an important element in southern literature of the growing-up process. The catalog urges its users to make choices, to decide—a privilege reserved for adults and sometimes a very difficult task considering the fact that the number of items offered, for instance, in 1942, amounted to an unbelievable 92,300.[6] The capacity to consider the offer and distinguish between what can be purchased or asked for, and what

---

[3] For a photocopy of the advertisement see Asher, *Richard Warren Sears*, 9.

[4] Quoted in Boris Emmet, and John E. Jeuck, *Catalogues and Counters: A History of Sears, Roebuck and Company* (Chicago: University of Chicago Press, 1950), 456.

[5] The term K Mart Fiction is sometimes used as a derogatory label, suggesting banality and consumerism, but it developed into a full-fledged stream of realism, close to minimalism, portraying the life of the lower class and informed by popular culture. See, for example, George Hovis, "K Mart Fiction," in *The Companion to Southern Literature: Themes, Genres, Places, People, Movements, and Motifs*, eds. Joseph M. Flora, and Lucinda H. MacKethan (Baton Rouge: Louisiana State University Press, 2002), 394-396.

[6] Emmet, and Jeuck, *Catalogues and Counters*, 473.

should be transferred, at least temporarily, into the realm of daydreams, denotes a sign of maturation.

But the catalog is not just a list of products and prices, as most of the items are introduced through illustrations in which models wear the garment, use the weapons, or handle the tools and the machinery. The quality of the illustrations gradually improved. While the early catalogs used exclusively woodcuts, in 1900 one fourth of the illustrations were halftones and zinc etchings made from pen-and-ink drawings. Halftones were utilized first for clothing and shoes, but their use increased rapidly in the 1920s, so that by 1929 even furniture and guns were shown in halftones.[7] In the early 1940s, the color pages of the Sears, Roebuck catalog were no longer marred with text but contained illustrations only, while "copy," descriptions of the products and ordering information, was set in black type on the facing pages.[8]

As in every successful advertisement, the illustrations are supposed to arrest attention and start an interactive game with the readers, who ask the cardinal question: Are the models like us? If not, what makes them different? If we buy the product, will we become more like them? And, last but not least, do we really want to become them? To find out, it is necessary to create a story featuring the models as protagonists. In this way, the catalog served as a sourcebook for creative thinking, able to teach people who never had storytelling ambitions to spin stories and find the urge in themselves to pass them on. Under this consideration, it seems to be a paradox that the founder of Sears, Roebuck, Richard Warren Sears, originally hated the idea of advertising through nice pictures and was heavily criticized for the lack of "picture, beauty, art and touching lines" in his advertisements. In his opinion, it was the quality of the product and its low price that sold it, no matter where the advertisement was placed and what it looked like: "[Y]ou are likely to get some reputation as an advertiser, whether you insert your ad, large or small, artistic or plain, in the Howling Wolf of Frozen Dog, Idaho, or the Desert Muse of Solitude, Texas."[9]

Fortunately, his co-workers and followers soon changed this policy. The mail-order catalog became a Wish Book for both children and adults who developed material desires otherwise unconsidered, a book that due to a clever strategy made people want even what they would never have craved under different circumstances. The use of illustration was liable to strict rules: distracting elements were removed to focus attention solely on the product, the items of merchandise were shown in use whenever possible, and trick layouts were forbidden. As Boris Emmet and John E. Jeuck write in their history of Sears, Roebuck & Company: "Illustrations had to flash their meanings instantly and compellingly. . . . Catalogue copy had to be able to arrest the attention of every reader . . . who might be interested in any given item, to stop the reader as he thumbed through the book, and to rivet his attention on that item."[10]

---

[7] Ibid., 258-259.

[8] Ibid., 476.

[9] Asher, *Richard Warren Sears*, 8. Titles of imaginary newspapers not italicized in the original text.

[10] Emmet, and Jeuck, *Catalogues and Counters*, 253.

As a side effect, however, recipients of the catalog realized their poverty much more acutely, which influenced their behavior and pushed forward both their dreams and depressions. Not even approaching the "compulsory" success postulated in the concept of the American Dream, they resorted to the catalog as to a Dream Book that enabled them to shake off their lives, to pass the limitations of their own existences onto the unknown models, and, in turn, to receive the models' undisclosed, but supposedly much better destinies.

William A. Owens in his autobiography *This Stubborn Soil* (1966) describes the family ritual of a country Texas family trying on the clothes delivered from Sears, Roebuck on the eve of Thanksgiving Day. Later he admits: "All my life I had wished on their catalogues." Nevertheless, when at the age of fifteen he starts working for Sears, Roebuck's Dallas branch as an order picker in the oilcloth (and later in the ladies' underwear) department, he faces the derision of his city colleagues who find out that his own clothes were purchased from the company; one of the boys even tells him: "I wouldn't buy anything made to sell to country folks."[11]

Another writer who deals with the Sears, Roebuck catalog as a Wish Book is Tim McLaurin. Having grown up in the small farming community of Beard, North Carolina, McLaurin recollects, in his autobiography *Keeper of the Moon* (1991), the era when each year in late November the catalogs began pouring in; not only Sears', but also K Mart's and J. C. Penney's. Those most easily seduced by the plentitude of products, especially toys, were children; there were five of them in the McLaurin family: "We'd rip through the pages, eyes bugging at the collection of trucks, bikes, games, cap pistols, and other cheap toys. Within the first week we wanted a hundred different things but then would have to narrow the list to fit the number of gifts my mother decided we could budget. . . . Each selection was made with careful thought and agony, hours spent poring over the slick pages."[12] After the children made their choices, they went through the catalogs again, worried that they "had not chosen the right toys." The possibilities of the choice were, for a child's soul, overwhelming and young Tim's preferences reflected his inclination to science—"plastic dinosaurs, a chemistry set, a battleship, and a launchable rocket."[13] The catalog helped to trasform this child from a poor farming family into a champion of scientific progress, the "keeper of the moon" who, several years later, became famous among local schoolchildren as the owner of a powerful telescope through which he looked at stars, a telescope not purchased through Sears, Roebuck but bought by an uncle in Europe. Even some of Tim's other gifts were not bought by mail, but in the local Woolworths or K Mart. McLaurin's personal memories correspond with the Sears, Roebuck annual reports which showed that in the South, especially from the Atlanta mail-order center, "toys sold poorly, even at Christmas."[14]

---

[11] William A. Owens, *This Stubborn Soil: An Autobiographical Chronicle of Frontier Life in Twentieth Century Texas—and the Story of a Boy in Search of Something Beyond a One-Room School* (New York: Charles Scribner's Sons, 1966), 241, 248.

[12] Tim McLaurin, *Keeper of the Moon: A Southern Boyhood* (1991; Asheboro, NC: Down Home Press, 1998), 58-59.

[13] Ibid., 62, 65.

[14] Emmet, and Jeuck, *Catalogues and Counters*, 471.

McLaurin was even more specific about the use of the Sears, Roebuck catalog in his short essay for *The Companion to Southern Literature* (2002). In this essay, he writes about country children looking forward to the arrival of the Christmas edition of the catalog. From the beginning of November they organized "watches," regularly waiting at the curve of the local road for the mailman to appear, while the rest impatiently gathered around the mailbox. The "scout" then had the privilege of getting hold of the catalog first, although just for a few seconds.

Without diminishing the role of the catalog as the Wish Book, he mentioned at the same time the common practice among farming families of placing a reading copy of the catalog in the outhouse. Harry Crews, who wrote about putting the catalog to this particular use even earlier, emphasized that in spite of all the jokes concerning its replacement for regular toilet paper, it was not utilized that way as "dried corncobs . . . served the purpose . . . with all possible efficiency and comfort."[15] However, McLaurin did consider the catalog useful for activities beyond reading and ordering merchandise: "It was by far the thickest book in our house. It made a good doorstep or could be used to weigh down the lid on a box of baby opossums my dad brought home from a hunting trip."[16]

While in 1961, at the age of eight, Tim McLaurin found the selection of toys more than sufficient, fifty-five years earlier, in 1906, fourteen-year-old Will Tweedy from the little town of Cold Sassy, Georgia, the protagonist of Olive Ann Burns's novel *Cold Sassy Tree* (1984) would like to add an item to the rich assortment from Sears, Roebuck, namely inflatable female breasts. To amuse friends, Will invents the story in which Aunt Lona bought rubber busts through this company and on the day of her wedding to Uncle Camp she asked Will to blow them up with a bicycle pump. Before the wedding ceremony, Will punctures the left breast with a needle, and it goes "*pssssssssssssst all through the weddin'*."[17]

Such a story, implying that there is nothing that cannot be bought from the company, could serve as a good advertisement for Sears, Roebuck. Will's imagination owes more to the local storytelling tradition than to leafing through the catalog, but in spite of that Sears, Roebuck signifies for him a bearer of progress even in the most private spheres of life. This is documented by historians as well: there were cases when customers asked Sears, Roebuck to select a wife for them or help them to name their child.[18] The authors of *Mr. Sears' Catalog*, a 1989 TV documentary, chose as an example the letter of a country teacher who wished to order the man "who appears on page 491 of your latest edition. If at the present time this particular man is not in stock, I leave the responsibility of choosing my future mate up to you."[19]

The connection of the catalog with the erotic does not necessarily involve a purchase. In Fred Chappell's "The Good Time," an episode from the novel, or rather

---

[15] Harry Crews, *A Childhood: The Biography of a Place* (New York, Harper & Row 1978), 54.

[16] Tim McLaurin, "The Sears Catalog," in *Companion to Southern Literature*, 761.

[17] Olive Ann Burns, *Cold Sassy Tree* (1984; New York: Dell, 1986), 182.

[18] See Emmet, and Jeuck, *Catalogues and Counters*, 254.

[19] *Mr. Sears' Catalog*, VHS, directed by Edward Gray, and Ken Levis (Boston: Corporation for Public Broadcasting, 1989). WGBH Boston premiered the film on November 14, 1989.

sequence of interconnected short stories, *I Am One of You Forever* (1978), ten-year-old Jess Kirkman tells the story of life on the family farm in North Carolina in the pre-war year 1940. That year, the eighteen-year-old Johnson Gibbs came from the town orphanage as a hired farm hand and gradually became a close friend of the Kirkmans, living with them on the farm. The farm work was tiresome and Johnson expressed the extent of his fatigue in the following way: "I have stopped dreaming about the underwear girls in the Sears catalog. . . . When I lay down to sleep, it's all pork chops."[20] Young Tim McLaurin was also aware of the allure of the Women's Clothing section of the catalog when he admitted that he was not interested in clothes "except the pictures of women in their underpants."[21] This section also insinuated its way into poetry. Randall Jarrell, in his poem "Sears Roebuck," created the poetic image of a southerner[22] who was supplied by the mail-order company with his garments, his house, and even his Bible, but now faces the temptation of the semi-nude models:

> But thumbing these leaves, I light upon a plasterer's hawk,
> A Wilderness of Women's Intimate Apparel,
> A girl slides to me in ribbed flannel panties. . . .
> Ah, gauds of earth! My heart catches in my throat:
> Beware! the rockets poised above the world!
> How even my oilskins, in the evil hour,
> Blaze up around me! Ah, the fire, the fire![23]

The Sears, Roebuck management was obviously aware of this sort of "inspiration" drawn from their mail-order catalogs. As early as in 1905, the era of halftones, the local distributors of the catalog were advised: "Do not give a catalogue to children; boys and girls under 18 years of age."[24] Although the primary reason for this rule was a business one, as it could not have been expected that children would place orders, it was not the whole truth; the children who leafed through the catalog often persuaded their parents to buy a product. The self-imposed censorship forbade illustrations "of women smoking and drinking . . . 'too full' brassières, 'sexy' legs in stocking advertisements, etc."[25] Occasionally there were crusades against offering books that dealt with sex, which, however, were never consistent; at the peak of the campaign in 1948, the company chose as its People's Book Club selection Erskine Caldwell's early novels.

Even though it was undesirable for the editors of the catalog, there was obviously enough ground to take the catalog one step further, to extend its role from a Wish Book to a Dream Book. As a Wish Book the catalog attracted the attention of

---

[20] Fred Chappell, *I Am One of You Forever* (Baton Rouge: Louisiana University Press, 1978), 14.

[21] Tim McLaurin, "The Sears Catalog," 761.

[22] In his own introduction to *Selected Poems*, he labeled such southerners as "heroes." See Randall Jarrell, *Selected Poems* (New York: Atheneum, 1964), xii.

[23] Ibid., 99.

[24] Emmet, and Jeuck, *Catalogues and Counters*, 94.

[25] Ibid., 479.

consumers to the quality, utility, and low price of advertised products, but as a Dream Book it addressed its audience mainly through aesthetic means. The tableaux with models and their prospective stories became of primary importance, while the merchandise turned into mere props. That is why people dreaming over the catalog made mediocre customers and the company tried its best to turn them back to wishing.

Both functions of the catalog are described in Harry Crews's autobiography *A Childhood: The Biography of a Place* (1978). There young Harry and an African American friend, Willalee Bookatee, played on the floor with the catalog, which they acquired from Willalee's younger sister by swapping a couple of fat worms: "Then we opened the catalogue at random as we always did, to see what magic was waiting for us there."[26] Crews points out that country people, especially in his native Georgia, were hardly able to afford anything from it, but could at least dream over it. The poorer the people were, the more it stirred their imagination and creativity. Crews acknowledges the formative effect of the catalog on his own future as a writer and praises the company for the regular portion of dreams delivered free of charge directly in people's mailboxes: "The federal government ought to strike a medal for the Sears, Roebuck company for sending all those catalogues to farming families, for bringing all that color and all that mystery and all that beauty into the lives of country people."[27]

Nevertheless, young Harry's approach to the catalog was a mixture of love and hate. First, the models in the catalog did not even vaguely resemble people he knew; while real countrymen had wounds of various kinds and very often even a limb missing, the people in the photographs were complete, unhurt, and beautiful. He came to the conclusion that they must at least have some spiritual trouble, and as they are all pretty, they must know each other, which automatically leads to violence and hostile feelings—the golden rule of human relationships in the South of the poor: "Young as I was . . . , I had known for a long time that it was all a lie. I knew that under those fancy clothes there had to be scars, there had to be swellings and boils of one kind or another because there was no other way to live in the world."[28]

In the next stage the models in the catalog turn into individuals in the boys' eyes. The boys make up stories about them, and Harry sincerely admits that his African American friend is better at it. In their stories the models have love problems, trouble with parents or children, or even a brush with the law. The Sears, Roebuck catalog becomes a textbook in psychology, civics, and the arts.[29] Like Chappell's Johnson Gibbs, the boys also open the catalog on the page with women in their underwear, but instead of their bodies, they admire their spotless garments. They imagine that one of models is the daughter of a man from another section of the catalog, the one "dressed in a red hunting jacket and wading boots, with a rack of

---

[26] Crews, *Childhood*, 53.

[27] Ibid., 54. Crews repeats this statement on camera in *Mr. Sears' Catalog*.

[28] Ibid., 54.

[29] Sears, Roebuck supported education in the South in a more institutional way as well when it gradually established 5,357 schools in fifteen southern states between 1917–1940. See Caleb, *Chicago Tribune*, 3 February 1940, rpt in Asher, *Richard Warren Sears*, 19.

shotguns behind him."[30] Then they invent a story about her no-good lover who, in spite of his white shirt, tie, and suit is stealing hogs from farmers, while her father's kin plot to get rid of the unwanted suitor. Harry and Willalee never consider the catalog or people in it as "foreign," and their fabrications are in full correspondence with real life in the rural South when they imagine that "the entire Wish Book was filled with feuds of every kind and violence, maimings, and all the vicious happenings of the world."[31]

However, the illustrations that stirred the imagination of children and adults alike were themselves, in David L. Cohn's words, "drawn not from the imagination but from the living model."[32] Emmet and Jeuck concede that the illustrations might have other values beyond those of selling the goods, e.g. aesthetic or historical, but add immediately: "If the men who performed all those tasks made history, or recorded it, in the process, that was incidental to their main purpose."[33] Nevertheless, even they must admit that "Sears, Roebuck and Company long since intrenched itself in the American mind, idiom, humor, and folklore to an extent certainly unequaled since Paul Bunyan and probably unsurpassed in the commercial history of the nation."[34]

The best elucidation of the use of the catalog as a Dream Book full of stories to be narrated can be found in Lewis Nordan's short story collection *All-Girl Football Team* (1986). In the story "The Sears and Roebuck Catalog Game,"[35] the Mecklin family from the fictional little town of Arrow Catcher, Mississippi (modeled after Itta Bena where Nordan spent his childhood years) never orders anything from the catalog; it is used only as an excuse to create stories. The narrator, fourteen-year-old Sugar Mecklin, often spends time over the catalog with his mother. She has invented a game in which they randomly choose pictures and try to build up stories about the models in them. Logically, the mother's stories closely correspond to her emotions at a particular time. When she considers herself emotionally deprived, the people from the catalog are unhappy and lonely, and shortly before she undertakes a suicide attempt, slashing her wrist with a kitchen knife in front of her son, she even announces a suicide in the Sporting Goods section. Spinning stories over the mail-order catalog could seem to be good therapy, but in Sugar's mother it works two ways. On one hand, it contributes to the development of her imagination, otherwise drowned in the sequence of everyday household chores and never-ending patience with her alcoholic husband. On the other hand, the stories she creates from the pictures are as depressing as those of her real life or even more so.

A good example is the invented story of her childhood in windy and chilly Canadian Saskatchewan, in a fifth-floor walk-up with thin walls, while in real life

---

[30] Crews, *Childhood*, 55.

[31] Ibid., 57.

[32] David L. Cohn, *Good Old Days* (New York: Simon and Schuster, 1940), xxxiv.

[33] Emmet, and Jeuck, *Catalogues and Counters*, 255.

[34] Ibid., 254. Sometimes the influence of Sears, Roebuck on Harry Crews showed itself in a more subdued way. In *The Mulching of America*, his 1995 novel, Crews introduced the character of a door-to-door supersalesman of toilet soap; such a test sale of soap was started by Richard Warren Sears as early as in 1890, see Asher, *Richard Warren Sears*, 5.

[35] For a different analysis of the story see Robert W. Rudnicki, "'I Think I'm Beginning to See': The Rustle of Lewis Nordan's Fiction," *Southern Quarterly* 41.3 (Spring 2003), 51-54.

her father was from sunny and moist Tennessee and she spent most of her childhood in the equally warm state of Mississippi. While the impulse for the story came from people in the catalog, in the end some of the objects that can be ordered from Sears, Roebuck serve for her as metaphors of harmful vanity and opulence. She deliberately chooses products that no southern lower middle-class family would ever want to order when she melodramatically tells Sugar that her "cruel father spent every penny of my mother's hard-earned money on a mahogany gold-handled walking cane and pointy-toed shoes made of kangaroo skin."[36]

As we find out later, Gilbert Mecklin, Sugar's father, keeps in his closet an assortment of even stranger and less useful objects, notably the sequined Rock 'n' Roll Music suit that in another story, "Sugar, Eunuchs and the Big G. B.," Sugar secretly wears in his attempt to get closer to his father's history. However, the depressed, heavy-drinking loser Gilbert, a house painter, is not endowed (at least in this story) with imagination; he lives in a state of intellectual poverty. That makes it more difficult for him to escape from day-to-day stereotypes, but at the same time it saves him from suicidal tendencies. Unfortunately, Sugar, who wants to save his father from the former, inflicts on him the latter.

After the mother's unsuccessful suicide attempt, Sugar and Gilbert, who stay in the house alone, decide to play "Mother's game" with the catalog. From a distance of many years and with the clear realization of the grave consequences of the game, Sugar tries to recollect whose idea it originally was: "The game must have been my idea. And yet I think I remember that it was my father who wanted to play." Gilbert Mecklin, despite his alcoholism, had been a classic example of a man at peace with the disharmonious world. This changes forever after Sugar's seemingly innocent question concerning a model standing alone and looking off into the distance, the embodiment of solitude and loneliness: "Who is she waiting for?" This question starts Gilbert's inner struggle—his unwillingness to enter new territory and at the same time the notion of the inevitability of crossing the border. This process, mediated by the Women's Clothing section of the Sears, Roebuck catalog, is a one-way street. Gilbert, who could not previously get beyond the idea that the model's coat would look nice on his wife, comes to the conclusion that the lonely model can look back at him. At that moment, his imagination is born and makes him, in Sugar's words, a liar, womanizer, and secretive person. Sugar's comment is: "The rest of his days he spent in misery."[37]

However, under Gilbert's misery, his son's fate is concealed. Sugar, who has all the imagination he can use and is used to playing the catalog game routinely, can surprisingly perceive the models in the catalog exactly as his unimaginative father saw them before he became immersed in the game—as lifeless two-dimensional objects, almost forgeries of human beings: "They seemed false. Nobody seemed alive. There was no geography to read from their faces, which were poses for a camera." At the very end of the story, Sugar, in an attempt to suppress his

---

[36] Lewis Nordan, *All-Girl Football Team* (Baton Rouge: Louisiana State University Press, 1986), 52.

[37] Ibid., 56, 57. Another of Nordan's characters inventing stories over the Sears, Roebuck catalog is Alice Conroy, a schoolteacher from his novel *Wolf Whistle*. See Lewis Nordan, *Wolf Whistle* (Chapel Hill: Algonquin, 1995), 156.

overwhelming sorrow, deliberately adopts the point of view of a model in the catalog. When he tries to pull the dead body of his father out from under the house, he reduces himself to a mere two-dimensional illustration: "I looked at my father through the eyes of the model in the picture and saw what she saw: the face of a yellow corpse beneath our house and in that face an emptiness too vast ever to be filled up or given meaning."[38] The image of his father's dead body in pyjamas in a place where long-forgotten things are hidden and come out only during a flood presents one more hint at the Sears, Roebuck catalog. The metaphor of Gilbert's death draws on the similarity between the color of a gravely ill man suffering from liver problems and the pages of an old catalog that, despite the nice pictures in it, was thrown away as useless, outdated, and expired.

In his fictional autobiography *Boy with Loaded Gun* (2000), Nordan confirms that inventing stories from the catalog was his mother's favorite armchair activity. In an upsurge of wild imagination aroused by the catalog, Nordan's mother even toyed with the idea of a career in showbusiness. Nordan himself admits that the game equipped him with creative capacities, and together with comic books, gave him powers to cope with the everydayness of his Mississippi childhood.[39] The Sears, Roebuck catalog game could stir emotions and fulfill the need for drama and sentiment people usually find in romantic movies or mass-market romance novels. The catalog's influence on Nordan was so powerful that we cannot even be sure whether Roebuck Lake in his fiction was named after the deer or after the co-founder of the company.

In 1940, David Cohn recognized poetry in the catalog, to him bearing similarities to the obituary poetry of the ancient Greeks, where "appear again and again the youth's hound, the fowler's snare, the fisherman's net, the farmer's plow. These values, too, are in the catalogue, and they are not less poignant because they belong to our times than to antiquity."[40] In his opinion, the real poetry comes not from the models in their underwear, but from the farming, hunting, and fishing equipment, which is needed for the most frequent activities, working or leisure, of most male southerners and which also illustrate the technical and economic progress of the South's rural areas at its best.

In the first story of Lewis Nordan's *Music of the Swamp* (1991), Sugar Mecklin wakes up on a beautiful Sunday morning and listens to the sounds of machinery in the fields: "Sugar Mecklin heard the high soothing music of the swamp, the irrigation pumps in the rice paddies . . . , he heard the wheezy, breathy asthma of the compress, the suck and bump and clatter like great lungs as the air was squashed out and the cotton was wrapped in burlap and bound with steel bands into six-hundred-pound bales, he heard the operatic voice of the cotton gin separating fibers from seeds."[41] Compare Nordan's music of the swamp with Louis Asher's diary description of the printing shop where the Sears, Roebuck catalog was made: "I enjoyed the smell of printer's ink, the pungent odor from the can of benzine used to clean type forms, the peculiar elusive effluvium of the big rolls of catalogue paper

---

[38] Ibid., 57, 58.
[39] See Lewis Nordan, *Boy with Loaded Gun* (Chapel Hill: Algonquin, 2000), 50-58.
[40] Cohn, *Good Old Days*, xxxii.
[41] Lewis Nordan, *Music of the Swamp* (Chapel Hill: Algonquin, 1991), 6.

fresh from the mills. The noisy clanking rhythm of the Langston typecasting machine as the two arms switched around finding the matrix characters as if they were sentient beings, soothed my ear like music."[42] The imagery of Nordan and Asher in these two excerpts is strikingly similar. In both cases not only the catalog, but also the machinery and its use (in Asher's case for the production of the Dream Book itself) acquire significant aesthetic qualities. It is evident that Asher recognized the potential of the catalog as a Dream Book, although as a proper businessman he was more interested in selling and buying. But even the narratives contained in his diary describing his successful road from an editor of the catalog to the business manager of Sears, Roebuck—for instance the story about his accidental misplacement of East by West in "Freight prepaid East of the Rocky Mountains" that cost the company millions—are stylistically very close to the oral folk tradition from which Lewis Nordan also drew inspiration.[43]

However, there were southern writers who never recognized the aesthetic qualities of the catalog and for whom Sears, Roebuck was a synonym for uniformity. Elizabeth Spencer, whose father was a rich businessman, and whose relatives owned farms in Carroll County, Mississippi, never dreamt over the Sears, Roebuck catalog. Still, even though the goods from the catalog do not bear for her any trace of innovation or imagination, she at least acknowledges their quality. In her 1978 story "Indian Summer," set in 1941, Marilee Summerall, an intelligent farm girl who inadvertently turned her cousin Andrew, a local teacher with a military background, into a would-be businessman, provides us with the following description: "He wore a coach's cap with a neat bill, a soft knit shirt, gabardine trousers, and gym shoes. He also wore white socks. All told, he looked to have stepped out of the Sears Roebuck catalogue, for he was as trim as could be, but he was too regulation to be real." His choice of attire goes hand in hand with his unfulfilled ambitions. Andrew would like to turn a part of the family estate into a profitable suburban housing colony. However, his father not only refuses to consider this suggestion, but gets angry and leaves the farm for several months to show who is boss in the family. After his father's return, Andrew felt "as if he [Andrew] wasn't there anymore. . . . Figuratively speaking, his voice had been taken from him."[44] Dreaming his managerial dreams, he sank into obscurity, not understanding that true dreams are born from the imagination and are incompatible with greediness.

Spencer used the catalog once before in her story "The Bufords," introducing a grotesque Mississippi family that might be a little too strange, but at least their members stick together and respect each other. The children from the Buford family are nightmares for all the teachers of the local school, especially for young Miss Jackson. Dora Mae Buford, who is currently the "ambassador" of the family in Miss Jackson's class, refuses to absorb any piece of knowledge directed at pupils, and lives in a world of her own. Once "at recess, she had jumped up and down on a Sears Roebuck catalogue in the dressing room behind the stage, creating such a thunder nobody could think what was happening." Although the teacher never tries to

---

[42] Asher, *Richard Warren Sears*, 50.

[43] Ibid. 50.

[44] Elizabeth Spencer, *The Stories of Elizabeth Spencer* (New York: Viking Penguin, 1981), 394, 400.

explain Dora Mae's behavior, it is obvious that the feeling of powerlessness the poor child experiences in front of a shop window, albeit a portable one, combines with the pride of any human being who does not accept the world as ready-made, but wants to make it better. That is why Dora Mae secretly uses the sewing machine installed in the school building for the students of the home economics class (and accidentally sews through her own finger), or holds her reader in the air between her feet. To make life more interesting, her older brother even brought a horse inside the school building once. The unhappy young teacher can feel nothing but a constant wonder: "The world you were dozing on came back with a whoosh and a bang; but it was not the same world you had dozed away from, nor was it the one you intended to wake up to or even imagined to be there. . . . Were you dreaming? Or were things meant to be this way?"[45]

Obviously not everyone responded in the same way to what, according to McLaurin, the Sears, Roebuck catalog could be heard as saying: "Open me, child. Look into your heart, wish and want and believe. The season of innocence and trust will pass too soon."[46] Little Dora Mae from Elizabeth Spencer's story showed an unrecognized sign of early maturation and reached a stage where the Sears, Roebuck catalog did not suffice either as a Wish Book or a Dream Book. All the writers and protagonists I have discussed came to the same conclusion and outgrew the catalog's magic—that is why the tales introducing the catalog are so often connected with childhood and youth. That, however, does not devalue the role of the catalog in the century-long formation of people's desires, which brought the unplanned side effect of igniting their fantasy and creativity.

---

[45] Spencer, *Stories*, 232, 233.
[46] Tim McLaurin, "The Sears Catalog," 762.

ERSKINE CALDWELL ANTICIPATES THE NEW SOUTH

Edwin T. Arnold

Given the state of Erskine Caldwell's present reputation, it comes as a surprise to many that for a time Caldwell stood as the leading liberal, progressive, even radical spokesman for the New South. For these ten or so years, from the early days of the Depression through the first years of World War II, Caldwell was constantly in the public eye, challenging the status quo, demanding reform, calling on the nation and its leaders to intervene in the South, which he presented as a third world region run by home-grown tyrants. If Caldwell's fiction sometimes left readers wondering about his attitude towards the comic and tragic characters he described—the impoverished peasant Lesters in *Tobacco Road* (1932), the landed but wasteful, doomed Waldens in *God's Little Acre* (1933), the hypocritical, lustful but still god-haunted denizens of Rocky Comfort, Georgia, in *Journeyman* (1935), the casually racist community of Andrewjones, Georgia, that lynches an innocent man out of mean desperation and despair and then stones to death his female accuser in *Trouble in July* (1940), just to name the novels Caldwell wrote during this time—then his non-fiction could not be clearer in its stance.

As a contributor to such publications as the *New Masses*, the *Daily Worker*, the *Nation*, and the *New Republic*, Caldwell was identified as the southerner who courageously spoke against his own region at a time when others were closing rank. For example, in December, 1933, the Arkansas poet and writer John Gould Fletcher wrote a letter to the *Nation* in response to articles critical of the convictions of the "Scottsboro Boys," nine black men accused of gang-raping two white women in Alabama in 1931. Despite serious doubts as to their guilt, eight of the nine had been sentenced to death, thus setting into motion a series of trials that would continue for years.[1] Although Fletcher acknowledged that there were questions surrounding these trials, he nonetheless avowed, speaking for southerners in general:

> We believe that under our system the great majority of the race are leading happy and contented lives. But our system, we admit, has one defect. If a white woman is prepared to swear that a Negro either raped or attempted to rape her, we see to it that the Negro is executed.

He then proclaimed:

> We will not suffer further dictation from the North as to what we are to do about the Negro. All that we built up again out of the ruins of Civil War and of Reconstruction is again at stake. Rather than permit our own peculiar

---

[1] The trials and retrials lasted until 1937. For further information on this convoluted judicial process, see Dan T. Carter, *Scottsboro: A Tragedy of the American South* (Baton Rouge: Louisiana State University Press, 1979). See also "The `Scottsboro Boys' Trials" website http://www.law.umkc.edu/faculty/projects/FTrials/scottsboro/scottsb.htm, which provides a useful timeline of the trials; and *Scottsboro: An American Tragedy* (PBS Video, 2001).

conceptions of justice to be questioned, we will take the law into our own hands, by a resort to violence. . . . We in the South alone can find the solution to that problem. We will never accept any solution that comes to us from the North. Rather than that, we will again take up arms in our cause.[2]

Caldwell answered Fletcher, speaking as another man of the South, but one prepared to refute such thinking. He wrote,

> I myself am a Southerner, I was born here, I have lived here most of my life, and I shall probably die here. But if being a Southerner carries with it the implications of Fletcher's letter, then I will renounce whatever birthright and heritage I may have, and give my allegiance to some other country. However, I prefer to remain here, and I shall do so; and if anyone would like to coin a name for those of us who are opposed to what Fletcher stands for, then under that name I shall live. I have taken my stand, and I intend to keep it; but to draw sharp this necessary dividing line, it is on the other side of the fence from Fletcher and his "millions of Southerners."[3]

The following year, Caldwell again inveighed against the practice of lynching in the South. In early 1934, he published two "reports" in the Communist publication *New Masses* describing the aftermath of a series of lynchings in Bartow, Georgia. The first was called "A Story That Got Lost"; the second "'Parties Unknown' in Georgia." In these first-person accounts, Caldwell's emphasis was on his moral confusion, his attempts to understand the behaviors of his kinsmen. He wrote,

> I was standing in the main street of Bartow trying to wonder what I was doing there. I was trying to reason why three Negroes could be put to death in such a quiet, peaceful town by white men who were at that moment in their homes asleep. Nobody was disturbed. Nobody was walking around in the dark with a flashlight trying to find evidence to convict the killers. Nobody was abroad offering protection to Negroes who wished to come out of their cabins. Bartow was as calm as any Georgia town at midnight. Georgia was as peaceful as any Southern state in January.[4]

There was clearly a degree of self-promotion in Caldwell's portrait; he stood as the only white man horrified by what had taken place. And the editors of the *New Masses* contributed to this image, telling their readers that "Caldwell himself is in danger"[5] and that "His personal safety is seriously threatened because of his

---

[2] John Gould Fletcher, "Is This the Voice of the South?" (Letter), *Nation* 137.3573 (27 December 1933), 734-735.

[3] Erskine Caldwell, "Caldwell to Lieber" (Letter), *New Masses* 10 (30 January 1934), 21.

[4] Caldwell, "'Parties Unknown' in Georgia," *New Masses* 10 (23 January 1934), 16. Rpt. in *New Masses: An Anthology of the Rebel Thirties*, ed. Joseph North, (New York: International Publishers, 1969), 137-141.

[5] "Editorial," *New Masses* 10 (16 January 1934), 3.

sensational revelations of anti-Negro terror in Georgia."[6] In this last editorial, the *New Masses* elaborated on the threats made against Caldwell:

> An unsolicited letter from Atlanta advises us: "If Caldwell sticks to his post and continues to fight, something will happen to him." But Caldwell has no intention of keeping silent. "It's my story and I stick to it," he replied when notified to appear before the grand jury in May to show proof of his charges that at least three innocent Negroes were put to death by Jefferson county whites. Solicitor-General Gross eloquently threatens to "put Caldwell in jail until he is ready to talk—" but both Caldwell and his father, Rev. I. S. Caldwell, are more than ready to talk right now; for the coroner's jury reported "death at the hands of parties unknown" and the lynchers right now are "walking the streets in heroic strides."

Caldwell, of course, wrote about more than the South. He traveled throughout the country, and as a self-identified writer of the political left, he took stands on numerous national issues. As Sylvia Jenkins Cook notes in her essay, "Erskine Caldwell and the Literary Left Wing," in 1932 he publicly supported the Communist Party's nominee for the Presidency, espoused "his own adherence to revolutionary and Communist ideals," and, as late as 1939, was still offering support to the Communist movement in the U. S. Cook recognizes that much of what Caldwell wrote was, indeed, "directly propagandistic."[7] His 1934 series of articles on the Detroit automobile industry that appeared first in the *Daily Worker* and was later included in his book *Some American People* is an example. According to Cook, these articles comprise "a savage satire of ["King"] Henry Ford's insulated industrial kingdom, where flower gardens cover the place where Ford's police gunned down his workers, and employees, mutilated by unsafe machinery, are turned out onto the streets to scavenge for what they can get."[8]

With titles like "The Eight-Finger City," "The School of Prostitutes," and "Where America Died," Caldwell fulminated against Ford, his private army, his "spy system," and his "man-killing" assembly line speed-up system, "the most inhuman system of extracting labor known in any industry." He described how Ford's motor plants have "taken a toll of fingers, hands, arms, legs, and crushed bodies." His examination of the assembly line system was sometimes intentionally exaggerated, but it was exaggerated in the same way Charlie Chaplin exaggerated the same industrial system in his film *Modern Times* in 1936. Indeed, one wonders if Chaplin was perhaps influenced by Caldwell, who wrote that the "speed up

---

[6] "Editorial," *New Masses* 10 (6 February 1934), 3.

[7] Sylvia Jenkins Cook, "Erskine Caldwell and the Literary Left Wing," *Pembroke*, 11 (1979), 132-39. Rpt. in *Critical Essays on Erskine Caldwell*, ed. Scott MacDonald (Boston: G. K. Hall & Co, 1981), 362, 370, 378.

[8] *Erskine Caldwell and the Fiction of Poverty* (Baton Rouge and London: Louisiana State University Press, 1991), 229.

system—of which Ford is the proud papa—drives men insane," exactly what happens to the Tramp at the beginning of Chaplin's film.[9]

Still, Caldwell was most often identified with issues of southern labor and poverty, especially as exemplified by the plight of the tenant farmers. In late 1934, Caldwell returned to east Georgia, the locale for his most popular novels. He had been hired by the New York *Post* to report on the effects of the Roosevelt Administration's experimental Agricultural Adjustment Act, which paid subsidies to farmers and land owners to leave the land uncultivated so that cotton production (the main southern crop) would be reduced and the price for cotton would increase. What Caldwell quickly realized was that while the landowners did, indeed, benefit from these experiments, the large number of sharecroppers or tenant farmers, who owned no land and depended on others who did, would find little benefit and even less work.

Caldwell's biographer Dan B. Miller has written that Caldwell's *Post* series "represented the boldest, most extensive piece of investigative reporting dealing with the South's poorest citizens."[10] The articles ran for four days, February 18-21, 1935, in the *Post* and they caused an uproar. These were sensational charges, with titles like "Georgia Land Barons Oust Dying Girl and Her Father" and, most striking, "Starving Babies Suckled by Dog in Georgia Cabin." In them Caldwell employed the most grotesque imagery and examples he could find, as he would also do in his "Detroit" essays the following year. He wrote:

> These are the unknown people of today, the tenant farmer of the South. These are the people who hide their nakedness behind trees when a stranger wanders off the main-travelled roads. Here are the deformed, starved, and diseased children born since 1929. Here are the men who strip leaves off trees, dig roots out of the earth, and snare whatever wild animal they can. . . . There is hunger in their eyes as well as in their bellies. They grasp for a word of hope. They plead for a word of advice. They have no friend or leader to help them.

He saved his most horrific examples for the last article. Here he described a six year old boy: "His legs were scarcely any larger than a medium sized dog's leg, and his belly was as large as that of a 130-pound woman. Suffering from rickets and anemia, his legs were unable to carry him for more than a dozen steps at a time; suffering from malnutrition, his belly was swollen several times its normal size. His face was

---

[9] Caldwell, "The Kingdom of Henry I," "The Eight-Fingered City," "The School of Prostitutes," "F.O.B.," and "Where America Died" in *Some American People* (New York: Robert M. McBride & Co., 1935): 158, 168. Caldwell went to Detroit in May, 1934. The articles appeared in the *Daily Worker* over five days, June 2, 4, 5, 6, 7, 1934; the series was then included in his book *Some American People*, published in October 1935. Chaplin worked on his script "between the summer of 1933 and August of 1934" and "shot the film between October 11, 1934, and August 30, 1935, after which he supervised the editing and scoring, which was finally completed on December 22." The film premiered in New York on February 5, 1936. See Charles Maland, "*Modern Times*" in *Film Analysis*, ed. Jeffrey Geiger and R. I. Rutsky (New York and London: W. W. Norton & Company, 2005), 245, 246.

[10] Dan B. Miller, *Erskine Caldwell: The Journey from Tobacco Road* (New York: Knopf, 1995), 216.

bony and white. He was starving to death." Even more shocking was his example of the starving babies "neither a year old, sucking the dry teats of a mongrel bitch. . . . The infants cuddled against the warmth of the dog's flank, searching tearfully for the dry teats. . . . The dog got up and shook herself and lay down several feet away. The babies crawled crying after her." In other places he described men eating tree bark, snakes, clay and "cow dung" to stay alive.[11]

Time magazine reprinted excerpts from the series in March of 1935. During the same month, the Augusta, Georgia, *Chronicle* began its own five-part series of investigations in an attempt to confirm or challenge Caldwell's portrait of this section of the state, concluding, finally, that there was truth to his allegations, although the examples they found were of "a relatively small number." "The *Chronicle* admits, without cheerfulness, that there is a wretched situation among a few of the poor whites of our section," the editors continued, but they faulted Caldwell for his implication that these "few" represented the majority, for his willingness to have "laundered our dirty linen and rattled the skeletons in our closet before thousands of people," and his failure to offer "a constructive remedy" for the situation.[12] In April, Caldwell followed up with a second series, relatively less sensational, in which he did offer vague suggestions for correction. "The landowner-tenant system should not be permitted to exist," he wrote. "A unionized wage-scale system would be ideal in theory for a capitalistic nation, but in practice it is difficult to imagine any such relationship succeeding between the present-day landowner and the worker. A far greater step would be the discarding of the landowner and the cultivation of the large farm on a collective basis, or else the breaking up of large fertile units of land into small parcels for intensive cultivation by one or two persons."[13]

The editors of the *Post* ended the second series with their own comments entitled "Hell on Earth," in which they noted that the South's "special problems . . . may be beyond the power of any one Administration to solve."[14] Nevertheless, they called on Commerce Secretary Henry Wallace to investigate the policies of the Agricultural Adjustment Administration and to make public the results. Like the *Post* editors, Caldwell also looked to a strong government to step in and solve problems, even if it imposed corrections unwanted by state or local authorities.[15] Thus he supported unionization of the tenant farmers and the conscription of land. He fiercely attacked Georgia Governor Eugene Talmadge as "the dictator of three million people who exercises more power than Huey Long" and claimed that Talmadge, the "self-styled `wild man'," was "riding to greater power" by "refusing to furnish food, clothing, or work to one-third of the population."[16] When Caldwell

---

[11] Caldwell, *Tenant Farmer* (New York: Phalanx Press, 1935), 5, 12-13.

[12] "The Caldwell Issue and Long Range Rehabilitation," Augusta *Chronicle*, 24 March 1935, 16; rpt. *Critical Essays*, 137.

[13] Caldwell, *Tenant Farmer*, 30.

[14] "Hell on Earth," New York *Post*, 22 April 1935, 10; rpt. *Critical Essays*, 152.

[15] Caldwell collected all eight articles as *Tenant Farmer*, a 30-page pamphlet published in 1935 by the left-wing Phalanx Press. It was the first of a series such pamphlets on social problems published by the press.

[16] *Tenant Farmer*, 3.

was asked, along with Sherwood Anderson, to provide an introduction to the program that accompanied the 1935 opening of "An Art Commentary on Lynching," a public showing in New York of paintings, sculptures, and etchings depicting the horrors of that practice, he wrote that lynching "should be dealt with as any other major crime" and called on "the Congress of the United States to pass the necessary legislation, and to place the enforcement of the law in the hands of the Department of Justice."[17] At his most extreme, Caldwell could consider even more radical actions. For example, he, like his father, contemplated government sterilization for "certain individual mental and physical cases" as a means to control incest, illegitimacy, and disease among the most impoverished, but he recognized that this was no long-term solution.[18] And in the early days of World War II, shortly after his return from the USSR where he and his wife Margaret Bourke-White had covered the beginning of the Nazi invasion, he questioned whether a democratic system could stand against Hitler. "We have a war on and we go along the street and you'd think it was July 1925. . . . A rolling army like Hitler's can swallow nations in a few hours. We think of 1943-44. They think of 3 p. m. to 5 a. m. . . . I'm not advocating Communism. I'm just being realistic. . . . Would you rather have a temporary dictator or be completely subject to Hitler?"[19]

Years later Caldwell distanced himself from such proclamations. As he told Michel Bandry in 1980, "People had an idea that I did have a purpose in mind, to popularize or to propagate communism, Marxism. It just happened that I had come along in a time, a climate, which was conducive to the same kind of feeling that Marxism was based on. . . . I have been sympathetic to the idea of, not so much spreading the wealth or revolution, but the fact that there must be some economic reason why people suffer as they do and have done continuously, and whoever can find the correct solution for it is going to get my sympathy, my understanding, and my faith." He concluded that "as a general rule I think the democratic process is still workable."[20] Cook observes, "Even at the height of Caldwell's public commitment to a radical left-wing ideology, there is a conservative counter-current in his writing that fears the takeover of individuals by the government just as strongly as it promotes the ideals of unions, power and fraternity."[21]

In later years, when he was no longer as respected as during the heady 1930s, Caldwell still was asked about the future of the South, most often in terms of race. In 1964 he was interviewed by Morris Renek for *Cavalier*, a poor cousin to *Playboy* and a sign of his diminished reputation. Nevertheless, he frankly expressed his views, stating that the South would change as a result of the dying off of old prejudices, continued education, and the growth of media. "It's the cruelty," he said,

---

[17] "A Note" in *Art Commentary on Lynching* (1935), unpaginated.

[18] *Tenant Farmer*, 16.

[19] "Erskine Caldwell's Lesson from Russia: America May Lose War," *P. M.'s Weekly*, 22 February 1942, 6-7; rpt. *Conversations With Erskine Caldwell*, ed. Edwin T. Arnold (Jackson: University Press of Mississippi, 1988), 24-25.

[20] Michel Bandry, "Interview with Erskine Caldwell," *Annales de la Faculte des Lettres et Sciences Humaines de Nice-Etudes Nord-Americanines* 4 (1982): 125-36; rpt. *Conversations*, 208.

[21] "Erskine Caldwell and the Literary Left Wing," 378.

commenting on racial unrest in the South. "The cruelty of the white man in the South taking it out on the Negro. . . . It's this combination of human cruelty, white prejudice, and his Southern heritage. Gradually this combination will evaporate due to TV, radio, magazines; especially education. We need a Peace Corps in the South. Yes, we do. The older people have to die off. They can't be changed. . . . Education is coming to the South. You can't have prejudice in a democracy. If the South wants to be a democracy, Southern prejudice will have to go."[22] He saw hope in the mixing of the races, stating, "It is so easy to recognize the vitality of this new breed of people, the people in between the white and black, these mulattoes and octoroons. And they are certainly going to have an effect. You can't escape it. They will be accepted because they are too vital. It's going to liven the whole civilization. . . . And it is the foundation of the future."[23] Caldwell was essentially optimistic about this future. In 1967, he predicted that "five years from now there's going to be an even greater acceptance of Civil Rights and a greater acceptance of integration than there is right now. And in ten years it's going to be even more so. It's a progressive kind of thing and will go on and on, until eventually segregation is wiped out."[24]

Throughout his career, Caldwell saw himself less as an artist than as a social reformer. In 1935, his father told a reporter from the Augusta *Chronicle* that "Erskine's interest in the class of people is with a motive of having something done to correct their condition and their future development. They say that through his writings he hopes to center attention on their deplorable lot and have a movement started to eradicate such conditions, and preclude the possibility of conditions of the like in the future."[25] Five years later Caldwell himself would say, "I represent the people. . . . I'm just like a Congressman asking for a WPA [Works Progress Administration] appropriation. I am citing facts, telling what there is, what exists, what these people are facing."[26] And again in 1984, shortly before his death, Caldwell would recall his motives, "I couldn't think of anything else to do except to write what my conscience told me about these people who were suffering. I thought other people could help somehow, either by medicine or by food—something. What else could I do but write about it? . . . It changed very rapidly during the administration of Roosevelt. I think he was the first one to recognize that these people had to have assistance, that they were at the end of their rope."[27]

---

[22] "'Sex Was Their Way of Life': A Frank Interview with Erskine Caldwell," *Cavalier*, March 1964, 12-16, 40-42; *Conversations*, 79-80.

[23] Alan Lelchuk and Robin White, "An Interview with Erskine Caldwell," *Per/Se* (Spring 1967): 11-20; *Conversations*, 102.

[24] *Conversations*, 101.

[25] "Erskine Caldwell," Augusta *Chronicle*, 14 March 1935, 1; *Critical Essays*, 130.

[26] "Who's Who in Darien: Erskine Caldwell," *Darien Review*, 5 September 1940, 1-2; *Conversations*, 20.

[27] Edwin T. Arnold, "Interview with Erskine Caldwell," *Conversations*, 275.

THE WAR ON THE HOME FRONT: JAMES AGEE
AND THE MAKING OF LET US NOW PRAISE FAMOUS MEN

Robert H. Brinkmeyer, Jr.

In his film reviews for the *Nation* during the 1940s, James Agee frequently attacks movies made purely for propaganda purposes. Commenting on *Mission to Moscow*, a film apparently produced at the urging of the federal government in order to enhance public opinion of the Soviets during World War II, Agee writes that the Soviet Union is presented as "a great glad two-million-dollar bowl of canned borscht, eminently approvable by the Institute of Good Housekeeping."[1] The film's message, Agee goes on, is finally that there are no significant differences between the Soviet Union and the United States, "except that in Russia everybody affects a Weber and Fields accent and women run locomotives and you get tailed by a pair of harmless comics who claim to be GPU men."[2] Agee scorned such films, which were flooding American theaters during the war, for their simplifications and manipulations of reality; propaganda films, Agee comments in another review, are made by fools and treat their audiences as fools. "The proof is in every commentator's voice, his phrasing, his abject mawkishness and political childishness," Agee writes, commenting on the typical American documentary made for propaganda purposes, "and in the puff-paste, onanistic, heartless quality of most of the camera work, whose nearest equivalent is the tradition Leni Riefenstahl froze in Germany."[3] Propaganda films, moreover, presume that their audiences are entirely passive; and as do mediocre feature films, they strive "to do all the work–the seeing, the understanding, the explaining, the understanding, even the feeling."[4]

At the same time that he was attacking propaganda films for their deliberate distortions of reality, Agee was also asserting that great art could be propagandistic, though in making this claim he clearly was defining propaganda unusually. "I do believe, to be sure," Agee comments in a 1944 review of the Russian film *The Rainbow*, "that a kind of propaganda is possible whose constant effort is to clarify rather than merely simplify, not to say falsify or exploit, issues and motives and causes and needs; to forge, in Joyce's words, the uncreated conscience of the race."[5] Probably one of the few readers of Joyce to see him as a propagandist, Agee brings together Joyce's ideas on epiphany, for perceiving and representing the fullness of reality, with his own ideas on propaganda. As suggested in his reference to Joyce's forging "the uncreated conscience of the race," Agee believes that art opens the reader to the luminous wonder lurking in the everyday world, what he characterizes

---

[1] James Agee, Movie Column from the 22 May 1943 *Nation*, in *Agee on Film* [1958] (New York: Modern Library, 2000), 19.

[2] Ibid., 21. Weber and Fields were vaudeville comedians who spoke in exaggerated German accents and whose comedy frequently relied on miscommunication and splintered language.

[3] James Agee, Movie Column from the 25 December 1943 *Nation*, in *Agee on Film*, 49.

[4] James Agee, "Undirectable Director," in *Agee on Film*, 425.

[5] James Agee, Movie Column from the 18 November 1944 *Nation*, in *Agee on Film*, 110.

in the Preface to *Let Us Now Praise Famous Men* as "the cruel radiance of what is."[6] To open the reader to this wonder, art must undo the reader's everyday structures for seeing and ordering the world; or as Agee puts it in a description of his effort to cleanse his own vision, art strives "to suspend or destroy imagination, [so that] there opens before consciousness and within it, a universe luminous, spacious, incalculably rich and wonderful in each detail" (11-12). For Agee that's the purpose–the propaganda–of art.

While from a modernist perspective there is nothing particularly unusual in Agee's conception of the transformative, epiphanic power of art, his characterization of that power as propagandistic and of high art itself as propaganda is both striking and noteworthy. Exploring the reasons behind and the implications of Agee's conceptualization of the propagandistic thrust of art–and most certainly Agee had his own work in mind–goes far, I believe, in explaining both Agee's radical narrative strategies for representing southern poverty in *Let Us Now Praise Famous Men* and his political intentions with that text.

Agee knew he faced a monstrous task in portraying the plight of southern tenant farmers to the American reading public, despite the fact that during the 1930s much public attention was directed at southern poverty and that a number of writers and photographers were publishing texts and images portraying the rural South's downtrodden. Most of these other works, however, such as Erskine Caldwell's and Margaret Bourke-White's *You Have Seen Their Faces*, Agee found patronizing and simplistic, catering to the passive reader by presenting stock images of the southern poor rather than by delving deeply into their complex and unique lives. It is largely for this reason that Agee, in the Preface to *Let Us Now Praise Famous Men*, claims that the reality of the southern poor in the 1930s remains for most Americans unknown and unimaginable; and announcing intentions that extend far beyond those of straightforward documentary, he writes that he wants "to recognize the stature of a portion of unimagined existence, and to contrive techniques proper to its recording, communication, analysis, and defense" (xlvi). Rather than catering to readers, Agee works to challenge them, or as he puts it, "to pry their eyes open" (208). Agee wants his readers not only to see the world of the rural poor in all its complexity but also to understand how that world is in the grips of a system of grinding oppression that reduces individuals, alive with "grand stature and natural warmth," into "social integers in a criminal economy" (100).

In making visible the world of the rural poor, Agee for the most part employs a two-pronged narrative strategy. One tactic involves Agee as narrator suspending his imagination in order to present as stark and unadulterated details of the tenants' lives as possible, in effect mimicking the camera work of his partner Walker Evans, recording details as a "bodyless eye" (187). "If I could do it," he writes, reflecting the impossible extremes of this strategy, "I'd do no writing at all here. It would be photographs; the rest would be fragments of cloth, bits of cotton, lumps of earth, records of speech, pieces of wood and iron, phials of odors, plates of food and of excrement. . . . A piece of the body torn out by the roots might be more to the point"

---

[6] James Agee and Walker Evans, *Let Us Now Praise Famous Men* [1941] (Boston: Houghton Mifflin, 1988), 11. Further citations are from this edition and will be cited parenthetically.

(13). To cut through the pervasive and demeaning stereotypes of southern poor whites, Agee closely examines all areas of the families' lives–their work, shelter, clothes, fields, routines, joys, sorrows, and whatever else comes before his eyes. In this mode, Agee writes simply and directly, stripping his writing of metaphor and his observations of judgment, as in his description of the area underneath the Gudgers' house: "The rear edges of the house rest in part on stacked stones, in part on the dirt; in part they overhang this dirt a little. Beneath the house this dirt sinks gently, so that the flanks and forward edges are lifted to level in part on taller stacks of stone, in part on thick rounded sections of logs. The porch floor, and the forward parts of the house, are about two and a half feet off the ground" (147). A world teeming in fact and intense in detail emerges.

Agee's other, quite different, tactic involves filtering the details of the tenant families' world through his rich consciousness, presenting rhetorically dazzling interrogations of his observations and experiences. Agee achieves several things with this tactic. To begin with, he imbues the details of the tenant farmers' lives with a beauty and significance that extends far beyond their own limited world, often by employing an eye-stopping rhetorical excess meant to shatter the reader's demeaning preconceptions and stereotypes of the rural poor. To those who think there is no beauty in the tenants' run-down houses, for instance, Agee comments that the grain marking the lumber of the Gudgers' home "goes into convulsions or ecstasies such as Beethoven's deafness compelled" (145). And in one of his most remarkable passages, Agee comments on the symmetry of the Gudgers' house:

> On symmetry: the house is rudimentary as a child's drawing, and of a bareness, cleanness, and sobriety which only Doric architecture, so far as I know, can hope to approach: this exact symmetry is sprung slightly and subtly, here and there, one corner of the house a little off vertical, a course of weather-boarding failing the horizontal between parallels, a window frame not quite square, by lack of skill and by weight and weakness of timber and time; and these slight failures, their tensions sprung against centers and opposals of such rigid and earnest exactitude, set up intensities of relationship far more powerful than full symmetry, or studied dissymmetry, or use of relief or ornament, can ever be: indeed, the power is of another world and order than theirs, and there is, as I mentioned, a particular quality of a thing hand-made, which by comparison I can best suggest thus: by the grandeur that comes of the effort of one man to hold together upon one instrument, as if he were breaking a wild monster to bridle and riding, one of the larger fugues of Bach, on an organ, as against the slick collaborations and effortless climaxes of the same piece in the manipulations of an orchestra. (144)

As Agee's comments suggest, beauty of the highest register punctuates the tenants' world; if outside observers typically do not see this beauty, it is because they are either not looking for it or are not looking for it with the proper focus and empathy.

Other of Agee's interrogations of his experiences in the tenants' world and his experiences within it focus on his tortured feelings as participant/observer, often centering on his recognitions of shared humanity with those observed and, more importantly, of shared responsibility, as an American enmeshed in the social and economic system, for their plight. Early on, Agee questions the rationale behind, together with the large-scale social implications of, the original journalistic assignment (for *Fortune* magazine) that had sent him and Evans into the southern countryside (and that had become the origin of *Let Us Now Praise Famous Men*):

> It seems to me curious, not to say obscene and thoroughly terrifying, that it could occur to an association of human beings drawn together through need and chance and for profit into a company, an organ of journalism, to pry intimately into the lives of the undefended and appallingly damaged group of human beings, an ignorant and helpless rural family, for the purpose of parading the nakedness, disadvantage and humiliation of these lives before another group of human beings, in the name of science, of "honest journalism" (whatever that paradox may mean), of humanity, of social fearlessness, for money, and for a reputation for crusading and for unbias which, when skillfully enough qualified, is exchangeable at any bank for money (and in politics, for votes, job patronage, abelincolnism, etc.); and that these people could be capable of meditating this prospect without the slightest doubt of their qualification to do an "honest" piece of work, and with a conscience better than clear, and in the virtual certitude of almost unanimous public approval. (7)

Here and in his other ruminations, Agee implicitly challenges his readers to engage in the same self-scrutiny and to recognize their own complicity for the inequities and suffering about which they are reading. Or put more dramatically, Agee declares that with *Let Us Now Praise Famous Men*, he wants "to blow out the brains . . . of you who take what it is talking of lightly, or not seriously enough" (307).

Both of Agee's narrative tactics focus on immediacy: the immediacy of the tenants' lives and the immediacy of his tumultuous consciousness. He wants to present a deadly-accurate portrayal of southern poverty as he experiences it and as the tenants live it. There is very little preachiness in the text, not only because Agee typically finds over-arching moralizing pretentious, patronizing, and ineffective, but because he believes that the details of the tenants' lives, together with those of his struggles to comprehend their plight, are themselves alone staggering indictments of the iron-heeled economic system that is crushing the southern countryside. It is precisely this ferocious fidelity to detail that Agee later finds in the best films depicting World War II; those details, rather than observations by a moralizing commentator or character, best communicate the film's message. Of *The Story of G. I. Joe*, Agee writes that in its purity and intensity the film is "as full an indictment of war as I ever expect to see," despite the fact that "nobody is accused, not even the enemy," and that "no remedy is indicated" for the war's horrors.[7]

Near the end of World War II, fearing a vengeful backlash against the defeated nations, Agee recommends that Americans watch the March of Time's *Report on Italy*, which he says portrays "enough suffering and unaccusable faces of human beings who happen to be Italians to blast the brains out of a script twice as stern as this one is, with its talk about 'the Italian penance.' If people of the peacemaking sort knew or cared in the least how to look at faces–or dared to–the exhibition of

---

[7] James Agee, Movie Column from the 15 September 1945 *Nation*, in *Agee on Film*, 163.

such films at the peace conference could supply more valuable evidence, and hope for the future, than anything else I can think of."[8]

Agee's praise of films that put a face on war and suffering looks back to his and Walker Evans's attempt in *Let Us Now Praise Famous Men* to put a face on the depleted world of the southern tenant farmer. But the connection between the combat films Agee reviewed during the war and *Let Us Now Praise Famous Men* extends beyond aesthetics, for Agee's commentary on southern tenantry is shaped by the same political issue undergirding these films: the conflict between democracy and fascism as highlighted by World War II. Indeed, despite his microscopic focus on the tenants' world and his own consciousness, Agee ultimately contextualizes that focus in terms of the European political crisis, underscoring a primary motive in the writing *Let Us Now Praise Famous Men*: Agee fears that the European conflict threatens to pull America away from the war that it should be fighting–a war closer to home, a war on poverty and against the exploitation of the poor.

During the time he was writing *Let Us Praise Famous Men*, from the late 1930s up through early 1941 (he made last-minute additions as late as April, 1941; the book appeared that September), Agee kept a close eye on political developments in Europe. While certainly no admirer of Hitler, Agee at the same time looked doubtfully upon the democratic nations that were lining up against him, ironically noting that at the same time these nations were publicly championing democracy, they were stomping on their own poor and lording over imperial empires. If fascist countries were authoritarian, the democratic nations were not all that different. "If I had better faith than I do in any of the 'democracies' themselves as humane nations I might be clearer in favor of war," Agee wrote to Father Flye in 1939; "as it is, I feel it is a rattlesnake-skunk choice, with the skunk of course considerably less deadly yet not so desirable around the house that I could back him with any favor."[9] He was also dubious about the Soviet Union, despite the fact that he frequently identified himself as a communist. Agee's professed communism, however, as his biographer has noted, was more emotional than ideological[10]; Agee was less a follower of Marx than a man appalled at the sufferings of humanity who looked favorably upon social systems that sought to end those sufferings. At the same time that he was expressing communist sympathies Agee was also voicing a profound anti-authoritarianism, sometimes even, as in a 1940 letter to Father Flye, identifying himself as an anarchist; he told Father Flye, furthermore, that if he weren't an anarchist, he would probably be "a left-wing conservative,"[11] an apt designation of Agee's deeply felt but terribly confused political positions when it came to the pragmatics of statecraft. Knowing full well the ideals in which he believed but less sure about how to implement them, Agee was far more effective attacking than constructing.

As the European crisis worsened, Agee fervently opposed American intervention, seeing the authoritarian menace at home, rather than abroad, as the gravest threat to American stability. *Let Us Now Praise Famous Men* takes aim at

---

[8] James Agee, Movie Column from the 24 February 1945 *Nation*, in *Agee on Film*, 133.

[9] James Agee, *Letters of James Agee to Father Flye* (New York: George Braziller, 1962), 113.

[10] Laurence Bergeen, *James Agee: A Life* (New York: Dutton, 1984), 193.

[11] Agee, *Letters to Father Flye*, 125.

this domestic threat, with Agee often configuring himself and the tenants as participants in a deadly war. Several times in the text he identifies himself as a spy, a designation suggesting not merely his role as observer of the tenants' lives, but more importantly his role as undercover double-agent in a time of conflict: once he began writing about his article for *Fortune* (which its publisher, Henry R. Luce, had once considered calling *Power*), Agee did what he could first to subvert the original assignment (he refused editorial demands that he configure his essay into conventional form), and then later, with the essay rejected, to expand the essay into a book that would subvert the very system which he himself, as a writer for *Fortune*, represented.

In his role as artist-as-spy in *Let Us Now Praise Famous Men*, Agee models himself broadly after André Gide's authorial positioning in *Travels in the Congo* (1929), Gide's influential travelogue exposing colonialist abuses in French West Africa.[12] In that book, Gide describes his and filmmaker Marc Allégre's journey to West Africa in 1926 while under hire by the French government to observe the working and living conditions in the French colonies. Keeping his official task secret during the travels, Gide found himself being drawn to the life and people of the native cultures, at the same time that he was growing increasingly appalled at the oppressive conditions enforced by colonial rule. As described in his book, Gide soon begins seeing himself as a spy undertaking important work that might end the abuses of colonialism; he hopes to publicize the humanity of the natives and the inhumanity of the system that enslaved them. After witnessing a particularly egregious punishment of rubber workers who did not meet their work quotas, Gide comments on his transformation into an activist: "When I accepted this mission, I failed to grasp at first what it was I was undertaking, what part I could play, how I could be useful. I understood it now and I am beginning to think my coming will not have been in vain."[13]

Agee shared Gide's activist vision, and, following Gide, he configures himself in *Let Us Now Praise Famous Men* as a spy who over time is drawn deeply and sympathetically into the world he is sent to observe and away from the world that has sent him on his mission. Indeed, Agee felt so close to Gide in this positioning that he tried, unsuccessfully it turned out, not to read any of *Travels in the Congo* while working on *Let Us Now Praise Famous Men*, fearing that Gide's book would stifle his own creativity.[14] In the end, Agee probably need not have worried so much,

---

[12] When translated into English, Gide's two books on his African journey, *Voyage au Congo* (1927) and *Le retour du Tchad* (1928), were published as one volume with the title *Travels in the Congo*. See: Andre Gide, *Travels in the Congo*, trans. Dorothy Bussy (New York: Knopf, 1929).

[13] Gide, *Travels in the Congo*, 71.

[14] After one occasion of returning to *Travels in the Congo*, Agee wrote in his journal: "With about one sentence in every two I knew the mistake I was making [and that] I was doing wrong, for I was disturbed as you are bound to be when you find even minute aspects of your mind, and methods, and technical ideas, anticipated or cut across. I must not touch this book again until I have finished mine, though my own thinking would in some obvious respects gain by it." After another failure of will, he commented: "I have thought of turning parts of the Congo into my own kind. Maybe I will try it." See: Michael A. Lofaro and Hugh Davis,

for even though he was clearly inspired by both Gide's stance as responsive, reformist narrator torn between conflicting loyalties, *Let Us Now Praise Famous Men* is quite different from *Travels in the Congo* in its specific narrative methods. Gide structures his text largely as a conventional travelogue that includes straightforward political commentary inserted at key points, precisely the type of commentary (as we have seen) that Agee generally eschews. Agee's text, in contrast, is anything but straightforward conventional travelogue, following the flow of Agee's fevered thoughts rather than being shaped by conventional structure. Moreover, rather than being direct, Agee's political commentary circulates in and out of Agee's narrative, as much a work of disguise as Agee's own role as spy.

As author/spy, Agee hopes to insinuate his text within the reader's consciousness, where it will do its subversive work. In a stunning description, Agee equates the text's penetration of the reader–and the consciousness-clearing effects of that penetration–with what he describes as the mind-collapsing and then mind-expanding experience of listening to loud music:

> Get a radio or a phonograph capable of the most extreme loudness possible, and sit down to listen to a performance of Beethoven's Seventh Symphony or of Schubert's C-Major Symphony. But I don't mean just sit down and listen. I mean this: Turn it on as loud as you can get it. Then get down on the floor and jam your ear as close into the loudspeaker as you can get it and stay there, breathing as lightly as possible, and not moving, and neither eating nor smoking nor drinking. Concentrate everything you can into your hearing and into your body. You won't hear it nicely. If it hurts you, be glad of it. As near as you will ever get, you are inside the music; not only inside it, you are it; your body is no longer your shape and substance, it is the shape and substance of the music.
>
> Is what you hear pretty? or beautiful? or legal? or acceptable in polite or any other society? It is beyond any calculation savage and dangerous and murderous to all equilibrium in human life as human life is; and nothing can equal the rape it does on all that death; nothing except anything, anything in existence or dream, perceived anywhere remotely toward its true dimension.
> (15-16)

Nowhere else are the violent extremes of Agee's narrative strategy made more clear, with Agee imagining the reader being penetrated–raped–by the text and emerging from that violation (which Agee configures as an explosive self- and world-destroying orgasm, the reader becoming one with the text) to turn that violence back upon the death-dealing forces of the world (which elsewhere Agee makes clear is the modern authoritarian state).

Crucial to Agee's strategy of penetrating and transfiguring the reader is his narrative tactic of drawing the reader into sympathy with the tenants while simultaneously revealing the tenants' exploitation and suffering at the hands of America's economic and political system. Perhaps the most striking image Agee

---

eds., *James Agee Rediscovered: The Journals of Let Us Now Praise Famous Men and Other New Manuscripts* (Knoxville: University of Tennessee Press, 2005), 82, 103.

uses to suggest the tenants' locked-down and -away lives is the inescapable bubble which encloses them. This globular confinement begins at birth, indeed even before birth, with Agee describing the conception of a tenant child as "a crucifixion of cell and whiplashed sperm: whose creature is our center, our nerve we spoke of; in this instant already his globe is rounded upon him and is his prison, which might have been his kingdom" (103). Once the child is conceived, the crippling of the developing consciousness begins; speaking of the damage inflicted upon the tenants, Agee writes that their "intellects died before they were born; they hang behind their eyes like fetuses in alcohol" (305). From the protective womb, the already-crushed baby emerges into a "sutureless globe" (104) pressed in upon by "poisons, monsters, all shapes of ruin, smiling jaws of traps" and "wherein human hope is buried alive, the power and blindness, stiffness and helplessness of habituation, of acceptance, of resignation so totally deep it has sailed beyond memory of resignation or thought of other possibility: a benumbing, freezing, a paralysis, a turning to stone, merciful in the middle of all that storm of torture, relatively resistant of much further keenness of harm, but always in measure of that petrifaction obtuséd ten times over against, hope, possibility, cure" (106).

Agee's imprisoning globe suggests the authoritarian state's overwhelming and omnipresent power to control its citizens, a power which Agee characterizes at one point as "silent, insinuous, and masked" (105) and against which the tenants are utterly helpless. Agee underscores both the state's power and the tenants' helplessness in his descriptions of the process of socialization–actually of exclusion– that tenant children undergo. As Lillian Smith would later do in *Killers of the Dream* (1949), Agee describes the socialization of southern children–in his specific case, of children of tenants–as a never-ending dance lesson that numbs the mind and cripples the body. The children dance in "grave mutations" (324), a characterization suggesting both the severity of the lessons and the death-in-life routine the dancers follow. "They are made into hopeless and helpless cripples," Agee writes of tenant children, "capable exactly and no more of doing what will keep them alive: by no means so well equipped as domestic and free animals" (306).

Using stark images that recall wartime propaganda posters from World War I and the Spanish Civil War, Agee implicitly urges his readers to join him in his war against the authoritarian system that was destroying tenant farmers and, by implication, all of America's poor. At one point, Agee portrays the tenants as air war victims, "bombarded, pierced, destroyed" (110). At another, he pictures the defenseless tenant cowering before "his grinning grincing machinearmed scorcheyed lovetaloned raving foes" (104). And at another, he describes the farmers as prisoners of war. "On this vast continental sorrowful clay it is I see you," Agee writes, "encamped, imprisoned, each in your pitiably decorated little unowned ship of home, ten million, patient, ignorant, grievous, ruined, so inextricably trapped, captured, guarded" (391-392).

Despite all the destruction and suffering that Agee describes, and despite the largely tragic tone of the text, Agee nonetheless looks forward to a more hopeful future, at one point describing the day when the forces of oppression will be defeated by the power of the world's enlightened people. "On the stone of this planet," he writes, addressing here specifically the tenants and more generally all of the oppressed, "there is a marching and resonance of rescuing feet which shall at length all dangers braved, all armies cut through, past, deliver you freedom, joy, health, knowledge, like an enduring sunlight: and not to you alone, whose helpless hearts have been waiting and listening since the human world began, but to us all, those lovable and those hateful all alike" (392). The forces liberating the southern poor, Agee suggests, will be made up of people like the narrator (and, Agee hopes, the newly enlightened readers) of *Let Us Now Praise Famous Men*, people agonizingly aware both of the individual humanity of the poor and of their own complicity in the poor's sufferings at the hands of an increasingly brutal authoritarian society. These liberators, returning to Agee's words on Joyce, will not represent "the uncreated conscience of the race," but instead the "created conscience of the race," forged by the complicated workings of Agee's propaganda–propaganda "whose constant effort is to clarify rather than merely simplify"–that undergirds *Let Us Now Praise Famous Men*.

"Let us now praise famous men, and our fathers that begat us" begins the Scripture with which Agee closes his text. Agee's famous men are not America's leaders who in 1941 were readying themselves for America's entrance into the European war, but its everyday folk whose lives would continue to be destroyed if America turned its eyes exclusively to European oppression while remaining blind to the oppression within its own borders. That's what Agee wants his readers to see, that's the thrust behind what he characterized as the "deep stealthfulness" (137) of *Let Us Now Praise Famous Men*. And besides showing his readers where to look, Agee's propaganda attempts to show them how to look, how to purify their vision so that they too could see with the clarity of sight that the photographs by Walker Evans exhibited. The opening lines from the poem addressed to Evans, which begins book two of *Let Us Now Praise Famous Men*, say it better than I can: "Against time and the damages of the brain / Sharpen and calibrate."

PROGRESS THROUGH RAYON:
THE NEDERLANDSE KUNSTZIJDEFABRIEK IN HOMINY VALLEY 1928-1940

Anneke Leenhouts

The history of the textile industry in the U.S. South, in particular its rapid expansion in the early twentieth century, has been well documented in studies such as George B. Tindall's *The Emergence of the New South*, and many more specialist works. The living and working conditions of the textile mill worker have likewise been the subject of wide-ranging attention, with W. J. Cash's descriptions of the "lintheads" in *The Mind of the South* remaining the most memorable. The following paper examines a hitherto largely overlooked Dutch contribution to North Carolina's textile industry, the building of the American Enka plant near Asheville by the Nederlandse Kunstzijdefabriek, and shows that its labor relations and social policies were less a copy of those prevailing at neighboring plants than based on tried and tested conditions in the Netherlands.[1]

In September 1928 plans were announced by the American Enka Corporation to build a rayon manufacturing plant on 2,000 acres in Hominy Valley, Buncombe County, some seven miles west of Asheville, North Carolina. The American Enka Corporation, or American Enka as it came to be known, was incorporated in May of 1928 by the Dutch limited liability company the Nederlandse Kunstzijdefabriek (the Netherlands artificial silk company), and indeed drew its name from the way its initials, NK, are pronounced in Dutch. The commercial production of artificial silk, or rayon as it is more commonly known, had started around 1900. The Nederlandse Kunstzijdefabriek was founded in 1911 by Dr. J.C. Hartogs, a Dutch chemist who had gained his practical experience at Samuel Courtaulds' manufacturing plant in Coventry, which had been spinning viscose-rayon yarn since 1905. Hartogs' first plant, in Arnhem, started production in 1913 with sixty employees, but by 1915 it was producing 72,000 kilograms of rayon, and by 1916 the company was turning a profit. The company benefited both from the greatly increased demand for rayon brought on by World War I and from the Netherlands' neutral stance during the conflict: a large part of the production was shipped to nearby Germany. The company was listed on the Dutch stock exchange in 1918 and continued to expand and prosper, paying out an average dividend of 26 percent between 1918 and 1926. In 1919 work started on the construction of a much larger facility in Ede, some 20 kilometers to the north of Arnhem. Ede, a town of some 5,000 inhabitants, provided soft water, cheap land, and the attraction of a large potential workforce to be drawn from the surrounding farm areas. By 1928 the company was looking abroad for further expansion, taking shares in companies in France, Italy, and the United Kingdom, and sending a group of experts on a tour of the U.S. to look at suitable

---

[1] See George B. Tindall, *The Emergence of the New South, 1913-1945* (1967; rpt. Baton Rouge: Louisiana State University Press, 1970), 70-110, 318-353, and W. J. Cash, *The Mind of the South* (1941; rpt. Harmondsworth: Penguin Books, 1973), 351-435.

sites there.[2] Building a plant in the U.S. was intended to counter growing American trade protectionism, which was leading to a decrease in the importation of rayon into the U.S., and in this the Nederlandse Kunstzijdefabriek may well have followed the example of the German Bemberg and Glanzstoff companies, which established American subsidiaries in Elizabethton, Tennessee, in 1926 and 1928, respectively.[3]

As in the case of Ede, which had won out over other potential sites in the Netherlands by selling land for the plant at the give-away price of Dutch 10 cents per square meter, the Nederlandse Kunstzijdefabriek drove a hard bargain before settling in western North Carolina. The Asheville area was one of six shortlisted after a first tour of inspection in the U.S., and the company negotiated for four months with Asheville's Chamber of Commerce and city leaders to have its demands met. When the contract was signed on September 22, 1928, the city of Asheville thus agreed to take full responsibility for the plant's acquisition and building even though it was to be located west of the city limits in Buncombe County.

To the Nederlandse Kunstzijdefabriek the main attractions of the Asheville area were its readily available pure, iron-free water and other natural resources, the proximity of the Southern Railway's Murphy Branch for the transportation of coal, wood pulp, sulfuric acid, and other raw materials required for the production of rayon to the plant and shipment of the finished product to textile mills for processing into clothes and hosiery, a temperate climate highly suited to the process of viscose-rayon production, and above all the presence of a labor force used to low wages. To Asheville's city leaders, faced with collapsing property values and the decline of the tourist industry as the depression took hold, signing the contract for the American Enka plant represented an initial outlay of sixteen million dollars by the Dutch investors, the greater part of which would be spent employing local contractors and construction workers working with locally bought materials.[4] In addition, the Chamber of Commerce hoped that, in the words of its president, American Enka would "call the attention of the industry world to the idea that Asheville and western North Carolina should be considered by any and all plants contemplating a change in location."[5] For this reason, it was stressed that average wages in Ashville were substantially lower than in most other places, reportedly because the city's cost of living was also lower, while at the same time American Enka's potential mill workers were claimed by the *Charlotte Observer* to be the best as they were neither

---

[2] All information about the Nederlandse Kunstzijdefabriek taken from http://www.enka-ede.com/kunstzijde-pagina.htm.

[3] Tindall, *New South*, 342.

[4] All data on the building of the American Enka plant taken from "The Story of American Enka: When the Dutch choose the South," http://southern.railfan.net/ties/1961/61-10/enka.html and Jennifer Chapman, "Rural to Modern: The Shift From Agriculture To Industry In The Enka Community And The Enka Plant's Uniqueness In Its Concern For Their Women Employees," senior history thesis, University of North Carolina at Asheville, 2003, unpaginated. According to W.J. Cash, Asheville at the time of the Enka negotiations "was in bankruptcy." (Cash, *Mind*, 367). As regards the benefits for local business, the website of David Steel Construction, an Asheville based company, lists work on the American Enka plant as one of its first large projects (http://www.davesteel.com).

[5] http://southern.railfan.net/ties/1961/61-10/enka.html

the "ignorant and radical" immigrant worker of the North nor the "incapable Negro" of the South, but instead were "intelligent, steady, home-loving, and pure-blooded."[6] Neither the boosterism nor the claims of racial purity were out of the ordinary, as Tindall has comprehensively shown in *The Emergence of the New South*. According to Tindall, "All through the Piedmont Crescent promoters were seeking new mills. Gaston County, North Carolina, adopted the slogan 'Organize a mill a week.' It was magnificently unrealistic, but the county had 105 mills by 1923 and in 1929 was the leading textile county in the South, third in the nation."[7] Similarly, low wages and the limitless supply of poor white farmers and their families prepared to work without complaint were stressed at every opportunity, to the point where they had become "one of the cherished Southern traditions, the great magnet for outside capital, the foundation of industrial growth."[8] Indeed, the southern textile barons could be said to have adopted their own version of the Anglo-Saxon myth of the South, one in which by offering "sanctuary to the impoverished whites of the farms and mountain coves . . . they had brought salvation to the purest stock of native Americans."[9]

In any case, it is tempting to say that American boosterism and Dutch business acumen combined to build what was to become the largest rayon plant in the world in Hominy Valley. In the company's opening balance sheet in 1928, the American Enka Corporation lists its assets as $15,295,000 in cash, with $705,000 declared for preliminary expenses and patents "pro memory." There had been 500,000 shares without par value authorized and 400,000 issued, bringing the company's total assets to $16,000,000.[10] In the Profit and Loss Statement of the American Enka Corporation for 1933, the President of the Corporation, F.H. Fentener van Vlissingen, announced a net profit for that year of $1,062,620 and informed the stockholders that "This is the first year since your Company began operations in the fall of 1929 that the results can be said to be satisfactory. The net earnings this year practically covered the total accumulated losses of the past four years while the company was being organized and established. During 1933 there was a substantial increase in the consumption of Rayon and Synthetic yarns and your Company increased its production by reason of certain changes and installation of new equipment."[11] The statement adds that the directors "declared a first dividend on the common stock of twenty-five cents per share, payable on April second, 1934," and "in compliance with the N.R.A. Code of Fair Competition for the Rayon and Synthetic Yarn Industry, your Company has added a considerable number of employees to its pay roll." The statement also noted that "the properties of the company were fully maintained throughout the year and a substantial sum was

---

[6] C.R. Sumner, "Largest Plant In World For Manufacture Of Rayon Is Located At Asheville," *Charlotte Observer*, 18 November 1928.

[7] Tindall, *New South*, 75.

[8] Ibid., 318.

[9] Ibid., 76.

[10] American Enka Corporation, *Opening Balance Sheet as of May 2, 1928* (June 18, 1928), Archives of Akzo Nobel Nederland B.V., Arnhem, the Netherlands.

[11] *Statement to the Stockholders of American Enka Corporation* for 1933, Archives of Akzo Nobel Nederland B.V.

expended for the improvement of its product and for supplementing manufacturing facilities."[12] Net profits for 1934 were considerably lower, amounting to only $151,089, due to a price reduction in May of 10 cents per pound and the need during the last half of 1934 to rebuild entirely the spinning equipment in order to achieve a higher product standard. No dividend was announced, but the overall tone continued to be optimistic, for, in the President's words: "All of these changes have been completed, the last machine being put into operation in January of this year and we trust that we can soon return again to a more satisfactory cost with a greatly improved product."[13] In 1935, despite the adverse effect on earnings of average lower prices over the year and the effort of achieving a higher standard of quality with the rebuilt spinning equipment, net profits passed the $500,000 dollar level again at $556,215 and in 1936 they came to $2,092,062, with dividends totalling five dollars per share. An additional investment in plant and equipment to further increase American Enka's production was also authorized. In the Statement for 1937, this investment is listed as "approximately $3,300,000 . . . spent for machinery and buildings to improve the quality of our product and carry forward the expansion programs authorized. . . ."[14] Expansion continued throughout 1938, with a further $1,980,000 spent, and despite a decline in the volume of rayon sales, which resulted in a curtailment of production in the industry generally, American Enka actually managed to ship a slightly larger volume in pounds in 1938 than it did in 1937. Nineteen forty proved another highly profitable year, when once again a five dollar dividend was paid out, this despite a "rather disastrous flood" on August 30, which resulted in a direct flood loss of $427,266 in addition to the loss of ten days of plant production. The Statement for 1941 observed that "Selling prices approved by the Government exist throughout the Industry" and refused to be drawn on future productivity "by reason of shortage of materials, equipment, supplies or transportation that would result solely from war developments."[15] However, despite government restrictions, American Enka continued in profit during the war years and continued to pay out dividends.

Clearly then, American Enka quickly became a profitable enterprise and remained one throughout the 1930s despite regular price reductions and production curtailments. The annual reports almost invariably speak of investment in new buildings and machinery, new employees added to the payroll, and the expectation of further increases in production. Shareholders obviously benefited from their investment, but it is equally obvious that American Enka brought material advantages to the surrounding area. As an immediate effect of the establishment of the American Enka plant, the community of Hominy acquired improved sanitary water and sewer treatment facilities, had its main road paved, and saw additional telephone lines installed. A station was built on the Southern Rail Road to provide

---

[12] Ibid.

[13] *Statement to the Stockholders of the American Enka Corporation* for 1934, Archives of Akzo Nobel Nederland B.V.

[14] *Statement to the Stockholders of the American Enka Corporation* for 1937, Archives of Akzo Nobel Nederland B.V.

[15] *Statement to the Stockholders of the American Enka Corporation* for 1941, Archives of Akzo Nobel Nederland B.V.

regular services to and from Asheville and the city's bus line was extended.[16] In due course the school system expanded to deal with the influx of new students and a new grammar school was built.

Moreover, within a year of the plant's opening, American Enka was building mill houses within walking distance of the plant to accommodate its increasing workforce. In building what was to become known as Enka Village, American Enka was following a common trend in the Carolinas. According to Tindall, "three quarters or more of the Southern textile workers lived in mill villages," and although he states that "by the late 1920s most company-owned homes were provided with lights, water, and inside toilets, while a smaller percentage even had fully equipped bathrooms,"[17] conditions varied widely. Thus W.J. Cash could write in 1941 that "the factory housing of Gastonia . . . to this day remains, very largely a slum" and Jonathan Daniels, travelling the South in 1937, commented on how the Cannon family in their company town of Kannapolis created "one pretty little park about the mill offices and left the village itself an ugly community of dirty clapboard and asphalt shingle."[18] At the bottom end of the scale were the Baldwin and Clinchfield mill villages in Marion, North Carolina, where "dilapidated millhouses, perched on brick pillars, lacked either running water or sewerage, and filth overflowed from outside privies."[19]

Whether American Enka looked at the standards or, in the case of nearby Marion, non-standards to which other Carolina mill villages were built is not clear. What does appear certain is that the company drew on the experiences of its Dutch parent company in Ede, which had built 330 homes for its workers near the plant between 1921 and 1925. The houses in Ede were built along the garden village model and spacious for their day, some having as many as five bedrooms to attract the large families the company preferred to hire. All had sizeable gardens to enable the workforce of former farm workers to grow their own potatoes and other vegetables. The tenants were provided with free running water from the factory and partial sewerage was installed. Initial rents ranged from FL 4.25 to FL 8.00 a month, at a time when weekly wages for adult male workers at the plant were about FL 18.00. The Nederlandse Kunstzijdefabriek used its quality housing to attract reliable, preferably large, working families and keep them in its employ.

American Enka practiced a similar policy. The houses in Enka Village were generous in size and would have been among the better worker accommodation on offer in the region: all had indoor plumbing, and the kitchens were equipped with electric stoves. These were modern conveniences generally absent from the small farms from which many of the workers were drawn and no doubt used as an inducement by management in its selection of suitable workers. Enka Village had a police force, a fire department shared with the plant, and a hospital with an operating room and two nurses on duty at all time, all paid for by the company. There was no company store with its attendant sharp practices, but businessmen, who considered

---

[16] *Asheville Citizen Times*, 23 September 1928.

[17] Tindall, *New South*, 325.

[18] Cash, *Mind*, 279; Jonathan Daniels, *A Southerner Discovers the South* (New York: MacMillan, 1938), 30.

[19] Tindall, *New South*, 347.

the Enka workforce an attractive customer base, opened various small shops and restaurants.

American Enka comes out favorably in terms of its welfare work. Tindall states that "only a few of the largest mills had extensive programs" and quotes Harriet Herring's 1926 study of 322 North Carolina plants, "only 49 [of which, for instance] employed community workers, and only 40 had group insurance plans."[20] American Enka, again following the example of its parent company in Ede, employed a welfare nurse to deal with sanitation and health issues, including regular inspections of the homes in Enka Village. In 1933 the Enka Credit Union was set up as "a not-for-profit organization to serve the financial needs of American Enka employees."[21] Reading was promoted through the funding of a library with over 2,000 books for children and adults; the building was also used for evening classes on such practical subjects as shorthand, which were offered free of charge to all interested employees.[22] American Enka also emulated its parent company's attempts at promoting a company spirit through sports and social activities and a company newspaper. The monthly *Enka Voice* was published from April 1930 and along with the employees' personal announcements of marriages, births, deaths, etc. provided advice by the editors on proper grammar (one lesson read "AIN'T—not an accepted word, say `I am not') and suitable reading matter for children. In the Netherlands a large number of Enka social clubs were founded between 1925 and 1927, including gymnastics, cycling, and billiards clubs, a dramatic society, a brass band, and a male choir. In North Carolina, the Enka Athletic Association was formed, which encouraged male and female employees to play volleyball, basketball, baseball, and softball on the plant's grounds. Opened in 1930 the Enka Country Club, on the shore of Beaver Lake, would admit workers for a $5.00 fee per quarter. The club offered tennis courts, a boathouse, a beach for sunbathing, and a diving pier. By 1938, the Athletic Association had expanded to include bowling, an indoor rifle range, and a dramatics club that staged plays and shows in the local school's auditorium. According to Mary Roberts, a forty-year Enka employee interviewed by Chapman, the women's basketball team "was good for many years" and an evident source of pride to the female employees.[23]

In the Carolina textiles industry the legally permitted age for factory work by 1931 was fourteen for day work and sixteen for night shifts, and workers tended to be hired on the understanding that all grown members of their families should work. At American Enka, as at its Dutch parent company, females formed the majority of the workforce. Women's softer, smaller hands were deemed more suited to changing cones on spinning machines and handling and sorting rayon yarns. Women's pay scales were, as a rule, also lower than men's. Out of 2,000 employees in Ede in 1920, some 1,350 were girls, and families with many daughters were given preferential treatment in regard to company-owned housing. According to the

---

[20] Tindall, 327; Harriet L. Herring, *Welfare Work in Mill Villages: The Story of Extra-Mill Activities in North Carolina* (Chapel Hill: University of North Carolina Press, 1929), 27-31, quoted in Tindall, 327 .

[21] See the Enka Community Credit Union website, www.enkacu.com.

[22] Chapman, "Rural to Modern."

[23] Ibid.

Asheville Citizen Times, the American Enka plant's "initial payroll would consist of two-thirds women and one-third men."[24] Jennifer Chapman notes in her senior history thesis that American Enka, unlike many American companies, was prepared to promote women to supervisory positions and pay them the same as male supervisors. A considerable number of women reached such positions.[25]

Although sources are scarce and company records scant, relations between the workforce and American Enka's initially Dutch management seem to have been fairly good. American Enka's workers did not take part in the great textile strike of 1934, which saw an estimated 20,000 out of 25,000 mill workers in nearby Gaston County participate and involved as much as two-thirds of the South's textile workers. The company's workforce did not join the United Textile Workers Union until 1939. American Enka's continued expansion and general profitability throughout the 1930s is another indicator of stable labor relations. What is harder to establish, is the extent to which American Enka's Dutch style of management was responsible for this stability or, at any rate, contributed to it. American Enka provided good-quality housing, and electric stoves and indoor plumbing that unquestionably made life easier for working women, but the company also employed a welfare nurse to check that homes were properly kept, which could be interpreted as interference in employees' personal lives and setting rules and regulations well beyond the workplace. The fully equipped hospital in Enka Village might suggest potentially dangerous working conditions. By funding the library and its contents, American Enka could be said to have controlled what all but its most independent-minded workers and their families read. The *Enka Voice* published workers' contributions only if they were positive in tone. A country club membership of five dollars per quarter probably restricted membership along intended lines. Then again, it could be argued that children reading adaptations of the classics with the encouragement of the *Enka Voice* on the grounds that "As a rule the best literature is that which has stood the test of time,"[26] is far better than children not being encouraged to read at all. Nor is there much to be said against promoting the use of proper English and providing employees with greater opportunities in the form of night classes. There is no mention in the annual reports of any serious accidents other than the flooding of 1940. By contemporary standards, the country club was by no means elitist, with everybody free, in theory, to join. Free playing fields were provided on site, and the company actively sponsored various teams, including women's teams. In an age of automobile ownership and consequent easy labor mobility, obituaries in the Asheville and Charlotte newspapers frequently mention that the deceased was employed by American Enka for thirty years or more. In short, Dutch management practiced a form of paternalism that was imported at least as much as it derived from southern industrial tradition, but was by no means the worse for that. Rayon brought progress to a largely deprived area, and the benefits by and large offset any drawbacks.

---

[24] *Asheville Citizen Times*, 23 September 1928.
[25] Chapman, "Rural to Modern."
[26] "Books for Children," *Enka Voice*, April 1930, 9.

PART II FIGHTING FOR RIGHTS

JUNETEENTH:
THE EVOLUTION OF AN EMANCIPATION CELEBRATION

Elizabeth Hayes Turner

In 2005 in the nation's capital, observers came together to celebrate the 140th anniversary of what one journalist has called "an obscure Texas celebration." Others are calling it a "National Freedom Day," the "Second Emancipation," "America's Second Independence Day," and "Juneteenth Independence Day." Going global, Elissa Russell, an African American teacher living in Taiwan, made sure that Juneteenth would be celebrated there for the second year in a row. Juneteenth festivities were held that year in France, Germany, Spain, England, Italy, Czech Republic, Israel, Kuwait, Japan, South Korea, Ghana, Trinidad, Barbados, Honduras, Puerto Rico, and Guam. In the United States, supporters are petitioning Congress to have Juneteenth declared a national holiday. Celebrations have spread from Alaska to Florida, from California to Delaware. Sixteen states have granted the nineteenth of June state holiday observance status; ten states have proclaimed legislative or gubernatorial resolutions in favor of Juneteenth. In 1997, Congress at the instigation of two Republicans (one of them Trent Lott of Mississippi), "recognized Juneteenth as Independence Day for Americans of African Descent." Two states, Texas and Oklahoma, have made the nineteenth of June a state (paid leave) holiday. In Galveston and on Capitol Hill in Austin bronze Juneteenth monuments are scheduled to be unveiled. In 2005, in over 200 Texas cities, small towns, and neighborhoods, Juneteenth parades, picnics, barbecues, worship services, and all kinds of music, theater, and cultural events joyfully unfolded.[1]

---

[1] Julia Moskin, "An Obscure Texas Celebration Makes Its Way Across the U.S." *New York Times*, 18 June 2004. Farai Chideya, "Interview: Elissa Russell Explains How Taiwan's Juneteenth Celebration Helps Advance Understanding of Black Culture," National Public Radio broadcast, transcript, 16 June 2005, internet, http://nl.newsbank.com/nl-search/we/ Archives?p_action=doc&p_docid=10BBE3E587288 . . . , accessed 10 August 2005. Tavis Smiley, "Interview: Pam Tilley and Al Edwards on the Juneteenth Celebrations in Texas," National Public Radio Broadcast, transcript, 19 June 2003, internet, http://nlnewsbank.com/nl-search/we/Archives?paction=doc&p_docid=0FBC83120A045 . . . , accessed 10 August 2005. Liane Hansen and Adam Hochberg, "Profile: Historical Sites in Several States Offering a More Realistic Portrayal of Slavery and Plantation Life," National Public Radio Broadcast, transcript, 19 June 2005, internet, http://nl.newsbank.com/nlsearch/we/Archives?p_action =doc&p_docid=10ADB47CD9AB, accessed 10 August 2005. The sixteen states that recognize Juneteenth as a state holiday observance are: Alaska, Arkansas, California, Connecticut, Delaware, Florida, Idaho, Illinois, Iowa, Kentucky, Louisiana, Michigan, Missouri, New Jersey, New York, and Wyoming, as well as Washington D.C. The ten states that have recognized Juneteenth through state assembly or gubernatorial resolutions are: Oregon, South Dakota, Mississippi, Massachusetts, Pennsylvania, Montana, Wisconsin, Maryland, Virginia, and Colorado. In 1997, Congress passed a historic resolution through *Senate Joint Resolution 11* and *House Joint Resolution 56*, recognizing the "19th of June as Juneteenth Independence Day in America." http://www.19thofjune.com/calendar/index.html, accessed 10 January 2005. Sponsors of the joint congressional resolution were Senator Trent Lott (R. MS) and Representative J. C. Watts (R. OK). On June 7, 1979, the 66th Texas

It was June 19, 1865 when 250,000 Texas slaves—the last within the Confederacy—learned of their freedom via Union soldiers. Despite the tardy news, Juneteenth came to symbolize the emancipation of an entire people after centuries of slavery. Of course, many slaves had been freed earlier than 1865—much earlier—in the long and painful history of slavery. And there were other emancipation day celebrations, but Juneteenth has surfaced to take national stage and is emerging as the *nation's* emancipation day celebration.[2]

---

legislature designated June 19 as "Emancipation Day in Texas," and in 1980 Juneteenth became a legal state holiday. Avis Thomas-Lester, "For Many, Today is Independence Day," *Washington Post*, 18 June 2005. Linda Wheeler, "Juneteenth Supporters to Lobby Here," *Washington Post*, 17 June 2000. Liane Hansen, "Commentary: African-Americans Should Look to Jewish High Holy Days for an Example of How to Celebrate Juneteenth," National Public Radio broadcast transcript, 19 June 2002, http://nl.newsbank.com/nlsearchwe/Archives ?paction =doc&pdocid =0F827400B 8830. . . , accessed 10 August 2005. Ronald V. Myers, Sr. to President George W. Bush, 10 July 2005, National Juneteenth Observance Foundation, National Juneteenth Christian Leadership Council, internet, http://www.juneteenth. us/bush.html, accessed 8 August 2005. For Texas legislation regarding a Juneteenth monument on state capitol grounds see Acts 1997, 75th Leg., ch. 563,§ 1, effective September 1, 1997. The purpose of the state legislation is to "coordinate state and local activities relating to the . . . celebration of Juneteenth; . . . and to establish a Juneteenth memorial monument on the grounds of the State Capitol. . . ." Government Code: Chapter 448: Texas Emancipation Juneteenth Cultural and Historical Commission. Bids were sent forth by the State Preservation Board, with instructions that the monument's granite base was to be constructed and ready for the placement of bronze sculptures by May 20, 2005; *Houston Chronicle*, 12 June 2003. Plans had already been made for a monument to be placed at Ashton Villa in Galveston, the alleged site of the reading of General Orders No. 3, proclaiming the end of slavery; *Houston Chronicle*, 25 September 2003, 10, 17 June 2004.

[2] For histories of northern antebellum emancipation celebrations see Shane White "'It Was a Proud Day': African Americans, Festivals, and Parades in the North, 1741-1834." *Journal of American History* 81 (June l994): 13-50. For emancipation celebrations in other southern states see Kathleen Ann Clark, *Defining Moments: African American Commemoration and Political Culture in the South, 1863-1913* (Chapel Hill: University of North Carolina Press, 2005). For a sociological perspective on freedom celebrations see William H. Wiggins, Jr., *O Freedom! Afro-American Emancipation Celebrations* (Knoxville: University of Tennessee Press, 1987). For a discussion of symbolic protest as a vital part of African American identity see James Oliver Horton, *Free People of Color: Inside the African American Community* (Washington: Smithsonian Institution Press, l993), 164. See also Kathleen Clark, "Celebrating Freedom: Emancipation Day Celebrations and African American Memory in the Early Reconstruction South," in W. Fitzhugh Brundage, ed., *Where These Memories Grow: History, Memory, and Southern Identity* (Chapel Hill: University of North Carolina Press, 2000), 107-32; and W. Fitzhugh Brundage, "Whispering Consolation to Generations Unborn: Black Memory in the Era of Jim Crow," in Winfred B. Moore Jr., Kyle S. Sinisi, and David H. White Jr., eds., *Warm Ashes: Issues in Southern History at the Dawn of the Twenty-First Century* (Columbia: University of South Carolina Press, 2003), 341-56. In the years before the Civil War, blacks held emancipation parades and festivals in northern cities even as blacks continued in bondage in southern states. For a time after the Civil War, January 1, the day the Emancipation Proclamation took effect in 1863, seemed to captivate liberation enthusiasts. For others April 16, (1862), the day slavery ended in the District of Columbia, brought forth freedom festivities.

Curiously, forty years ago, blacks struggled to keep Juneteenth celebrations alive in cities across Texas. So why has this regional event become today the nation's premier emancipation day? And has this critical historical moment, wherein all the nation's slaves were finally freed, taken on an altogether different meaning in the twenty-first century? These are the central questions addressed in this chapter. Juneteenth evolved through five discrete stages. Its earliest manifestations came in the form of community gatherings with worship services, parades, addresses, recitations, songs, recreation, and barbecue suppers. Former slaves and Union soldiers were honored as the newer generations voiced their connection to a bonded past and to notions of freedom. These celebrations set the stage for Juneteenth festivities in the years to come and were filled with allegorical symbols both familiar and powerful.

The second stage emerged by 1919, when segregation laws were firmly in place and a rising nativism engulfed the country. Juneteenth festivities were marginalized by white city officials even as celebrants combined messages of freedom with rights of citizenship. In the years between the two world wars, Juneteenth became more commercialized, an occasion for advertisers to sell clothing and for theme parks, dance halls, and night clubs to entice revelers. As the headlines proclaimed slow but measured progress for blacks in education, civil rights, and economics, the pace frustrated black leaders who continued to editorialize the meaning of emancipation, heroism in combat, and full rights of citizenship while recognizing its illusive reality in the face of rising racism, Ku Klux Klan terrorism, and discrimination in New Deal agencies and war-time jobs,

During the 1960s—Juneteenth's third phase—publicly announced celebrations virtually disappeared behind headlines that heralded on-going freedom struggles. Juneteenth's decline came as the result of unrealized expectations from the partial success of *Smith* vs. *Alwright, Brown*, the Montgomery Bus Boycott, and lunch-counter sit-ins. Although victorious in gaining a Civil Rights Act in 1964 and a Voting Rights in 1965, the end to discrimination was not at hand as white Americans acted with reprisals and violence. Juneteenth celebrations became synonymous with diminished hopes, reminding African Americans of segregated parades and festivities based on disappointment.

Juneteenth in its fourth stage returned in the 1970s, but its resurrection was more than the celebration of a victory by a repressed and long suffering people. Juneteenth, as it evolved in the past thirty years, has managed to transcend racial barriers; whites, blacks, Asians, Mexican Americans now participate together. The bond, so long recognized as a true and indigenous cultural contribution is African American culture, music, and art. Jazz and blues concerts swell the programs of Juneteenth festivities, carrying the idea of freedom—and reconciliation—on the sound waves of black artists. To be sure, the subject of slavery and emancipation are there, but they are muted compared to the celebration of African American talents, heritage, and culture. It is this shift from the painful subject of historical bondage to black cultural roots that has brought Juneteenth to a wider audience with a universal message.

In the years since 1979, another aspect of Juneteenth's evolution has emerged, contributing to its politicization. The result of the civil rights movement is apparent in state houses and in the U.S. Congress today. The push to create the commemoration of Juneteenth as a state and national holiday has been driven by politicians who see the chance to honor the past and in the process gain the good will of voters.

The story of this evolutionary path began when Major General Gordon Granger, Union commander of the Department of Texas on June 19, 1865, read General Orders No. 3 from a balcony in Galveston. His orders came as a proclamation from the "Executive of the United States" that read in part "the people are informed . . . that all slaves are free. This involves an absolute equality of personal rights and rights of property, between former masters and slaves."[3] In many quarters jubilation erupted. It was an event that marked a profound change for a people whose lives had been supervised, challenged, and restricted. Juneteenth became for freedpeople a site of memory; it allowed sojourners between slavery and freedom to remember a point in their lives that bonded them together as a people and that provided identity. Juneteenth's commemoration instructed children in the collective memories of their parents, grandparents, and relatives. It introduced a heroic history essential to identity in a region and in a nation that had often labeled itself a white man's country.[4] And celebrating Juneteenth represented a courageous act of political will for a people whose emancipation was resented by just about every white native Texan. Thus, each year, beginning in 1866, in either public or private gatherings, Texans of African descent celebrated Juneteenth as their independence day, becoming as one reveler put it "a red spot on the calendar."[5]

One of the most important features of these early celebrations was the inclusion of a sacred component. In church services, pastors reminded freedpeople of the solemnity of the occasion, of their duties as emerging citizens, and of their right to the pursuit of legal equality.[6] In 1892, the Reverend D. A. Scott, printed four

---

[3] Compared to other departments in the South, the military presence in Texas was comparatively weak. Granger may have anticipated difficulties in transition from slavery to freedom, thus he announced, "The Freedmen are advised to remain at their present homes and work for wages. They are informed that they will not be allowed to collect at military posts; and that they will not be supported in idleness either there or elsewhere." *Galveston Daily News*, 21 June, 1865. Robert W. Shook, "The Federal Military in Texas, 1865-1870," *Texas Military History* 6 (Spring 1967): 3-53. Carl H. Moneyhon, *Texas after the Civil War: The Struggle of Reconstruction* (College Station: Texas A & M Press, 2004), 6-8. Alexander T. Pratt, "The Day the Slaves Got the News," *Broadsides* (Spring 1996): 20-21, 27.

[4] Pierre Nora, "Between Memory and History: Les Lieux de mémoire," in Geneviève Fabre and Robert O'Meally, eds. *History and Memory in African-American Culture* (New York: Oxford University Press, 1994), 284-300. William H. Wiggins, Jr., *O Freedom! Afro-American Emancipation Celebrations* (Knoxville: University of Tennessee Press, 1987), xvii.

[5] Paul Darby, a Juneteenth celebrant, said "even if the American people in the United States didn't really set that day aside for us, I believe they owe it to us anyway . . . they ought to give the colored man a day for his freedom. It should be a red spot on the calendar and really took aside for." William H. Wiggins, Jr. "Juneteenth: A Red Spot Day on the Texas Calendar," in Francis E. Abernethy, Patrick B. Mullen, Alan B. Govenar, eds., *Juneteenth Texas: Essays in African-American Folklore* (Denton: University of North Texas Press, 1996), 237-52, 247-250. See also Steven Hahn, *A Nation under Our Feet: Black Political Struggles in the Rural South from Slavery to the Great Migration* (Cambridge: Harvard University Press, 2003), 2.

[6] Wiggins, *O Freedom!*, xx; David A. Williams, *Juneteenth: Unique Heritage* (Austin: Texan African-American Heritage Organization, 1992), 18. [Houston] *Informer*, 18 June 1938.

consecutive announcements in the *Sunday School Herald* encouraging Baptists to prepare for "a grand reunion of the old and young freedmen in the great Baptist ranks of Texas" to remember "the day when we were emancipated." That year, Juneteenth fell on a Sunday, and Reverend Scott wanted all the faithful to meet at 5 a.m. "Have the bell rang [sic] by the oldest member of the church for covenant meeting in grand thanks offering." This would be followed by Sunday school, preaching, and a reunion of former slaves to rejoice in the "religious and educational advantages" of the day. Spirituals and hymns of liberation accompanied the worship.[7]

Juneteenth celebrants looked forward to lengthy parades complete with marching bands, militia units, decorated horse drawn carriages, floats, and singing Sunday school children. In towns and cities, Juneteenth parades entered public space, giving African Americans a presence that was confrontational, political, and often feared or resented by whites. This celebration elicited a memory of emancipation, brought discussions of freedom to the streets, and countered any ideas that enslavement was either preferred by freedpeople or that it better suited them, an idea often maintained by whites.[8] In Galveston in 1904, women played equal roles in the celebration. The Women's Nineteenth of June Committee planned the program; beginning with a "magnificent parade," organized into five divisions: of mounted police, a Grand Marshal, the Island City Brass Band, and the Hawley Guards. In the following divisions came the assistant marshals, a young woman dressed as the Goddess of Liberty, and her maids of honor. Then came the floats "representing the race's progress in industrial, educational, commercial and laboring pursuits followed by . . . decorated vehicles, and the flower parade." Businessmen, members of labor unions, school teachers and children participated. These dignitaries represented for the African American community their most respected individuals, saluted by the sound of horns and protected by black guardsmen. The pride of the black community was all there on display.[9]

---

[7] [Austin] *Sunday School Herald,* 28 May, 4 June, 11 June, 18 June, 1892. William H. Wiggins, Jr., "'Lift Every Voice': A Study of Afro-American Emancipation Celebrations," *Journal of Asian and African Studies* 9 (July and October 1974): 184-85. Izola Ethel Fedford Collins, interview by author, tape recording, Galveston, Texas, 4 January 2005. "Free at Last," "Go Down Moses," and "Many Thousands Gone" prevailed among the spirituals. They sang secular songs, such as "John Brown," patriotic songs, such as "America," and the national anthem. After 1927, celebrants sang James Weldon Johnson's poem set to music, "Lift Every Voice," now the black national anthem.

[8] White, "'It Was a Proud Day' ," 13-50. Mitch Kachun, *Festivals of Freedom: Memory and Meaning in African American Emancipation Celebrations, 1808-1915* (Amherst: University of Massachusetts Press, 2003), 233-35. Clark, "Celebrating Freedom," 109-13. See also Elizabeth Hayes Turner, *Women, Culture, and Community: Religion and Reform in Galveston, 1880-1920* (New York: Oxford University Press, 1997), 250-51. In 1896, the year of the *Plessy* decision, the Juneteenth parade in Austin proceeded down the main avenues of the city [Congress Avenue to Sixth Street]. Observers spoke of marshals with cockhats, streaming sashes, and prancing steeds. A Cornet band led the carriage parade filled with clergy and their wives, followed by a float featuring the exalted Goddess of Liberty and her maids. [Austin] *Herald,* 27 June 1896.

[9] [Galveston] *City Times,* 11 June 1904. For a description and analysis of Juneteenth parades in San Antonio see Judith Berg Sobré, *San Antonio on Parade: Six Historic Festivals* (College

The parade ultimately ended in a park, often purchased for such occasions. Buying land for emancipation celebrations constituted an act of independence for which freedpeople were willing to make great sacrifices. Borrowing or begging space from white officials contradicted the intention of the celebration; thus in cases where land and funds were available, groups often negotiated the purchase. In Houston, in 1872, two pastors raised $1,000 to buy ten acres of land and called it Emancipation Park. In Mexia in 1898, a "Nineteenth of June Organization" also bought ten acres next to the Navasota River and called it Booker T. Washington Park. Juneteenth celebrations continue in these parks to this day.[10]

There the celebration included an enormous feast featuring barbecued beef that the men had roasted in underground pits through the night. One reveler recounted, "In the early Juneteenth morning in our community, we could always smell the mixed aroma of food coming from every house. . . . roast beef, spare ribs, fried chicken, collard greens, turnip greens, mustard greens, pork chops, purple hull and blackeyed peas, pastries, breads, roasted wild game, fish, and chitterlings."[11] Others remembered the delights of red soda water. Former slaves and Union soldiers over fifty were given special attention, and after the meal baseball games, fishing, boating contests, or dancing ensued.[12]

It was the program, however, that memorialized Juneteenth with the symbols of their freedom: the Emancipation Proclamation and the Goddess of Liberty. A reading of the Proclamation, usually by a young woman, centered the audience on the fact that Abraham Lincoln, a United States president, the highest elected official in the nation, had declared them free. In 1876, on the occasion of the nation's centennial, France had given to the United States the Statue of Liberty, which finally

---

Station: Texas A & M Press, 2003), 51-72. The presence of the Hawley Guards, a black militia, was exceedingly important to the black community, for it symbolized the privileges of freedom and citizenship and ensured protection. In 1906, at the height of segregation, the legislature removed the right of African Americans to bear arms in black militias. The Hawley Guards and all Texas black militias were disbanded and required to return all state property to Austin. [Galveston] *New Idea*, 15 July 1905; [Galveston] *City Times*, 28 April 1906.

[10] The two pastors were the Reverend Jack Yates, of Antioch Baptist Church, and the Reverend Elias Dibble of Trinity Methodist Episcopal Church. Patricia Smith Prather, "Juneteenth: A Celebration of Freedom," *Texas Highways* 35 (June 1988): 2-8, 4-5; Lorenzo Thomas, "Texas Tradition," *Houston City Magazine* 5 (June 1981): 103-105; Doris Hollis Pemberton, *Juneteenth at Comanche Crossing* (Austin: Eakin Publications, 1983), 205-12. The significance of land ownership cannot be overestimated especially in light of the memories of the alleged promises of forty acres and a mule. The purchase of land and its ownership, even for community purposes, equated with freedom. In Houston, Emancipation Park, which held annual Juneteenth celebrations, remained independently owned until 1916, when the city absorbed it into its park system. In Galveston, the Women's Nineteenth of June Committee by 1904, had "accumulated nearly $200 for the purpose of buying a celebration grounds of their own in the corporate limits of the city." [Galveston] *City Times*, 28 May 1904.

[11] Williams, *Juneteenth*, 18.

[12] "Early celebrants claimed that they lived from one year to the next just waiting to drink red soda water on Juneteenth. Prather, "A Celebration of Freedom," 2-8. Marjorie L.B. Allen, interview by author, tape recording, Houston, Texas, January 8, 2005; Izola Ethel Fedford Collins, interview.

stood in New York harbor in 1886. It became a beacon to immigrants but a hope for independence to the dispossessed in every corner of the nation. Adopting allegiance to the Proclamation and to the new national symbol of Liberty constituted a monumental break from white southern orthodoxy and thus established for African Americans their own identity, their own history, their own icons—beacons of hope in a racist age.[13]

This notion that African Americans were in fact more American than their southern white neighbors found its way into the black press, accompanied by strong declarations on the meaning of citizenship. What did it mean to be free in a republic where responsibilities for self-governance prevailed, they asked openly? During the Civil War, free blacks and former slaves had joined the Union army and fought for freedom. Reconstruction governments demonstrated that democracy could be carried out amongst a black voting populace. Tied to this were examples of black Republican legislators and appointed office holders in Texas. African American soldiers volunteered for service in the Spanish American War, and blacks gave their lives in World War I. Questions of rights as citizens reached a crescendo in the black press as Juneteenth celebrations in cities across Texas found their access to public space barred. Thus the marginalization of Juneteenth and its implications for citizenship commenced the second stage of Juneteenth's evolution.[14] A telling example of this came in 1919, when black soldiers returned from Europe. Houston city fathers ignored Decoration Day, May 30, which would have included honoring African Americans, yet they fully celebrated Jefferson Davis's birthday (June 3). Then for Juneteenth, these same city fathers relegated the Juneteenth parade to side streets. An angry C. F. Richardson, editor of the black owned Houston *Informer*, wrote,

> For the first time in the city's history the colored citizens of this community were refused a permit to route their Juneteenth parade over. . . . Main Street, . . . but [were] shunted . . . to . . . a route never before employed by any parade . . . but we were black and that meant shunting us off to a back and out-of-way street. . . . We are citizens of Houston and as such shall not be discriminated against.[15]

Adding to the insult, the white owned *Houston Post* ran an editorial that seemed to belittle the meaning of Juneteenth and the soldiers' honorable sacrifices. The editor of the *Post* indicated that blacks, after all, deserved little for their valor. He wrote, "Every Negro soldier who fought in France should have been rewarded

---

[13] Only later did Congress and the states through the constitutional amendment process validate what Lincoln had wrought. [Austin] *Herald,* 22 June 1895. [Galveston] *City Times,* 28 May, 11 June, 1904; Marina Warner, *Monuments and Maidens: The Allegory of the Female Form* (New York: Atheneum, 1985), 14-15; Turner, *Women,* 251; Horton, *Free People of Color,* 164.

[14] In the years following the close of the war, citizenship meant voting, political party membership, and political office holding. David W. Blight, *Race and Reunion: The Civil War in American Memory* (Cambridge: Harvard University Press, 2001), 354-62.

[15] [Houston] *Informer,* 28 June 1919.

with a watermelon on Juneteenth for his individual use."[16] C. F. Richardson returned this salvo:

> the above utterance . . . shows the average white Southerner's idea of what our race deserves for its unparalleled and unprecedented record in the late world war. . . . The black man responded to the call, firstly because he was an *American* citizen; secondly, because he knew that the world could not be made and maintained safe for democracy without at least bursting asunder some of the fetters that bound his race in 'democratic' America. . . . The black soldier fought for democracy—and not for a little measly, mushy watermelon.[17]

Richardson continued, "Take our creditable Emancipation Day celebration in this city June 19 and then see how the white papers endeavored to ridicule the race."[18] Black spokesmen had seldom before used Juneteenth as a forum to address white oppression so directly, but with police intimidation, lynchings, and race riots unfolding in cities across Texas and the nation, editors responded with growing stridency.

Although confined to the margins of urban life, by the 1920s and 1930s, Juneteenth celebrations, began to appear more commercial as a consumer culture spread across the United States. Newspaper advertisements suggested an array of items to buy for the festivities. Shop owners and department store chains, now appearing in Texas cities, reaped ready profits, as stores such as Foley Bros. in Houston sold dresses "Just in time for June Nineteenth."[19] Innovative Juneteenth celebrations also brought in needed revenue as air shows, stock car racing, and swimming exhibitions entranced audiences. Beauty pageants added glamour to the event, and tap dancing contests competed for space with sports events. Sports had always been a part of the recreation of Juneteenth, but semi-professional black baseball teams competed against each other. In Dallas' Steer Stadium the Dallas Black Giants and the Waco Black Cardinals played in "one of the biggest 'Juneteenth' celebrations ever arranged." Band concerts, wrestling matches, and carnival parks–such as Fair Park in Dallas–drew celebrants away from their jobs to a day of enjoyment. By night, bars and juke joints–especially in renowned Deep Ellum in Dallas–kept revelers out until all hours of the night. Juneteenth changed; it became a medium for mass entertainment, a day off from work, a chance to meet and greet and play and eat. Its historical meaning did not appear at the center of the annual gatherings as it once had.

---

[16] *Houston Post*, 22 June 1919.

[17] C. F. Richardson, "Is Watermelon to Be Our Only Reward for Great Service in Democracy's Martial Conflict?" [Houston] *Informer*, 28 June 1919.

[18] Ibid. David A. Williams notes that from 1866 to 1979, Juneteenth was "called many things (coon-day, nigger-day, etc.). . . ." Williams, *Juneteenth*, 21. [Houston] *Informer*, 29 September 1923.

[19] [Houston] *Informer* 16 June 1923, 16 June 1928, 15 June 1929, 16, 19 June 1937, 17 June 1939, 14 June 1941.

Two events, in the 1930s brought black history and culture back into focus. Folklorist J. Mason Brewer in 1932 published "Juneteenth," a collection of tales gathered from former slaves. Then the 1936 Texas Centennial Exposition in Dallas included a Hall of Negro Life among its exhibits, allowing black Dallas leaders to fill the $50,000 hall with murals and artifacts depicting "Negro progress" since emancipation. The hall was dedicated on June 19, 1936, and that day 46,116 African Americans attended the Centennial Exposition.[20]

With the advent of World War II African Americans questioned the extent to which they were regarded as full citizens. In 1943, just days before Juneteenth in Beaumont, three thousand whites rioted against blacks working at the shipyards, killing three people, and burning, and looting black homes. Novelist Ralph Ellison captured the betrayal when he wrote, "they called it Juneteenth . . . *The celebration of a gaudy illusion.*" In the war's aftermath it became increasingly clear that the old shibboleth "separate but *equal*" brought nothing but second-class citizenship, intensifying the drive for full equality. In context Juneteenth also seemed to bring little beyond reminders of the inequalities and unrealized dreams of true freedom in the South. What had once been a celebration that brought out the whole black community to parades and parks was now observed in private gatherings or at the occasional theme park. Public parades and commemorations were not to be found in most cities, and many black newspapers stopped reporting on Juneteenth. This third stage of Juneteenth's evolution, or devolution, might have brought about its complete demise, except for the fact that Juneteenth resided in collective memory. By legitimating black history and by gaining rights and citizenship for African Americans, the civil rights movement ultimately opened the door for the return of Juneteenth to public space. [21]

---

[20] "Juneteenth Observed By Negroes of Dallas*," Dallas Morning News*, 20 June 1929; "Plan Big Juneteenth Celebration at Ball Park; Game Features," *Dallas Morning News*, 17 June 1931; "Juneteenth Observance Delayed Because Sunday Is Not Workday Anyhow," *Dallas Morning News*, 20 June 1932; "Three Celebrations Regale Negroes for Juneteenth Holiday," *Dallas Morning News*, 21 June 1932; "Negro Nines Face In Juneteenth Go," *Dallas Morning News*, 17 June 1934. "Juneteenth Passes Quietly; One Killed, Twelve Jailed," *Dallas Morning News*, 20 June 1935; "Negroes Stage Big Juneteenth At Centennial," *Dallas Morning News*, 20 June 1936; "Two Dedications," *Dallas Morning News*, 20 June 1936. J. Mason Brewer, "Juneteenth" in J. Frank Dobie, ed. *Tone the Bell Easy* (Austin: Texas Folklore Society, 1932). On Brewer's scholarship see [Houston] *Informer*, 16 June 1932. Thomas, "Texas Tradition," 103-105. See also Brundage, "Whispering Consolation to Generations Unborn," 341.

[21] Ralph Ellison, *Juneteenth: A Novel* (New York: Random House, 1999), 115 (italics in the original). [Houston] *Informer*, 19, 26 June 1943. *Dallas Morning News*, 19 June 1968; Thomas, "Texas Tradition," 103-105. David A. Williams writes that young African Americans involved in the struggle for civil rights thought that "Juneteenth was antiquated or inept . . . archaic," Williams, *Juneteenth*, 20. Amy Grey, "Juneteenth: A Historical Perspective," unpublished research paper, 1991, Vertical File "Juneteenth," Center for American History (University of Texas at Austin, Austin, Texas), 12. Marjorie L.B. Allen, interview. According to Patricia Smith Prather, "Austin blacks revitalized Juneteenth in 1976, after a 25-year hiatus." Prather, "Juneteenth: A Celebration of Freedom," 7. From 1960 to 1967 no mention of Juneteenth was made in the *Dallas Morning News*. Between 1961 and 1970 no Juneteenth celebrations were recorded in the [Houston] *Informer*. In the *Houston*

Once hope began to return with civil and voting rights acts, leading to the election of black representatives to the Texas statehouse and to Congress, then Juneteenth evolved to a fourth stage. But this time it came back in different form. In 1973, Houston pastor, C. Anderson Davis, civil rights activist and former president of the Houston National Association for the Advancement of Colored People (NAACP), organized the National Emancipation Association and thus began a renewal process. In Houston, the Black Arts Center also sponsored Juneteenth festivities that glorified black culture through jazz, blues, spirituals, gospel, theater, art, crafts, and traditional designs.[22]

When Houston Representative Al Edwards (D-Houston), introduced House Bill 1016 to the Texas legislature in February 1979, he did so on the heels of the civil rights movement. He began his campaign to make Juneteenth a legal state holiday as soon as he entered the statehouse. Five months later, Edwards and a coalition of black, Tejano, and white legislators convinced both houses to pass the bill. In 1980, Texas celebrated Juneteenth as the first legal (paid) state emancipation holiday. This historic event moved Representative Edwards to proclaim, "it's a time when white, brown, and blacks can celebrate freedom together."[23]

Since that day Juneteenth has taken off as a celebratory event featuring African American culture and African roots. In 1981 in Houston, Juneteenth continued for four days, with concerts of jazz and blues performed at Emancipation Park and the city's Miller Outdoor Theater. Two thousand spectators came to listen to the Juneteenth Blues Festival. In Austin in 1985, the Black Arts Alliance, created to foster appreciation for black cultural arts, sponsored a four-day celebration called Juneteenth *Bluezfest*. Today, Juneteenth celebrations fan out all over the cities offering plays, concerts, "gospel explosions," festivals, art exhibits, dance performances, and food of every kind. Each year communities that had never before held Juneteenth celebrations announce they are starting them. As African Americans move to the suburbs and to small communities on the outskirts of cities like Houston, Juneteenth parades, exhibits, and celebrations unfold in places where they have never before been offered.[24]

Negro Labor News, however, a radio station KYOK sponsored a "Century of Progress" celebration on June 19, 1963 at Playland Park in Houston. The station advertised a similar Juneteenth celebration in 1964. *Houston Negro Labor News*, 15 June 1963, 13 June 1964. On June 26, 1971, the [Houston] *Informer* noted that, "June 19 all across the nation was celebrated by small groups and families in all Negro communities. . . . In the early days big celebrations were held all over the states but now only smaller minority groups seem to stick with the old trend of barbecuing and drinking red soda water. . . . the people seem to get further and further away from the celebration of June 19 . . . ." Frances Imon, "No Plans Made: Emancipation Day Fete Fading Away," *Daily Oklahoman*, 18 June 1965.

[22] Prather, "Juneteenth: A Celebration of Freedom," 7. *Houston Post*, 5 June 1980, 18 June 1989.

[23] *Houston Post*, 21 May, 5 June 1980. Williams, *Juneteenth*, 26-29. Despite voting rights, gerrymandering continued to be a problem, requiring many subsequent legal battles. Prather, "Juneteenth: A Celebration of Freedom," 8. *Houston Post*, 20 June 1989.

[24] *New York Times*, 19 June 1989; Austin *Chronicle*, 14 June 1985; Flier, "Emancipation Week, 1987, Organized by the Texas Association for the Study of Afro-American Life and History," Vertical File "Juneteenth," Center for American History. By 1989 three

When Juneteenth returned in the 1970s, it focused on celebrating freedom *and* the arts. Memories of emancipation include thoughts of slavery, and some hoped to avoid the pain, guilt, or sense of resentment associated with the pre-Civil War past. African American culture—music, dance, and the visual arts—brought another emphasis, a universal message that invited people regardless of race to join the celebration. Now Juneteenth has been transported all over the world in large part by American troops, but international audiences enjoy the celebrations and learn of African American culture and history.[25]

There is a postscript, however. Juneteenth has encountered another aspect to its revival, one that calls for its politicization. It involves politicians who find they can use Juneteenth to further their own ambitions in Austin and in the nation's capital. Juneteenth began to be celebrated in Washington D.C. sporadically by 1979 in churches, museums and art centers, such as the Kennedy Center. In 1989 the Smithsonian's Anacostia Museum and Center for African American History and Culture sponsored a Juneteenth family day.[26] Juneteenth moved from Washington D.C. museums and cultural centers to a larger forum in 2000. This came with the creation of the National Juneteenth Observance Foundation, started by the Reverend Ronald V. Myers, Sr. and endorsed by Congressman Danny K. Davis of Illinois in 1999. Their Juneteenth programs took place from 8 a.m. to 5 p.m. at the Lincoln Memorial and included a worship service, a march, and a rally. Today, Reverend Myers and the Foundation are beseeching Congress to make Juneteenth a national holiday, with the important goal of promoting greater understanding "through a national day of reconciliation and healing from the legacy of slavery."[27] For years the National Juneteenth Independence Day program has featured a reading of the

---

organizations had emerged to sponsor Juneteenth celebrations in Houston alone: the National Emancipation Association founded in 1973 by Reverend C. Anderson Davis; the Juneteenth Blues Festival under the sponsorship of SumArts, an underwriting organization for the arts in Houston; and Juneteenth USA organized by Representative Al Edwards. *Houston Chronicle*, 25 February 1982; *Houston Post*, 18 June 1989; Houston *Chronicle*, 12, 19 June 2003.

[25] Carroll Parrott Blue, *The Dawn at My Back: Memoir of a Black Texas Upbringing* (Austin: University of Texas Press, 2003), 85. She recalls the criticism of Houston women in the 1950s who did not like art that "highlighted slavery, a period regarded by the women as being 'too dark.'" For an artistic rendering of Houston's Juneteenth celebrations after 1977 see Tracy Daugherty, "Burying the Blues," in Tracy Daugherty, *It Takes a Worried Man* (Dallas: Southern Methodist University Press, 2002), 150-200.

[26] Jean M. White, "Mall Bearings," *Washington Post*, 14 June 1979; Anne Simpson, "D.C. Juneteenth Celebration," *Washington Post*, 23 June 1988; Ed Ward, "Celebrating Juneteenth," *Washington Post*, 9 June 1991; "On Tap at the Texas Festival," Washington Post, 16 June 1991; Vanessa Williams, "Texas-Born Observance at Home in D.C.—Juneteenth Event Celebrates News of Emancipation," *Washington Post*, 14 June 1998; "Juneteenth Celebration is Planned," *Washington Post*, 20 June 1991; Retha Hill, "Juneteenth, A Day of Jubilation," *Washington Post*, 23 June 1991.

[27] Linda Wheeler, "Juneteenth Supporters to Lobby Here," *Washington Post,* 17 June 2000. Avis Thomas-Lester, "For Many, Today is Independence Day," *Washington Post*, 18 June 2005.

names of the victims of lynching. The result was that Congress finally apologized on Juneteenth 2005 for never passing a federal anti-lynching law.[28]

Organizers of a national Juneteenth Day are angry that President George W. Bush will not give a Juneteenth Proclamation or attend the Washington D.C. festivities, although his website did congratulate the nation and acknowledged the significance of Juneteenth. Congress, led by Danny K. Davis, unanimously passed House Concurrent Resolution 160, urging President Bush to "issue a Presidential Proclamation concerning Juneteenth, and "calling on the people of the United States to observe Juneteenth Independence Day." Thousands of individuals have sent letters requesting a presidential proclamation making Juneteenth a national holiday, similar to Flag Day.[29] But so far, President Bush has not bent to the pressure. No doubt, Juneteenth organizers will continue to push for a national day of observance, and the process will give them political visibility.

Back in Texas disputes have erupted over the Juneteenth monument to be unveiled in 2005. State assemblyman Al Edwards won approval for a Juneteenth monument on capitol grounds. The Texas assembly created the Texas Emancipation Juneteenth Cultural and Historical Commission and named Edwards as permanent chair until the committee disbands. The legislature also budgeted 1.4 million dollars to fund the project.[30] Now there is considerable outrage over the use of the funds and the design of the monument. Most galling of all to legislators—some of them black—is that the central figure of the monument, "The Lawmaker," bears a striking resemblance to Representative Al Edwards. Editors at the *Austin American-Statesman* were blunt in their appraisal of the likeness. The "monument . . . is nothing more than glorification of state Rep. Al Edwards' oversized ego."[31] The eleven-foot "Lawmaker" will not be holding forth over the south lawn of the capitol, but instead will be recast. Rodney Ellis, a Texas state representative, raised the issue not to embarrass anyone, he said, but to warn commission members that "'a tribute to our tortured history' is the butt of Capitol jokes." It would seem that Rep. Edwards had used Juneteenth for his own advancement, but at the price of dissent among his former supporters. This may have cost him his seat in the House, for on

---

[28] Avis Thomas-Lester, "For Many, Today is Independence Day," *Washington Post*, 18 June 2005; "Juneteenth," *Austin American-Statesman*, 19 June 2005. Sadly, the two senators from Texas were among the fourteen who did not sign the resolution.

[29] Ronald V. Myers, Sr. to President George W. Bush, July 10, 2005, National Juneteenth Observance Foundation, National Juneteenth Christian Leadership Council, internet, http://www.juneteenth.us/bush.html, accessed 8 August 2005.

[30] Acts 1997, 75th Leg., ch. 563,§ 1, effective September 1, 1997. Its purpose is to "coordinate state and local activities relating to the . . . celebration of Juneteenth; . . . and to establish a Juneteenth memorial monument on the grounds of the State Capitol . . . ." [Government Code: Chapter 448: Texas Emancipation Juneteenth Cultural and Historical Commission]. According to bids sent out by the State Preservation Board, the monument's granite base was to be constructed and ready for the placement of bronze sculptures by May 20, 2005. *Houston Chronicle*, 12 June 2003. Plans had already been made for a monument to be placed at Ashton Villa in Galveston, the alleged site of the reading of the freedom proclamation. *Houston Chronicle*, 25 September 2003, 10, 17 June 2004.

[31] "Give Juneteenth Proper Honor," *Austin American-Statesman*, 10 July 2005.

April 11, 2006, Al Edwards lost the primary election, ending his twenty-six year career as a state representative.[32]

Inevitably celebrations and holidays change over time; some grow larger and more well organized, depending on leadership, commitment to the ideals of the event, and the place they occupy in a national culture. Juneteenth has emerged out of its segregationist past to become an all American holiday. The proponents accomplished this in part in the 1970s by universalizing the event, celebrating black history, art, music, and culture and by minimizing the guilt producing history of slavery. The change in emphasis drew in thousands of whites and other ethnic groups to the party. But with Juneteenth's popularity have also come divisions and power struggles among its advocates. Juneteenth has provided a vehicle for the advancement of political careers. Increased commercialization competes with the more meaningful aspects of the event. But commercialization is bound up with its "success." Thus, an ethnic celebration in order to become a national holiday, it seems, must adapt to America's consumer culture. It is difficult, however, to avoid the subject of slavery, and slavery is not easily commercialized. In 2005, which saw the 140th anniversary of Juneteenth, the rallies, parties, and parades still captured much of the joy of the event. There is evidence that meaningful ceremonies and thoughtful reflection ask once again about the historical relevance of slavery and freedom to all Americans. In the midst of the glitz, African Americans are willing to think about their place in history—as slaves, as survivors of Jim Crow, and as citizens in a nation whose experiment with democracy is far from over.

---

[32] Tavis Smiley, "Interview: Pam Tilley and Al Edwards on the Juneteenth Celebrations in Texas," National Public Radio broadcast, transcript, 19 June 2003, internet, http://nl.newsbank.com/nlsearch/we/Archives?p_action=doc&p_docid=0FBC83120A045, accessed 10 August 2005; Kristin Mack, "Fellow Dems Question Rep. Edwards' Priorities," *Houston Chronicle*, 24 March 2005; Michelle M. Martinez, "The Face of Juneteenth? It Looks a Lot Like Colleague, Legislators Say," *Austin American-Statesman*, 19 March 2005; "Edwards' Follies*,*" *Austin American-Statesman*, 23 March 2005; "Not a Fitting Memorial," *Austin American-Statesman*, 26 April 2005; Laylan Copelin, "Makeover Ordered for Juneteenth Bronze Icon . . . ," *Austin American-Statesmen*, 7 July 2005; "Give Juneteenth Proper Honor," *Austin American-Statesmen*, 10 July 2005; *Houston Chronicle*, 12, 13 April 2006.

THE NEVER-ENDING CYCLE OF POVERTY:
SARAH E. WRIGHT'S *THIS CHILD'S GONNA LIVE*

Sharon Monteith

In Georgia Douglas Johnson's play *Plumes* (1927), a poor black woman's daughter lies sick and dying. A white doctor offers an "operation" for $50 but the coffee grounds she and her neighbor read that morning predict a funeral. The mother has buried all her other children and takes in washing to survive. Her anguished decision about her remaining daughter turns on balancing the cost of the child's death against the doctor's vain or spurious hope that she may live. The woman chooses a $50 funeral complete with horses with plumes on their heads so that she may pay this final child a tribute: a dignified death. The child dies.[1] This one-act southern "folk play," as Johnson calls it, shows that extremes of poverty in the midst of systemic racism can often promote resignation rather than revolution. Sheer survival takes its toll; in southern narratives black children often die needlessly because of poverty, from slave narratives in which mothers mourn their children to Alice Walker's "Strong Horse Tea" (1973) in which a poor black woman's desperate search to find a "real doctor" for her child recalls *Plumes*.

Sarah E. Wright's 1969 novel *This Child's Gonna Live* is an angry and bitter "folk novel" about a 23-year-old black mother's desperate love for her children who are dying of TB, and suffering from malnutrition, pellagra, and hookworm in the Depression South. By the end of the novel two children are among the dead. Set in 1929-1930, the novel's Upshur family shucks oysters, digs potatoes, and skins tomatoes in an effort to survive. The Upshurs—Mariah, Jacob, and their three boys—exist in "a place of standing still and death," poverty-stricken Tangierneck on Maryland's Eastern shore.[2] Mariah is about to give birth to another child, their daughter Mary having died two years earlier because, unable to afford a hospital birth, an unhygienic make-do midwife made a tragic mistake. Mariah's overwhelming desire is to escape the rural South for the city—Baltimore or Philadelphia—so, she believes, the child she is carrying may live, if only she can "get on that speeding Route 391 and run" (17). However, Jacob believes they should stay because "a man is his land," and he is intent to reclaim his family's rightful acreage for Mariah and their children (12). Jacob has inherited his faith in land ownership from his father, Percy Upshur, who owned scores of acres in Tangierneck which he mortgaged and rented to the rest of the black community. As the Depression hits, he loses the land to a white woman—Bannie Upshire Dudley—who lends him money, raises the interest, and forces him to foreclose, bankrupting him.

The Upshurs and the Upshires stand at the miscegenated heart of what remains of the plantation economy. Wright's black characters are landless on the land, trapped in a system of peonage, or plantation agriculture, unable to accumulate with

---

[1] Georgia Douglas Johnson, "Plumes" in *Plays by American Women, 1900-1930*, ed. Judith E. Barlow (New York: Applause, 1985), 162-170.

[2] Sarah E. Wright, *This Child's Gonna Live* (London: Paladin, 1988), 16. Subsequent references will be included in the text.

Miss Bannie still behaving like the plantation mistress. Bannie is "rooting up [black] family trees" (49), not only in dispossessing the Upshurs of their land inheritance but because her own clandestine relationship with Jacob's father is unraveling. Jacob's ("black") grandmother and his ("white") great aunt grew up on the Upshire plantation and their sisterly friendship continued until Jacob's grandmother was murdered by disapproving Upshire men. Disapproval is not limited to the white community though and one resentful relative taunts Jacob for his family's historical association with whites: "They still think they related to them white dogs. . . . Like one big happy family" (60). First drawn together by their mothers' interracial friendship, Bannie and Percy have a secret son who has returned to Tangierneck as the local doctor, Dr. Grene "the kind of white-looking colored man that colored women get excited over" (162). It is to Dr. Grene that Mariah turns in debilitating grief at her daughter's death. The new child Mariah is carrying as the novel opens is Dr. Grene's child, the child of his half-brother about whom her husband Jacob knows nothing. Wright shows that this black family is strong enough to overcome adultery and guilt. Mariah and Jacob name the child after the grandfather common to both brothers; she is Bardetta Tommetta after Bard Tom whose courageous stance against land-grabbing Upshires presages his early death. In this way, Sarah E. Wright explores African American resistance to the "long shocks"[3] of slavery and the long-term effects of plantation economy. One of the last places Jacob and Mariah find work is Hillards' strawberry farm where workers are housed on a run-down, filthy plantation but by the end of the novel, the Upshurs are living in their own plantation house, a place that Mariah calls "home." The black family has adapted and survived.

Sarah E. Wright's novel has received less attention than it is due, despite being rarely out of print. Wright is missing from studies mapping the African American literary tradition, such as Claudia Tate's *Black Women Writers at Work* (1983), Sandi Russell's *Render Me My Song: African American Writers from Slavery to the Present* (1990) and Ann duCille's *The Coupling Convention: Sex, Text, and Tradition in Black Women's Fiction* (1993) and is referenced only in a single footnote in Deborah E. McDowell's classic essay "'The Changing Same': Generational Connections and Black Women Novelists" (1987).[4] Wright is missing too from surveys of southern literature and one reason for this may be her novel's setting in a so-called "border" state. Those critics who have examined the novel discuss the characters' poverty only to the extent that it fits within the framework of their thesis. For example, Patricia Yaeger refers to *This Child's Gonna Live* in the Prologue to *Dirt and Desire* (2000) to show how southern women write "dirt-eating, finger-sucking fiction" via Mariah's avowal to "eat that dirt and hustle on," while digging as many potatoes as she can to earn money for her family (8). Yaeger's concerns are mainly feminist and relate to the southern grotesque as a "space of

---

[3] Richard Wright, *12 Million Black Voices* (New York: Thunder Mouth Press, 1988), 31.
[4] Deborah E. McDowell, "'The Changing Same': Generational Connections and Black Women Novelists" in *Reading Black, Reading Feminist: A Critical Anthology*, ed. Henry Louis Gates (New York: Meridian, 1990), 113, n.27.

political obsession," so Wright functions as a swift though pointed illustration.[5] A more detailed focus on dirt and desire in *This Child's Gonna Live* could have revealed so much more about the sexual desire inside marriage and out of it that makes Wright's characters feel transcendent when little else can. Jennifer Campbell provides a more detailed consideration of author and novel in her bid to bring Sarah E. Wright to readers' attention in a 1997 article in *African American Literature Forum*, but in an introductory survey she finally chooses to emphasize Black Power politics in the era of the novel's first publication over the poverty at the novel's center.[6]

When acknowledged at all, the artistry of Wright's 1969 novel is typically overlooked in the search for sociological data. For example, it is the only fiction included in a list of sociology books recommended by Beverly Smith in "Black Women's Health: Notes for a Course" (1982).[7] The salient factor that critics have so far failed to note is that when Sarah E. Wright enters the southern literary tradition, it is as a neglected novelist of despair and survival and as an exponent of rural black southern speech, following Zora Neale Hurston and Richard Wright, and preceding Alice Walker and Ernest Gaines. Wright is missing, for example, from Marianne Hirsch's "Maternal Narratives: 'Cruel Enough to Stop the Blood'" (1990). Reading Morrison's *Sula* (1973), Hirsch argues that "The mother's discourse, *when it can be voiced at all*, is always repetitive, literal, hopelessly representational. It is rooted in the body that strives, hurts, bleeds, suffers, burns, rather than in the eyes, or in the voice, which can utter its cries of pain."[8] To read Sarah E. Wright is to alter this assessment and also to alter Deborah McDowell's idea of the literary tradition as the "changing same." The baby's kicking hurts Mariah's bowels, her head thumps and her hands bleed as she shucks oysters. In pain, she drags her heavy body across fields of potatoes but, most importantly, Mariah's "mother's discourse" is rooted in her voice. Mariah's voice is often funneled through the kind of "nauseous pain fog" that she experiences before the new child Bardetta Tommetta is born (148). This is not to imply that the prose is muffled or thick; it is spiky and feisty. Mariah's experience is embedded in the language she uses, and in this way Wright creates a powerfully disturbing story of "the folk." Mariah's voice is very different from Janie Crawford's in *Their Eyes Were Watching God* (1937), for example, because the weight of economic factors risks overriding her sense of herself as a lover or a wife.

---

[5] Patricia Yaeger, *Dirt and Desire: Reconstructing Southern Women's Writing, 1930-1990* (Chicago: University of Chicago Press, 2000), xii. Similar illustrations are present when Yaeger returns to the novel in "Ghosts and Shattered Bodies, or What Does it Mean To Still Be Haunted by Southern Literature?" *South Central Review* 22: 1 (Spring 2005): 87-108.

[6] Jennifer Campbell, "'It's a Time in the Land': Gendering Black Power and Sarah E. Wright's Place in the Tradition of Black Women's Writing on Racism and Sexism" *African American Review* 31 (Summer 1997): 211-222.

[7] Beverly Smith, "Black Women's Health: Notes for a Course" in *All the Women are White, All the Blacks are Men, But Some of Us Are Brave: Black Women's Studies* (New York: The Feminist Press, 1982), 45.

[8] Marianne Hirsch, "Maternal Narratives: 'Cruel Enough to Stop the Blood'" in *Reading Feminist, Reading Black: A Critical Anthology*, ed. Henry Louis Gates, (New York: 1990), 426.

Only her responsibilities as a mother penetrate the unrelenting "pain fog," and when she beats her children out of frustration borne of love, her self-hatred is overwhelming. Sarah E. Wright extends the "map of Dixie" that Zora Neale Hurston said she had on her tongue through simile and invective as well as the "everyday affair" of name calling and signifying.[9] In *This Child's Gonna Live*, violence— verbal as well as physical--endows this excoriating exposé with a power that renders it all the more graphic, in language that is as crude as it is poetic. Mariah talks to God about her poverty but, unlike Celie in Alice Walker's *The Color Purple* (1985), she rants and swears at a "stern and troubled" God (64).

Mariah's signifying is not only a mark of resilience in the fight against poverty and racist oppression. Words are often her only weapons. She steels herself to "sic her big bad word doggies" on Bannie's "ass-licking poor white" overseer who resents paying her what she has earned for digging potatoes out of the parched land. Mariah's "word doggies" can be vicious:

> "Jam your dick up your turd hole, cracker, and bust from the hot air you bloated with. You believe that every colored person that's getting a-hold of something's stealing. I believes in working for my money." If he said half a word back to her she was gonna grab his squelched-down corn-colored head and twist it to the east and the west and the north and the south so he could get a good look at all the scores of acres that used to be in Jacob's papa's hands. (9)

Rehearsing what she aches to say releases something of the anger that she feels because her chances to escape penury are being closed off in every direction. Similarly, her fantasy of killing Bannie Upshire energizes her temporarily precisely through her rage and resentment. Mariah wishes she had "a razor on her like most white people thought colored carried" (9), and she differentiates herself from others precisely through the thoughts that she would voice in unequivocal hatred: "I ain't like the rest of the niggers you and Miss Bannie got, saying your shit don't smell bad when you use them for a toilet. I ain't saying tiddely-toe and grinning when you fart in my face no more" (9).

Mariah's angry refusal to equivocate distinguishes the novel not only from those published in the 1930s but also from later representations of black women in novels set in the Depression South.[10] It also indicates another way in which the novel has been elided from even the most groundbreaking essays on African American—and southern—literary history. Hortense Spillers makes a very convincing case for *Sula* as the novel that breaks open the literary tradition in its imagining of a new black woman rebel who forges a place for herself outside of patriarchy, and in counterpoint to prevalent images of the black woman in fiction. Spillers reads *Sula* through Margaret Walker's *Jubilee* (1966) and Hurston's *Their*

---

[9] Zora Neale Hurston, *Dust Tracks on the Road* (London: Virago, 1982), 143-144.
[10] For example, Wright's Mariah is markedly different from black women as imagined by white writers such as Berry Morgan in *Pursuit* (1966). Her black character, Roxie Stoner, tells about black life in "Kings Town" (Port Gibson), Mississippi in the 1930s but is calmly stoical in her endurance.

Eyes Were Watching God as the closest Toni Morrison has to predecessors.[11] However, reference to *This Child's Gonna Live*, to Mariah's rebelliousness, and to her endless tussles with God would have contributed to Spillers's critique of Christian salvation in African American writing and underlined her claims for an insurgent woman character.

Sarah E. Wright grew up on Maryland's eastern shore, the daughter of an oyster farmer father and factory worker mother.[12] The significance of the hard, brutal descriptions of black poverty in the novel should be understood in the light of Wright's dual historical emphasis on the 1930s of her childhood and the novel's moment of production, the 1960s. The novel was published in 1969 following the dismantling of Lyndon Johnson's War on Poverty program with its mission statement to eradicate poverty among the nation's peoples—black and white. The program highlighted malnutrition as a fundamental problem for blacks in the South—not for the first time and not for the last—but its focus was inner city and urban poverty. Inaugurated in 1964 with the Economic Opportunity Act, Johnson's "war" accomplished much, including a significant downturn in the percentage of Americans living in poverty, from around 18 percent in 1960 to an estimated 12 percent in 1969, but the perception that Johnson's reforms were designed primarily to empower a black minority contributed to the conservative backlash that led to Nixon's victory in 1968. This context is as significant an element of the novel's critique as is its setting's exposé of Depression-era poverty in the South of the New Deal, dedicated to providing economic security "from the cradle to the grave," and of the South as "the Nation's No. 1 economic problem" as President Roosevelt went on to describe it in 1938.[13] Wright's novel reminds the reader that white fears of black gains in the 1930s segregated South were echoed in the 1960s across the nation, as in the Kerner Commission's warning in 1968 that despite reforms, white racism ensured that the nation was moving toward "two societies, one black, one white—separate but unequal." Striking at the causes of deep-rooted inequities, as Johnson had envisaged the Great Society programs would, was too radical a shift for many Americans even in the tumultuous 1960s.

In my reading there is a metaphorical knot at the heart of Sarah E. Wright's unflinching representation of poverty that recalls Richard Wright's description of the legacy of slavery as an "uneasily tied knot of pain and hope whose snarled strands converge from many points of time and space."[14] The Upshurs' precise location in the first winter of the Great Depression is vital to the folk history that Sarah Wright creates; by 1930-1931 poverty had become entrenched in places such as

---

[11] Hortense Spillers, "A Hateful Passion, A Lost Love," *Feminist Studies* 9: 2 (1983): 293-323.

[12] Wright's novel may be read as a homage to another neglected local writer. Water Turpin's 1937 novel *These Low Grounds* explores four generations of a single black family living on the same eastern shore where *This Child* is set.

[13] "The President's Council Reports on Southern Economic Conditions, 1938," in *Major Problems in the History of the American South Volume II: The New South*, eds. Paul D. Escott and David R. Goldfield (Lexington, MA: D. C. Heath, 1990), 389.

[14] Wright, *12 Million Black Voices*, 11.

Tangierneck. However, Depression Maryland is also a semantic field, like Richard Wright's "knot of pain," in which time and space are interdependent and operate as a literary x-ray to reveal the folk memory at the heart of the text.[15] The story of the Upshur family acts as synecdoche for a particular time (the 1930s) and place (the rural South), but the social forces that charge the fiction are those that characterized the War on Poverty and the expressive fictions of Black Cultural Nationalism of the late 1960s. In Sarah E. Wright's context, collecting the "snarled strands" that Richard Wright describes, involves a journey back not only in time but, like Hurston and Alice Walker, back figurally, if not literally, to the South of her childhood.[16] Sarah E. Wright's critical realism emphasizes the novel's movement through material deprivation and psychological trauma to the discovery of a proud selfhood grounded in the love and endurance of the black extended family.

The novel opens in a rural backwater in Maryland on the day of the stock market crash, October 30, 1929. In immediately yoking the local so specifically to the national, Wright signals from the outset that this story of a single poor family in a poor community will encompass wider social concerns:

> Hard as times were after that Wall Street, where they sent out the money from, crashed, many was already forecasting another green winter. A-many a poor soul done dropped dead from the starvation in spring as it was, in the rising of the sap. Looked like a-many a more wasn't gonna take the strain of the falling. (217)

The first significant change Wright's characters note over the first months of the Depression is an increase in southern migrant workers traveling north and an attendant upsurge in the community's resentment of their presence: "we ain't never had nothing round here like that drinking mess 'til them migrant workers come along. Place had a respectable name" (61). Wright ensures that by the novel's close, the Upshurs have experienced life as migrants themselves, "living like dogs" in a place called Chance, working the oyster season on Kyle's Island, and picking up work wherever it may be found.

To begin with though, little seems to change for a community already eking out a living and fearing another "green winter" will produce a "fat graveyard" (141). The family subsists at the mercy of the seasons; the previous summer was "the hottest summer anybody in the nation could remember and everything else dried up" (51), except the worms that blight the Upshurs' paltry crops. However, the Depression is soon revealed as a contributing factor in Bannie's decision to prise the

---

[15] Deploying Bakhtin's idea of the chronotope, Peter Hitchcock makes a similar point about community memory. See Peter Hitchcock, "Radical Writing" in *Dialogics of the Oppressed* (Minneapolis: University of Minnesota Press, 1993), 55; M. M. Bakhtin, "Forms of Time and Chronotope in the Novel" in *The Dialogic Imagination*, trans. Michael Holquist and Caryl Emerson (Austin: University of Texas Press, 1981), 84-258.

[16] In *Specifying: Black Women Writing the American Experience* (London: Routledge, 1987), Susan Willis asserts: "If there is one thing that predominates in contemporary writing by black America women, it is the journey (both real and figural) back to the historical sources of the black American community. . . . [which] probably originates with Hurston's flight from the city back to the South to drive the back roads" 57.

last few acres of land she can from the Upshurs, to shore up her son's future at the expense of theirs. Bannie bankrupts her son's black father to ensure their son will become an economically safe member of a black middle class, less easily "taken" by white powerbrokers such as members of her own family: "every last cent I could get out of anybody, I gave to him. . . . Wanted to give him the whole of Montipiro County" (133). The internecine machinations of white landowners and thieves ensure that this can never be an uncomplicated inheritance.

In their obsession with her theft of their family's lands, both Jacob and Mariah imagine murdering Bannie. In Jacob's case, "For a minute he had a vision of himself squeezing the wind out of Bannie's soft, pink throat, closing those impatient eyes. . . Miss white money-grabbing Bannie got her hands stuck down in my pockets squeezing my manhood" (49). Bannie Upshire's power is underwritten by the white power structure. The bank refuses loans to blacks unless on Bannie's cousin Haim Rawford's say-so (26) and a Mrs. Cramston refuses welfare to Mariah because she is seen as fraudulent. By putting names to the bankers, white welfare police, and slum landlords and describing them, Sarah E. Wright personalizes Richard Wright's "Lords of the Land" in *12 Million Black Voices*. When one night Mariah finds Bannie beaten up at the side of the road, Bannie accuses her former lover Percy Upshur of attacking her. Shocked by the idea that Jacob's father and she could be lovers, and intent to protect Percy whatever he may have done, Mariah is tempted to crush the frail frightened white woman because she is "lynch-bait": "Ought to take one—just one white person with me when I go. *Ought to take a million. Clear the earth of them*" (131). She settles on drowning Miss Bannie. She even takes her as far as the beach before she recalls her maternal responsibilities: "Ain't got no business mixed up in no shit like this. Got to save my baby" (131). Although reason overcomes Mariah's resentment of the white woman and she leads her home, by the morning Bannie Upshire is dead. The wider Tangierneck community has much to gain from Bannie's demise and Wright ensures that the reader is unable to extricate who killed her from who had reason to. For example, Mariah's father, Pop Harmon, the only man to pay his land debt to Percy Upshur before Percy lost the lands to Bannie, is in and out of the house on the night she is attacked and he boils with anger when asked where he has been (143). In another novel the machinations would collapse into melodrama, but there are myriad possible assailants among those who resent Bannie precisely because the poverty that determines the Upshur family dynamic also determines the community's survival.

Bannie's death sparks a train of violent repercussions in a community characterized by white-on-black violence: a poor migrant worker is accused of a murder he did not commit, taken from the jail, and beaten and killed on the courthouse lawn (197). Soon after, Bannie's cousin leads a group of men to Jacob's house in the middle of the night. The threat of lynching is pervasive in *This Child's Gonna Live* and the nightriders' visit recalls Jacob's grandfather and grandmother murdered in 1875 by members of the same white Upshire family hidden by their Klan robes. As their mother is dragged to her death, a young Percy ran helplessly after the cart trying to raise help, "to raise a commotion to get the people up but the people lived a considerable distance from each other in that day and time" (107). The literal distance is undergirded by the communal distance that fear engendered in the Reconstruction South. In 1930, however, the effectiveness of the white mob

cowing the black populace is less assured. Rather than ambush Jacob as they did his
grandmother on an isolated road, or publicly humiliate him as they had his father,
the nightriders enter Jacob's home. The Tangierneck community—"the people"—
rallies to scare the white men away from Jacob's home and family. It is a temporary
stand-off between black and white, broken when Jacob's father disappears and is
found murdered, but it is a rare scene in a fiction set in the 1930s: the fear of the
poor black community gives way to anger and translates into resistance. Despite
being portrayed in the early sections of the novel as a "wind-beaten, life-beaten
going nowhere man" with "a sickness of his going-nowhere self" (31),[17] Jacob is
important because he transcends the threats of those whites who seek to keep his
family locked in a plantation economy. He will not give up on the land or his family
even when he fears he may be lynched.

In this sense the representation of black anger owes much more to black
cultural nationalism in the late 1960s than it does to the Depression era, but the
many murders in the novel do recall a cycle of racist violence between 1929 and
1930, as well as descriptions of civil rights murders perpetrated in the 1960s. As
Philip Dray has shown, eleven (recorded) lynchings occurred in the South in 1929,
but the number doubled to around 22 over just the first eight months of 1930. Walter
White became convinced that the Depression and attendant unemployment was the
catalyst for worsening race relations. Dray also points to The International Labor
Defense's platform in 1930 which emphasized the connection between racist
injustices, economic depression, and global struggles for minority rights.[18] In the
novel murders proliferate: Jacob's aunt Cora Lou is murdered in the road by a
carload of white boys as she walks the miles to bring the doctor to see pregnant
Mariah. That it is a racist murder is left in little doubt when it is reported that state
troopers have never seen a road accident like this one: "she looked worse than
people killed in a war. . . . Brains was all spilled out" (138).

Sarah E. Wright looks through a prism of the 1960s back to the 1930s. By the
end of the 1960s, lynching was generally assumed to be a crime of earlier decades.
Tuskegee published its last annual report on the phenomenon in 1962, and the
murder of three civil rights workers, Schwerner, Chaney and Goodman, in 1964 was
beginning to be talked of as the final lynching of the civil rights era. That is to say,
the last in which complicity between police officers and the mob made racist murder
seem to belong to a disappearing past in which racist violence would be condoned—
if not perpetrated—by the law in the rural South. In *This Child's Gonna Live*, Percy
Upshur tries to use the law against the Upshires and their "klan" but the sheriff and
his deputies drag Percy out of the courthouse. A black witness describes the scene:
"They had done beat him. You could see the blood running out of his nose. And they
put him in a pick-up truck with some road cops. . . . And they drove off" (213).
Weeks later his body is identified only by remnants of his clothes. There is no

---

[17] In this he could also be read as a forerunner of Alice Walker's Grange Copeland in the
1973 novel who, beaten down by sharecropping, becomes "unnaturally bland" like a stone
and, finally, "an object, a cipher" cowed by the ever-present threat of racist violence and by
rural penury, *The Third Life of Grange Copeland* (London: The Women's Press, 1984), 9.

[18] Philip Dray, *At The Hands of Persons Unknown: The Lynching of Black America* (New
York: Random House, 2002), 303-304.

recourse to the law. The novel is a potent reminder that in periods of economic depression and political change black southerners have consistently been made scapegoats. This was the same concatenation of political beliefs that underpinned Sarah E. Wright's political activism in the 1960s and that is textured in the novel.

Reading the novel through a dual temporal lens reinforces Sarah E. Wright's wide focus as a Maryland writer who was a Member of the Harlem Writers' Guild throughout the time of writing. Vice-President of the Guild, having moved to New York in the 1950s, Wright was a member of the Old Left. Nevertheless, the organizations she joined or founded also made inroads into the New Left and connections with radical black alliances. Wright founded the Cultural Association of Women of African Heritage, which organized the 1961 demonstration at the United Nations protesting the assassination of the Congolese President Patrice Lumumba. She was also an inaugurating member of On Guard For Freedom which later, like SNCC, foundered on black radical vs. integrationist disagreements. She was prescient in discussing the tensions between black men and women and launching a critique of the male-centered aesthetics of black cultural nationalism.[19]

The members of the Harlem Writers Guild were mainly southerners whose writings aimed to capture the agony of the black experience in similar terms to those spelled out by Richard Wright. However, looking back on the Guild as it was in 1960, Sarah E. Wright remembered:

> The gaze of the Harlem Writers' Guild was focused not only on the South. We were also at one with the seething ghettos of the North, our ears attuned to Malcolm's message. And it was the year of Africa. We threw ourselves into solidarity work for the great freedom movements.

She noted Lumumba in the Congo, the South African anti-apartheid struggle, the fight for independence in Angola and Mozambique, and the fact that she and her husband Joseph Kaye founded an anti-colonial newspaper.[20] They also visited Cuba in 1960 with a group including Harold Cruse, Julian Mayfield, and LeRoi Jones (Amiri Baraka), all members of the Lower East Side coterie of socialists and cultural activists. When Fidel Castro was made to feel unwelcome at a Manhattan hotel during his visit of September 1960, he moved to the black-owned Hotel Theresa in Harlem and Wright and her group were there to welcome him.

Wright was just beginning to work on her novel in 1960, but in 1993 looking back she remembers the social ills that traverse the historical arc she creates in *This Child's Gonna Live*:

---

[19] See for example, Alice Childress, Paule Marshall and Sarah E. Wright, "The Negro Woman in American Literature" in *Freedomways Reader: Prophets in Their Own Country*, ed. Esther Cooper Jackson (Boulder: Westview, 2000), 291-298; James Edward Smethurst, *The Black Arts Movement: Literary Nationalism in the* 1960s *and* 1970s (Chapel Hill: University of North Carolina Press, 2005), 118-121.

[20] Sarah. E. Wright, "The Lower East Side: The Rebirth of World Vision," *African American Review* 27 (1993): 593-596.

what remained for me [is] what has always remained . . . many of our youth deprived of any chance in life, as I am confronted by the ugly swamp of poverty in our communities, the ever more insolent racism, the upsurge of murderous hate, the rampant and still growing unemployment and hopelessness, the death that increasingly comes too soon.[21]

The "ugly swamp of poverty" is a symbolic landscape that stretches across the decades and Wright extends it in *This Child's Gonna Live*. The Dismal Swamp was the image Zora Neale Hurston turned against Richard Wright when she reviewed *Uncle Tom's Children* in 1938, arguing that his stories of black southerners were so grim and unrelenting that "the Dismal Swamp of race hatred must be where they live."[22] The "long-tailed Dismal Swamp" (8) is the same maze of wetlands that William Styron's Nat Turner dreamed of as a possible escape. Wright's novel was published shortly after *The Confessions of Nat Turner* (1967) created a furor and members of the Harlem Writers Guild were so vociferous in their condemnation of Styron that John Henrik Clarke edited *William Styron's Nat Turner: Ten Black Writers Respond* (1968) as a polemical rebuttal. No black women writers contributed. Yet, *This Child's Gonna Live* signifies on Styron's book in the sense that her black characters are neither crazed nor isolated. Even when Mariah veers into her most alienating and suicidal fugues, as when the white angel of death speaks to her in tongues of flame, she finds solace in her son who "flung himself all slobbering on to the pillow. Just a-kissing her and chasing away that cold angel" (151).

Black anger is livid in this book, over the loss of land to whites, and the loss of social ground made up in the Reconstruction South. It is in this sense that *This Child's Gonna Live* is a "neo-abolitionist" novel, following Jack Temple Kirby's recognition that in the 1960s a "neo-abolitionist professional and popular history probably tarnished the sentimentalist images of plantation and slavery beyond recovery."[23] Neo-abolitionism was popularized through southern narratives, such as the 1969 movie *Slaves* based on a novel by Sarah E. Wright's mentor John. O Killens, and Ernest Gaines's *The Autobiography of Miss Jane Pittman* (1971) which was also filmed.[24] Similarly, Sarah E. Wright debunks any notions of a black pastoral that would reshape the plantation myth in the pre- or post-Civil Rights South and she borrows from Black Nationalist discourse in the texture of some of her descriptions. Mariah's father's apocalyptic pronouncements, for example, could

---

[21] Wright, "The Lower East Side," 596.

[22] Zora Neale Hurston in the *Saturday Review of Literature* 2 April 1938 in *Richard Wright: Critical Perspectives on Past and Present*, ed. Henry Louis Gates and K. A. Appiah, (New York: Amistad, 1993), 3.

[23] Jack Temple Kirby, *Media-Made Dixie: The South in the American Imagination* (Athens: University of Georgia Press, 1986), 165.

[24] Socially conscious fiction and film did not always send out unequivocal political messages. Despite Killens's emphasis on the deleterious ways in which black women were objectified in slavery, theater posters and press books publicizing the film of *Slaves* aimed at exploiting beautiful black slave Dionne Warwick, posing almost nude to lure audiences into the cinemas.

apply to each decade in American history from Reconstruction on. But, they resonate with the rhetoric of the 1960s:

> It's the time of a storm all over for the colored man. They lynching colored men every day by the whole-sale lot just south of this swamp, and up there in them cities, too. But in a different sort of way. (13)

He believes that the Tangierneck community should be at the forefront of black liberation struggles; he wraps his ideas up in apocalyptic biblical imagery—they are trapped in the reign of the first (white) horseman, but he will soon give way to the second (red) horseman who prophesies the coming of war, and out of that war and a plague of wars will come the third (black) horseman. Pop Harmon's interpretation of the Book of Revelations is that the black nations that emerge in the wake of wars will bring peace to the world's nations but that there remains work to be done in combating poverty: "[O]ur time has not yet come. We got to accumulate enough money for to go into business our ownselves. Build up something for the coming of the black nations of the world" (167-168).

Wright's context, then, involves liberation struggles and the debates about "the black family," and its history and future in such struggles that came to a head in the mid 1960s. Jacob's refusal to rely on welfare to feed or clothe his family because he sees it as the Democrats' "free disease" (67) may be read as a reaction against those debates. Following E. Franklin Frazier whose critique of the black family was an influence on his report "The Negro Family: The Case for National Action" (1965), Assistant Secretary for Labor, Daniel Patrick Moynihan sparked widespread black resentment for his neoconservative critique of the black family as matrifocal and the black father as emasculated.[25] In its unflinching portrait of a black woman's despair, Wright's 1969 novel responds to and counters Moynihan's Report and speaks to the furor it created among African Americans. Toni Morrison's 1970 novel *The Bluest Eye* has often been read in this regard, with critics reading the Breedlove family as "a perfect illustration of the black family model portrayed in the Moynihan Report."[26] However, Sarah E. Wright also engages with the ubiquitous phrase "the tangle of pathology" that Moynihan borrowed and reworked from sociologist Kenneth Clark's *Dark Ghetto* (1965). In this, she is a literary precursor of those feminists and historians whose cultural work on the black family dominated the early 1970s—Carol Stack and Angela Davis, for example—and who pointed to the resilience of African American women in the face of Moynihan's thesis and, by extension, Lyndon Johnson's primary focus on black men's access to employment.[27]

---

[25] The actual title of Moynihan's report speaks to Sarah E. Wright's literary project. The report was manipulated often by the press, to "explain," for example, racial unrest in Watts in August 1965, and by Citizens' Councils, who sold copies to segregationists to "prove" black pathology. See for example, Steve Estes, *I Am A Man! Race, Manhood, and the Civil Rights Movement* (Chapel Hill: University of North Carolina Press, 2005), 118.

[26] See for example, Madhu Dubey, *Black Women Novelists and the Nationalist Aesthetic* (Bloomington: Indiana University Press, 1994), 33. Dubey's is another study that does not mention Sarah E. Wright.

[27] For example, Carol A. Stack, *All Our Kin* (New York: Harper Colophon, 1970); Angela Davis, "Reflections on the Black Women's Role in the Community of Slaves," *Black Scholar*

Wright addresses the so-called pathology deemed to characterize black women's sexuality and, by extension, their roles as wives and mothers, as infused into Moynihan's Report. This is not to say that Wright privileges one gender over the other in *This Child's Gonna Live*. Jacob does not blame his wife for the impotence he feels in his efforts to support his family himself. A close reading reveals children sucking the icicles that hang from shanties for sustenance, children gagging on molasses sandwiches every day, and Jacob reeling from the pain of hunger as he sets off to work. Even so, one of his sons offers Jacob his only meat sandwich despite the fact he is starving (54) and though Mariah has to decide how to dole out what little medicine she has across five members of her sick family, on one occasion Jacob is overcome when his wife gives all the worm medicine to him (55). Through it all a bitter, apocalyptic wind blows and beats against the old slave houses: "Wind split the sands of his earth apart. Wind gulped the earth's top crust" (52). The laborers barely cling to the land; they struggle to maintain their footing and to survive a hurricane that breaks open the waterlogged graveyard bringing decaying black bodies and their white bones to the surface. The struggle against the elements exacerbates all sharecroppers' efforts to scratch a living out of barren land, and the sea is too dangerous to afford oyster men a living. Jacob tries both but the whites knock him back and the wind is cold and merciless, "Wonder the wind don't unhinge this house and sweep it over this shifting-assed hill" (117). Mariah is a desperate mother but rather than kill her children out of desperation like Sethe in *Beloved* (1988), she is equally vehement that they should live. Although her son Rabbit dies with worms crawling out of his mouth and anus, it is neither worms nor TB that kills him but the erroneous belief that his mother's pills, hidden in the house because the option of suicide is always in her mind, will cure his ailments. Wright underscores that the pervasive cause of death is poverty as linked to Jim Crow racism but, in countering deleterious images of the black family, she refuses to present uncomplicatedly saintly black mothers, selfless black fathers, or a homogenous "folk."

In knotting together a plethora of social and political affiliations with nature's unpredictability in a modernist swirl of a text, Wright troubles the waters of the historical novel by making Mariah and husband Jacobs's Depression-era story politically intelligible and socially relevant for the angry riot-torn tail end of the 1960s. As Martin Luther King, Jr. stated in 1968 in *Where Do We Go From Here: Chaos or Community?*, his study of "a people torn apart from era to era" whose only option is to unite as families to resist oppression: "no society can repress an ugly past when the ravages persist into the present."[28] The problems with which Jacob and Mariah contend are shown to persist for the black family from one era to the next, but *This Child's Gonna Live* succeeds because "getting at how we feel about the past moves us far more than attempts at historical re-creation." The phrase is Pauline Kael's describing the evocation of the Depression 1930s in Arthur Penn's

---

3 (December 1971): 2-15; Toni Cade ed., *The Black Woman* (New York: New American Library, 1970).

[28] Martin Luther King, Jr. *Where Do We Go From Here: Chaos or Community?* (Boston: Beacon Press, 1968), 108-109.

Bonnie and Clyde (1967).[29] Wright's is not an historical novel; the contemporary style and tone are hard-hitting, and the language as violent as some of the graphic images that made Penn's film a countercultural hit. Like Penn's outlaws, Mariah is a modern heroine whose lack of restraint and flashing anger make her a rebel in Hortense Spillers's formulation, and a militant in her class and racial consciousness. While Penn envisaged *Bonnie and Clyde*—its southern folk heroes shot to death in an orgy of excessive violence—as a critique of the U.S.'s presence in Vietnam, *This Child's Gonna Live* is as critical of the distance still to be made up since the racially divisive application of New Deal programs in the 1930s, as it is of how much remains to be done at the end of the 1960s to win the War on Poverty.

Mariah stitches clothes out of feed sacks and makes cardboard soles for broken shoes, and yet when she applies for welfare, she is deemed not to be poor enough. Despite the fact that many of her own teeth have been lost to pyorrhea, she is simply not in need. The scene of her humiliation prefigures Alice Walker's "The Revenge of Hannah Kemhuff" (1973), a short story set in 1963 but with its key incident taking place much earlier in a Welfare Hall in the Depression year of 1931. Hannah is expected to provide proof that her family is starving in order for them to be issued with food stamps but her dignity has led her to dress her family in a white employer's cast offs. Miss Sadler, "a slip of a woman, all big blue eyes and yellow hair" refuses to help her because she resents Hannah's pride. Hannah's children die.[30] Miss Sadler's "mean moppet" is a version of Sarah E. Wright's Mrs. Cramston who "bucked her hard brown eyes at Mariah" and says, "Welfare don't give out free clothes to nothing but the poor. . . . Can't trust most of you niggers worth a damn" (186). Poverty as a literary theme does not belong to any particular writer or era but to elide Wright from the tradition of black southerners writing about poverty is to miss the anger and resentment being expressed in a livid language that Alice Walker avoids. While both Wright's Mariah and Walker's Hannah are thwarted in any attempt to retaliate by the threat of white violence in the Jim Crow South, Mariah's hatred of the white woman who judges her, not only in her poverty but in her dignity, is the more immediate and visceral:

> Wished she could take her pocketbook and lam that woman in the face! Wished she could take one of her blue pills and drop it into her drinking water. Poison the living shit out of her. Wished . . . stared at the poor-assed land lining the road all the way back to Tangierneck (186).[31]

---

[29] Pauline Kael, "Bonnie and Clyde," *New Yorker*, 21 October 1967.

[30] Alice Walker, "The Revenge of Hannah Kemhuff," *In Love and Trouble* (London: The Women's Press, 1984), 51.

[31] Gerda Lerner long ago pointed to the discrimination over New Deal Welfare payments: "Black people whose needs were usually greater, whose families were larger and whose chances of employment were worse than those of whites were the last to receive relief, the first to be cut off, and the last to be hired for work relief." Roosevelt was inundated with letters from those who were denied help when they believed themselves deserving. See *Black Women in White America: A Documentary History*, ed. Gerda Lerner (New York: Vintage, 1972).

The Upshur family survives a "tangle of pathology" on their own terms in a rural place cut off by the water and generally missed in the War on Poverty's focus on urban and inner city areas. Mariah begins the novel by attempting suicide and, maddened by poverty, hears voices throughout the novel telling her to kill herself and others. At the end she walks into the sea: "Just wade on in, Mariah . . . go on out into the ocean" (250). But she catches herself up and returns home with the simple statement, "Jacob, I forgot to put the dough in the oven so you and the children could have some nice hot bread for your dinner" (251). Mariah is finally one of the most robust of black southern women characters. The family she returns to bake bread for comprises the child who lives—Bardetta Tommetta—a girl named in memory of a lynched ancestor but whose Afrocentric name signals the pride in African ancestry that characterized the Black Arts Movement of the 1960s, and the development of revolutionary nationalism. The family includes a child of Jacob's born of another woman, and two more children, orphans whose mother is killed by a racist mob, as well as Jacob and Mariah's surviving sons: seven children and two parents. This extended black southern family will, it is made clear, be well cared for and nurtured, just as Jacob will nurture the new seeds he is planting in the few acres of land he has managed to buy back for his family as the novel closes.[32]

Mariah's powerlessness; heavily pregnant but welcoming death, is mediated into a form of resistance in *This Child's Gonna Live*. She is stubborn but, more importantly, she is anarchic, a rebel, and she is historicized as a southern woman, a descendant of other black women in the southern literary tradition. Mariah begins by scoffing at the history she inherits: "Ain't no history to this Eastern Shore worth telling, that I can see. All the history ever made left here when that Harriet Tubman left. History of this place ain't nothing but work, work, work" (28). However, in Wright's novel, history is a dialectical process in the way that Richard Wright described at the very end of *12 Million Black Voices*: "The seasons of the plantation no longer dictate the lives of many of us; hundreds of thousands of us are moving into the sphere of conscious history."[33] In a historical moment when African American writing was intensely political, not least in its aims to encourage a vision of greater depth, as well as equality for African Americans, Wright focuses on female vitality in her protagonist's struggle against poverty. In *The Autobiography of an Ex-Colored Man* (1912), the narrator asserts that "log cabins and plantations and dialect-speaking 'darkies' are perhaps better known in American literature than any other single picture of our national life."[34] But what was not adequately "known" was the humanity of the African American family and its ability to adapt. Narrativity is a feature of the history of black poverty, and the failure by the end of the 1960s to

---

[32] In this way, the Upshurs also recall Richard Wright's black kin who work together to make a crop, Wright, *12 Million Black Voices*, 59. This also reflects a shift in the intellectual history of the African American family from Gunnar Myrdal and E. Franklin Frazier to Herbert Gutman's *The Black Family in Slavery and Freedom, 1750-1925* (1976) in which the black family was no longer expected to replicate the white "American" family but was valued as part of a "widespread, adaptive, and distinctive kinship system." See Richard King, *Race, Culture, and the Intellectuals, 1940-1970* (Washington: Woodrow Wilson Center, 2004), 136.

[33] Wright, *12 Million Black Voices*, 147.

[34] James Weldon Johnson, *The Autobiography of an Ex-Colored Man* (London: The X Press, 1995), 145.

break the cycle of black deprivation does not equate with the failure of black cultural nationalism. This is a brave and a hopeful novel. In returning the reader to the dawn of the Great Depression at the moment when neo-abolitionism fuelled 1960s fiction, Wright invokes the experience of Depression in the rural South as relevant to African American social struggles continuing into the late 1960s and beyond. Sarah E. Wright integrates two historical moments and embeds them in the rhetoric of the 1960s; Mariah and Jacob have to "keep on marching" and, as Mariah's father warns, "build up something for the coming of the black nations of the world" (167-8). Such a novel makes pressing demands on collective memory, on the nation's capacity to withstand the "long shocks' of slavery, and the violent and destructive forces that continued to haunt the South and American race relations in the late 1960s. It portrays the black southern family as adaptive and progressive in the face of poverty and the thrall of progress.

LYNDON JOHNSON AND ALBERT GORE:
SOUTHERN NEW DEALERS AND THE MODERN SOUTH

Tony Badger

Jack Robinson, the young man from Carthage who ran Albert Gore's Senate office from 1956 to 1964 remembered:

> [A]fter Johnson was sworn in, just a few days later, he [Gore] comes to the office and says, "Jack R. I've got the call from the President and he wants to see me." Which means why don't you drive with me over to the White House. He says, "I won't be long, just wait here," at the south end you know. And again, you know, it's not Lyndon, it's the president. So he comes out, it didn't take long. And I said, "Well, what happened?" He said, "Well the president said, 'Albert, you know we're both old school teachers, and what I would like to do is to take the eraser and wipe the slate clean.'" And I said, "Well what did you say?' He said, "Mr. President I agree." He was so serious, you know. Well it wasn't two weeks that each was smacking against the other again.[1]

Lyndon B. Johnson (LBJ) and Albert Gore were elected to Congress within a year of each other in 1937-38. They were elected in the old style of patronage-oriented southern Democratic Party politics in which a plethora of candidates with few issues to divide them contested primary elections. Both circumvented the local county seat elites who usually delivered their counties' votes by taking their case directly to the people, mounting vigorous campaigns to establish their name recognition. Johnson reached out to the tiniest and most isolated communities in his district and completely overturned the "leisurely pace normal in Texas elections." Gore played the fiddle with a small band to attract a crowd on Saturday afternoons in courthouse squares across his district.[2]

But if they started their political lives in the traditional, old, rural South, their careers—LBJ until he stood down from the Presidency in January 1969 in the face of the intractable war in Vietnam, Gore until he was defeated as the number one target of the Nixon Southern Strategy in 1970—spanned the creation of the modern South. They themselves contributed to the collapse of the poor, rural, white supremacy South and the creation of a prosperous, urban, biracial South. Their careers saw the replacement of the props that had underpinned the Old South: a rural one-crop region mired in poverty became a booming industrialized, urbanized society with a diversified agriculture; a rigidly segregated South became a desegregated society in which African Americans enjoyed full civil rights; a politics which excluded disenfranchised African Americans became a bi-racial democracy in which African Americans voted, held office and shaped public policy; a one-party

---

[1] Jack Robinson, Sr., interview with the author, 23 January 2003.
[2] Robert Dallek, *Lone Star Rising: Lyndon Johnson and His Times, 1908-1960* (New York: Oxford University Press, 1991), 125-156. Robert Caro, *The Years of Lyndon Johnson: The Path to Power* (New York: Knopf, 1982), 389-444. *Carthage Courier*, 5 May 1938.

system in which the Democrats monopolized power became a two-party system in which a lily-white Republican Party routinely won the region's presidential votes.

Gore and Johnson were very similar. They were born within a year of each other in the hill country of Tennessee and Texas. Both struggled to go to college: Gore would raise enough of a crop to pay for tuition for a semester or two at Middle Tennessee State Teachers College, then go back to the farm, raise another crop and return to college. Johnson scrounged a bewildering variety of jobs at South West Texas State and taught Mexican Americans for a year at Cotulla to enable him to complete his degree at San Marcos. Both taught—Gore in one-room schools in Smith County, Johnson in Houston—but not for long. Both were natural politicians. Gore's classmates recall that he would stay in his room on a Saturday night at college to write postcards to people back in Smith County because he knew he would be running for office one day, and Johnson was a political whirlwind even at San Marcos. Gore was elected Superintendent of Education for Smith County, then served as campaign manager for rising Tennessee politician, Gordon Browning, and became Browning's Commissioner of Labor. Johnson went to Washington as Congressman Richard Kleberg' secretary and then became State National Youth Administration director for Texas.[3]

After election to Congress, both Johnson and Gore served in the war for strictly limited periods—Johnson at the start in the Far East, Gore near the end in Europe. Bryce Harlow, future Republican top-ranking official in the Eisenhower and Nixon administrations, worked in General Marshall's office and remembered that he had been given the task of getting service experience for New Deal congressmen who were up for re-election and had voted for the draft but not served themselves, though of draft age:

> So I had the task of giving a hand-conducted tour through the armed forces in time of war. . . . to get them in for a special basic training, and in for a little advanced training, and then for a special shipment to a combat area, and a special escort through a combat area, special return to the United States and special discharge. So then they would be veterans who had served in combat, so they could approach the voters unassailably the following year.

Harlow certainly exaggerated: Gore, for example, only enlisted after he was re-elected in 1944, and he had to resign his congressional seat, unlike Johnson. But although both Johnson and Gore would appeal to fellow veterans after the war, neither had the sort of tough war-time experience that profoundly shaped so many southerners, white and black.[4]

But if Gore and Johnson had been elected in the old-style of local, patronage-oriented politics in which the prime purpose of political office was to control jobs, they came to represent a new style of issue-oriented politics in the South, heralded

---

[3] Albert Gore, Sr., *Let the Glory Out: My South and Its Politics* (New York: Viking, 1972), 38-42. Albert Gore, Sr., Interview, Southern Historical Collection, University of North Carolina, Chapel Hill. Dallek, *Lone Star Rising*, 62-92.

[4] Bryce Harlow, Oral History Interview, 28 February 1979, by Michael Gillette, Lyndon B. Johnson Library, Austin, Texas.

by the New Deal and an activist federal government, in which politicians sought power to put liberal policies into action. They were typical of "a new generation of leaders" whom President Franklin D. Roosevelt (FDR) identified in the region and who were elected to state legislatures, statehouses, and Congress in the late 1930s and 1940s. Johnson and Gore would be elected to the Senate in 1948 and 1952: Johnson would defeat the rigidly conservative, popular governor, Coke Stevenson; Gore would defeat the veteran chair of the Senate Appropriations Committee and ally of Boss Crump, Kenneth McKellar. Both would do so by dauntingly vigorous personal campaigns. While Johnson used a helicopter to follow a punishing schedule across the state, the stately Stevenson deigned to give one address in each county seat. While Gore criss-crossed Tennessee in a relentless daily schedule of stump speeches and television broadcasts, the enfeebled McKellar largely remained in his hotel while supporters hit the campaign trail as surrogates.[5]

The Tennessee Valley Authority (TVA), the New Deal's massive flood control and power program, was the key factor in a new politics. To a new generation of southern politicians the TVA was a model for what the federal government might do for the poorest region in the country. They became, in north Alabaman John Sparkman's words, TVA liberals. Just as the federal government had rejuvenated a whole valley, so the federal government could rejuvenate a whole region: federal assistance through flood control, cheap power, and water resource development could be the engine of economic growth, modernizing agriculture, and stimulating industry; aid to education could transform the schools; federal assistance could provide everything from hospital construction to rural telephones.

Of course all politicians in Tennessee were in favor of the TVA. Senator McKellar, the bitter foe of TVA chairman, David Lilienthal, claimed to have been the founder of TVA and bitterly resented any claim that George Norris might have had anything to do with it. But McKellar did not see TVA as a model for federal intervention in the region's economy—he saw it as a piece of pork barrel and a source of jobs that he wished to control, whereas the new young politicians fought to preserve the independence of the TVA from political interference.[6]

---

[5] Tony Badger, "Whatever happened to Roosevelt's 'New Generation' of Southerners?," Robert A. Garson and Stuart Kidd, eds., *The Roosevelt Years: New Perspectives on the United States, 1933-1945* (Edinburgh: Edinburgh University Press, 1999), 122-138. Tony Badger, "'Closet Moderates': Why White Liberals Failed, 1945-1972," Ted Ownby, ed., *The Role of Ideas in the Civil Rights South* (Jackson: University Press of Mississippi, 2002), 86-88. Dallek, *Lone Star Rising*, 298-348. Robert Caro, *The Years of Lyndon Johnson: The Means of Ascent* (New York: Knopf, 1990), 179-302. David Lilienthal, *The Journal of David Lilienthal, Vol III, The Venturesome Years 1950-55* (New York: Harper and Row, 1964), 256, 333. James B. Gardner, "Political Leadership in a Period of Transition: Frank G. Clement, Albert Gore and Estes Kefauver in Tennessee Politics, 1948-1956" (Ph.D. diss., Vanderbilt University, 1978), 158-175, 239-276, 302-326. Nashville, *The Tennessean*, 1 July-31 July 1952.

[6] Steven M. Neuse, *David E. Lilienthal: The Journey of an American Liberal* (Knoxville: University of Tennessee Press, 1996), 155-59. Erwin C. Hargrove, *Prisoners of Myth: The Leadership of the Tennessee Valley Authority, 1933-1990* (Princeton: Princeton University Press, 1994), 58.

What Gore saw in the Tennessee Valley, Johnson saw when rural electrification came to the Hill Country and when he could see what the great projects on the Lower Colorado River could achieve. Whereas for southern conservatives the federal government was the problem, for southern New Dealers like Johnson and Gore the federal government was the solution. Federal aid, they believed, was essential to solve the region's health care and educational problems. Cheap credit from the Reconstruction Finance Corporation would liberate the region's entrepreneurs. In the battle to develop the region's infrastructure, Johnson and Gore would be allies from the late 1930s to the Great Society: most notably, on interstate highways, federal aid to education, and Medicare.

Gore, with Johnson's backing, was the main congressional sponsor of the Interstate Highway Act of 1956. His time in Germany convinced him of the value of the *autobahns*. And at the end of the war there was a dramatic increase in car ownership. As Al Gore recalled:

> I remember seeing as a child the long, long, long lines of red tail lights stretching out of highway 70 at night and the equally long line of headlights coming in the opposite direction. And at that time with only one, two-lane road going representing the main east-west corridor for Tennessee but also nationally. Highway 70 north was the principal east-west route for the whole midsection of the country.

Al Gore remembered that the six to eight round trips a year between Carthage and Washington became "a much longer ordeal." The lesson his father learnt from those regular trips was that these two lane roads were no longer adequate.[7]

Albert Gore took great pride in his leadership of Senate forces in support of the interstate highway system, what he and his House co-sponsor called "the greatest construction program in the history of the world." As chair of the Subcommittee of Public Roads of the Senate Public Works Committee he followed up on President Dwight D. Eisenhower's initiative and, even before General Clay's task force reported, introduced legislation for federal funding over the next six years of an interstate system. He believed that, without it, "national economic development would be seriously impaired." Given his head by the alcoholic and unfocused chair of the Committee, Dennis Chavez, Gore secured Senate passage of his bill in 1955. In 1956 the House tackled the source of funding—user taxes paid into a Highway Trust fund—and the Interstate Highway Act passed that summer. Gore consistently led the fight to ensure that there was no "stretch-out" of the program, to ensure that spending on the program was not cut back in the late Eisenhower administration and throughout the 1960s.[8]

---

[7] Al Gore, interview with the author, 9 April 2005.

[8] *New York Times*, 27 June 1956. Remarks, Governors' Forum, 4 May 1955. Albert Gore to Wilbur Mills, 6 October 1959. Remarks before the American Road Builders Association, 6 March 1961. Gore to R. Beatty and G. Davidson, 4 October 1968, Albert Gore Senate Papers, Gore Research Center, Middle Tennessee State University, Murfreesboro, Tennessee. Richard F. Weingroff, "Creating the Interstate System," *Public Roads* (online Summer 1996). Richard Weingroff to Mike Martin, 14 December 2001 (in author's possession).

The South led the nation in securing federal funds for interstate construction and led the nation in devoting its state budgets to highway construction. In 1965 every southern state but North Carolina exceeded the U.S. level of highway spending per thousand dollars of personal income. Mississippi spent twice the national ratio.[9] Al Gore illustrated the dramatic impact of the interstates at home in Tennessee:

> Last year, this past year, Nashville was the number one city in the nation for the recruitment of new industries and the relocation of industries and businesses from other places to Nashville. Number one in the entire nation. Nissan located here, Saturn located here, Dell Computer located here, not all of those three in the last year, but why? And why has Nashville been so prosperous even during the downturn? Because there's interstate 40, interstate 65, interstate 24. And if you look at the market of the United States there's the eastern two-thirds and then the scarcely populated Rockies and then the west coast, Nashville is at the center, the center of gravity, particularly as the population has shifted towards the Sunbelt. . . . And the confluence of those three major interstates right here has made it one of the most attractive places to locate businesses in the nation.[10]

Johnson and Gore had particular enthusiasms for special aspects of federal investment in the South.

For LBJ it was the space program which brought such spectacular benefits to Alabama and Florida, but above all Houston. The powerful Houston congressman, Albert Thomas, the only congressman LBJ was allegedly afraid of, actually opposed the space program as chair of the Appropriations Subcommittee that controlled space spending. But once the Soviets launched Sputnik, LBJ saw the potential to embarrass the Eisenhower administration and rally Democrats. He and Sam Rayburn got Thomas onside, together with another Texan, Olin "Tiger" Teague, chair of the House Space Committee, and led the fight to establish the National Aeronautics and Space Administration. NASA awarded fifty of its 130 research grants and contracts to southern universities. When it was announced that the Manned Spacecraft Center would be built in Houston, twenty-nine companies had located there within a year, even before construction started.[11]

For Gore it was atomic power. FDR had made him privy to the developments at Oak Ridge. Gore was as enthusiastic about the peaceful use of atomic power as he was for the TVA. In his senate campaign in 1952 he vowed to make Tennessee the "atomic capital" of the nation. Despairing of the slowness of private industry to develop nuclear reactors on the scale of the British, he secured passage with

[9] Bruce Schulman, *From Cotton Belt to Sun Belt: Federal Development and the Transformation of the South, 1938-1980* (Durham, NC: Duke University Press, 1994), 200.

[10] Al Gore interview.

[11] Schulman, *From Cotton Belt to Sunbelt*, 147-149.

Johnson's help of a Senate bill in 1956 for government financing of reactor construction. The bill floundered in the House.[12]

Scholars such as Alan Brinkley and Numan V. Bartley argue that this growth-oriented liberalism represented a backtrack from the redistributionist politics of the New Deal. Commercial Keynesianism was the characteristic of American post-war liberalism and failed to challenge the structural inequalities in American society. It is possible to cast Johnson's War on Poverty in such terms—interested more in creating access to jobs and services rather than putting a floor under people's incomes or giving them jobs. It was also a program that local elites in the South sought to co-opt. Whereas New Dealers saw the lack of economic growth in the region as inextricably linked to poverty, southern political leaders of the late 1960s and 1970s did not see rural and urban poverty as an obstacle to economic growth. Thus the spectacular growth of the Sunbelt coexisted, as it does today, with the persistence of severe, Third-World style poverty.[13]

Yet it is difficult to ignore the welfare explosion in the South in the 1960s, the increased transfer payments of the War on Poverty, the access to educational opportunity that facilitated the dramatic increase of the black middle class, the empowerment of local black activists and politicians as they sought the control of the new federal programs, or the benefits of Medicaid and Medicare. Gore supported Johnson fully in these endeavors.

Gore may have been more of a Populist on economic issues than LBJ: he distrusted tax cuts, pushed for tax reform and constantly lamented policies of high interest rates. But both men admired and cultivated rich and successful businessmen: for Johnson, George Brown of Brown and Root and some of the independent oilmen, for Gore, Bernard Baruch and Armand Hammer. Raised in economic insecurity, both strove to achieve financial success. Johnson made his money while in office through his radio and TV empire in Austin. Gore had more modest goals while in office—he set up a local food and feed mill with Grady Nixon, which gave him enough financial security to contemplate the senate race in 1952. He also set up a cattle breeding business with Hammer. They consoled each other over the loss of their prize Angus bull, the 382, and Hammer suggested they place an obituary of the

---

[12] Campaign Speech, 7 June 1952, Box 12, Gore to *Memphis Commercial Appeal*, 31 October 1951, Albert Gore House Papers, Gore Research Center, Middle Tennessee State University, Murfreesboro, Tennessee. *New York Times*, 17, 18 April 1951. Albert Gore to Clinton Anderson, 14 December 1956, copy in Box 44, LBJ Congressional File, Johnson Library. Albert Gore to Ben West, mayor of Nashville, 8 March 1957. B53, Legis. Gore Senate Papers. Gore statement, provided to Mrs. T. Roy Reid for *Democratic Women's Club Newsletter*, February 4, 1957, B11, Dept., "AEC—General," 1957, Gore Senate Papers. Gore to *St. Louis Post Dispatch*, 29 June 1956. B51, Legis., "AEC--S2725," 1956, Gore Senate Papers.
[13] Alan Brinkley, *The End of Reform: New Deal Liberalism in Recession and War* (New York: Knopf, 1995), 265-271. Numan V. Bartley, *The New South: 1945-1980* (Baton Rouge: Louisiana State University Press, 1995), 38-73. For persistent social democratic trends in Congress in the 1950s see Roger Biles, *Crusading Liberal: Paul H. Douglas of Illinois* (DeKalb, IL: Northern Illinois University Press, 2002), and Meg Jacobs, "The Politics of Purchasing Power: Political Economy, Consumption, Politics and State-building in the United States, 1909-1959" (Ph.D. diss., University of Virginia, 1998), chap. 4, 5.

382 in the *American Angus Journal*. But Gore made serious money after he left office. Setting up as a lawyer in Washington with Hammer's Occidental as one of his clients, Gore became chair of the Island Creek Coal Company, one of Hammer's subsidiaries, and he traveled the world negotiating one to one with foreign heads of state like Ceausescu of Rumania and with the Chinese.[14]

Southern liberals believed that federally-sponsored economic development would eventually solve the region's racial problems. Economic growth would eventually lessen the need for competition between lower-income whites and blacks and eliminate poor white racism. The race issue was a conservative red herring designed to divert poor whites from supporting New Deal-style policies. Such sentiments were both genuine and prudential. They accorded with social science predictions but also enabled the politicians to focus on the economic issues which united their bi-racial lower-income coalition of supporters and to avoid the racial issues which divided them. When the race issue could not be avoided in the 1950s, most leading southern liberal politicians—like Lister Hill, John Sparkman, and William Fulbright—became "closet moderates" running for cover. They argued that they had no alternative but to espouse segregationist views in deference to the mass white racist sentiments of their constituents. In the words of Lewis Killian, they surrendered to the mob before it even gathered.[15]

Gore and Johnson were cast in this southern liberal New Deal mode on race but for personal and political reasons freed themselves from the fatalism and resignation on the race issue that affected so many other white southern liberal politicians. Both favored economic measures as the key to gradual racial change. As State National Youth Administration director in Texas, Johnson had worked behind the scenes at night with black leaders to ensure that African American students could take full advantage of the NYA. Both Johnson and Gore supported the drive to abolish the poll tax. Both claimed to have an epiphany on segregation as a result of their drives to and from Washington. Johnson lamented that his cook had to squat in the bushes to relieve herself because there were no colored rest rooms at the filling stations. Gore dated his awareness to his first drive to Washington, DC, in 1939 with their new baby and African American nanny. Unable to find a motel that would house them for the overnight stop, they detoured to a cousin's in the east Tennessee mountains. Subsequently he came to an arrangement with a motel whereby they could all be housed, provided they arrived after dark and left before other guests rose in the morning. Mrs. Gore outraged the wife of another Tennessee congressman during the war by addressing an African American woman with the prefix "Mrs."[16]

---

[14] Dallek, *Lone Star Rising*, 189-192, 247-52, 409-416. Albert Gore, Sr. and Mrs. Pauline Gore, interview with the author, 1 December 1990. Albert Gore interview with Jack Bass, Southern Historical Collection, Chapel Hill, 1974, Albert Gore Oral History Interview, John F. Kennedy Library, Boston, Massachusetts. Gore, *Let the Glory Out*, 143-47, 187-191.

[15] Badger, "'Closet Moderates': Why White Liberals Failed, 1945-1972," 88-93.

[16] Dallek, *Lone Star Rising*, 138-43. Robert Mann, *The Walls of Jericho: Lyndon Johnson, Hubert Humphrey, Richard Russell and the Struggle for Civil Rights* (New York: Harcourt Brace, 1996), 64-68, 84-86. Albert Gore, Sr. and Mrs. Pauline Gore, interview with the author, 1 December 1990.

Gore considered himself "personally upfront" on the race issue, but if he and Johnson had any doubts about segregation, they carefully avoided sharing these doubts with their constituents. They made no effort to prepare the voters for the *Brown v. Board of Education* decision. Indeed, Johnson after his narrow Senate election victory in 1948 strove to ingratiate himself with both Texas conservatives and Richard Russell and the older southern senators with flamboyant segregationist speeches attacking the specter of federal government interference with southern race relations. Even when the *Brown* decision was handed down, they both contented themselves with asserting that implementation was a matter for the courts and men and women of goodwill at the local level. Johnson instinctively wanted to avoid the civil rights issue. Like his mentor Sam Rayburn he saw it as a sectional issue that could only divide the Democratic Party: he disliked the fire-eaters on both sides, the segregationist diehards from the South and the civil rights "bomb throwers" from the North.[17]

But both were young enough to have national political ambitions. Both saw themselves as possibly the first modern southern president. Before his heart attack, Johnson had ambitions for the presidential nomination in 1956 and never entirely gave them up. Gore had his eyes on the vice-presidential slot in 1956, and he had the example of his fellow Tennessee senator, Estes Kefauver, who ran another strong bid for the Democratic nomination in 1952. So when the South started to resist the *Brown* decision, both demurred. Neither Gore nor Kefauver signed the Southern Manifesto. Both sponsors and many constituents assumed Kefauver would not sign in the midst of his presidential bid. But they assumed Gore would. To put Gore on the spot and leave him no alternative, Senator Strom Thurmond of South Carolina invited Gore to sign on the floor of the Senate, brandishing the Manifesto and jabbing him in the chest. "Hell No," Gore replied, then looked up to the gallery to see the southern pressmen, all primed in advance, witnessing the confrontation.[18] A former classmate of Pauline Gore warned that people felt Gore had "actually betrayed the South because people felt that you were on their side." Gore faced, he threatened, "almost certain defeat in 1958." In fact Gore survived comfortably in 1958. Estes Kefauver would also defeat conservative segregationist opposition two years later.[19]

Johnson, anxious to establish his civil rights credentials to win over northern Democrats and to show that the Democratic Party, contrary to Republican charges, was not paralyzed on civil rights, masterminded the passage of the 1957 Civil Rights Act, the first since Reconstruction which essentially opened the way for the Justice Department to protect the right to vote in the South. As Robert Caro has shown compellingly at great length, and Evans and Novak showed more concisely almost forty years ago, Johnson had to make the bill moderate enough to avoid a southern

---

[17] Tony Badger, *Race and War: Lyndon Johnson and William Fulbright* (Reading, England: University of Reading Press, 2000), 6-8.

[18] Tony Badger, "Southerners Who Refused to Sign the Southern Manifesto," *Historical Journal*, 42.2 (1999): 517-519, 525-526.

[19] Sims Crownover to Albert Gore, 19 April 1956, Gore Senate Papers. Hugh Davis Graham, *Crisis in Print: Desegregation and the Press in Tennessee* (Nashville: Vanderbilt University Press, 1967), 29-90. Robinson interview.

filibuster, yet strong enough to retain northern support. His brilliant maneuvering, softening enforcement provisions through jury trials and co-opting western Democrats with promises on pet western projects, stunned the Republicans.[20]

Gore was able to support the 1957 Civil Rights Act, (as he would again in 1960), once he had managed, he claimed, to eliminate its worst coercive elements. He was unequivocal in his defense of the right to vote. In 1958 at the last minute former Governor Prentice Cooper ran against him and specifically campaigned on the issue of the Manifesto. Cooper waved a copy of the Manifesto at every opportunity and announced that he would have signed it. There were tense campaign stops for Gore in western Tennessee, the cotton plantation, black majority area of the state, but he made no apology for supporting the right to vote of people who had been prepared to serve their country in World War II.[21]

As vice-president, Johnson made substantial progress jawboning defense and government contractors to open up equal employment opportunities for African Americans. When Kennedy finally introduced strong civil rights legislation in 1963, Johnson advised him not to be scared of the southerners. As President, Johnson had the measure of the southern opposition. He knew he had to get the strongest possible bill through to win over northern liberal doubters and legitimize his nomination in his own right as President. He faced down the southern filibuster and retained the loyalty of Republicans by demonstrating that he was not going to compromise. That Republican support was crucial to the final passage of the 1964 Act. Having dismantled overnight de jure segregation and laid the basis for massive school desegregation and the ending of job discrimination, Johnson was anxious to move on to end black disfranchisement. His landslide victory in 1964 and the violence at Selma gave him the leverage to drive through the 1965 Voting Rights Act. The effect was dramatic. Freedom Summer had registered less than a thousand voters in Mississippi. Less than 6 percent of the voting age black population was registered. Within three years of the passage of the Voting Rights Act, 60 percent of Mississippi blacks could vote.[22]

It was to be LBJ's last major civil rights victory. The long hot summers of race riots strengthened northern hostility to further civil rights concessions. Congress was increasingly unsympathetic to black demands. Jobs were harder to legislate for than voting rolls. The Vietnam War distracted Johnson and took money away from social programs. He shied away from Martin Luther King, Jr. and could not deal with younger black militants. He was prey to the poison that J. Edgar Hoover put in his ear about King, revolutionary black radicals, and communist conspiracies. He reacted angrily to the Kerner Commission on the riots which he took as a personal affront to all he had tried to do.[23]

Yet all the time he worked away at doing what he did best, trying to get legislation through. He kept pushing for civil rights measures even when the odds were stacked against him. He understood black impatience and understood how little

---

[20] Badger, *Race and War*, 12-13. Rowland Evans and Robert Novak, *Lyndon B. Johnson: The Exercise of Power* (New York: New American Library, 1966), 119-40.

[21] Robinson interview.

[22] Badger, *Race and War*, 13-15.

[23] Ibid., 16.

had been done for the black poor in the ghettoes. He retained the closest relationships with black leaders like Roy Wilkins, James Farmer, and Whitney Young, and when King was assassinated, he seized the chance to get through Open Housing legislation. He cemented the loyalty of African American voters, north and south, to the Democratic Party. And what he did for black civil rights remained his proudest achievement until his death in 1973.[24]

For Albert Gore, balancing racial moderation with white constituency pressure was harder in the 1960s when African American protesters started dictating the timetable of racial change. In 1963 and 1964 Gore hoped to repeat his tactics of 1957, i.e. getting concessions to enable him to support civil rights legislation. But his constituency mail ran overwhelmingly against the legislation, and Gore faced tough opposition from Republican Dan Kuykendall from Memphis at a time when Barry Goldwater was attempting to win over disaffected white segregationists. Gore voted against the bill. He himself focused on the lack of guidelines or standards in Title VI—he feared unelected bureaucrats in the Department of Health Education and Welfare would arbitrarily cut off funds to Tennessee school districts. He no longer had the protection of Estes Kefauver alongside him. Some argued that Pauline Gore, alerted by brother Whit LaFon in Jackson, was fearful of the political fall-out in western Tennessee in the election. But Gore's pattern of behavior was not uncommon amongst southern moderate congressmen. Jim Wright, Jack Brooks, and Dante Fascell all followed the same path—refusing to sign the Southern Manifesto, voting for the 1957 Act, but against the 1964 Act. The right to vote was one matter, local school districts were another.[25]

But re-election and the violence at Selma resolved dilemmas more easily. While many constituents blamed King and the protesters for the violence and feared that Johnson's bill would create a "watered down replica of the Russian monstrosity," Gore found Johnson's address to Congress "inspiring" and from the start indicated that he would support the Voting Rights Act. "Freedom of the ballot box is the very essence of democracy," he proclaimed. Indeed, as someone who had supported anti-poll tax legislation in 1942, he supported the efforts to add the abolition of the poll tax by legislation in 1965 rather than constitutional amendments.[26]

White disillusionment with such civil rights grew in western Tennessee over the next five years. The specter of Communism loomed large in correspondence from Gore's constituents. "The Communists are our most deadly enemies, our boys died by the 1000s in Korea and now over 400 in South Vietnam so far, why let these boys down by letting these Communist agitators create chaotic conditions as exist in Selma today?" A repeated refrain was the double standard applied to whites and to civil rights protesters. King was a lawbreaker "who violates any law he wishes,

---

[24] Ibid.

[25] Graham, *Crisis in Print*, 235, 264. John Seigenthaler interview with the author, 18 February 2003. Robinson interview. Badger, "Southerners who did not sign the Southern Manifesto," 534.

[26] Albert Gore to Larry McHee, 16 March 1965, to Mrs. Curtis E. Fort, 24 March 1965, to Mary Walton Collier, 12 March 1965, C 17 Legis. J. R. Philyaw to Gore 16 April 1965, Mrs. H. R. Parotte to Gore, 10 April 1965, A 47 Issue Mail, Gore Senate Papers.

according to his conscience, while no one else is allowed to." Is it right "for us to be taxed to support the negs to raise bastards. Negro preacher's daughter down here has six bastards. And the US News shows that Washington is full of bastards."[27]

Gore was unmoved and supported the Open Housing Act in 1968 and opposed the Supreme Court nominations of conservative white southerners Clement Haynesworth and Harold Carswell. These votes won him much praise from the black political organization, the Tennessee Voters Council. Gore received overwhelming black support. But there was always a certain distance between black voters and Gore. David Halberstam noted Gore's "failure to make special gestures, his belief that his record speaks for itself." Gore himself acknowledged that "while black leaders almost unanimously supported me, some of them were not all that enthusiastic. For they never felt I was quite their man. While I had supported civil rights legislation generally, I was not the kind of person to "clear things in advance with black leaders—or any other kind of leader." Gore's relations with African Americans reflected the general pattern of southern moderates of his generation. They campaigned for black support at one remove, dealing through intermediaries with black leaders who were expected to deliver the black vote. That style of campaigning for black support made it hard for Gore to pick up some of the immediacy and impatience of black demands and to enthuse the black electorate.[28]

Johnson and Gore therefore had much the same political agenda on economic development and racial change. They were natural allies. They worked hard to like each other. Gore rejoiced in Johnson's Senate victory in 1948. They flattered each other and joked about their respective herds of cattle. They visited each other's ranches. Their wives got on well. Gore gave Johnson a much-appreciated pig for his ranch, and they spoke in each other's states. In particular, Johnson called Gore over to Texas to speak in the last week of the 1956 campaign as he and Rayburn tried to keep the state in Democrat hands. Johnson cast Texas votes for Gore's vice-presidential bid in 1956. Gore had the greatest admiration for Johnson's legislative expertise. He supported the Great Society legislation enthusiastically.[29]

Yet in many ways they were too similar. Both saw themselves as potential southern presidents, Gore was never a member of the southern caucus, and he was never part of Johnson's inner circle. He was too uncompromising for the majority leader, who was always anxious to compromise. As Harry McPherson recalled:

He [Johnson] had a terrible time with Gore. They had a lot in common politically, but Gore had the damnedest ability to offend through a kind of righteous pomposity that would drive Johnson right up the wall and me too. I used to just despise it. He always looked like a Baptist bishop standing back

---

[27] Tony Badger, "Albert Gore, Sr. and Civil Rights," Paper at the Gore Research Center, 8 November 1997.

[28] David Halberstam, "The End of a Populist," *Harpers*, (January 1971): 42. Robinson interview. Gore, *Let the Glory Out*, 276.

[29] Albert and Pauline Gore to Lyndon Johnson, 6 October 1948, Gore to Johnson, 10 December 1957, Johnson to Gore, 19 December 1957, Johnson to Gore, 6 November 1956, Box 44. Johnson to Gore, 30 August 1956, Johnson to Gore, 16 June 1959, Box 71, U.S. Senate Master File, Johnson Library.

there speaking of the outrageous thing that had just been perpetrated on the people by the Establishment. Then Gore was also terribly ambitious.

As Gore's admirer, Adrian Fisher recalled, Gore was "a hard man to put pressure on," and Johnson wanted to be able to pressure everybody. Whereas Johnson was a friend of J. Edgar Hoover, Hoover targeted Gore with characteristic single-mindedness from 1953, when Gore had criticized the treatment by FBI agents of one of his constituents. Gore was far friendlier with Johnson's Texas nemesis, Ralph Yarborough, than with Johnson. He was close also to other senators whom Johnson often humiliated—like Paul Douglas of Illinois and Herbert Lehman of New York—or tough men Johnson could not control—like Gore's closest ally, Mike Monroney of Oklahoma.[30]

Johnson kept Gore off the Finance Committee for a long time. He undercut Gore's efforts to investigate campaign finances in 1956. From 1958 onwards, the conservative Buford Ellington, whom Gore regarded as a "dolt," was Johnson's point man in Tennessee. Much as Gore needed Johnson's support, he chafed at the deference required to the majority leader. In 1960 he led an effort to undermine Johnson's absolute control of the Democratic Policy Committee. Gore invited all the likely Democratic presidential candidates to Tennessee in 1960. He saw no reason to feel inferior to any of them, and he supported Kennedy rather than Johnson for the presidency in 1960. He thought that Johnson was too subservient to the big money interests. He also thought that Johnson was the meanest man in Washington, and he meant "mean" as in cruel. When Kennedy was elected and Johnson became vice-president, Gore must have thought that his days of having to defer to Johnson were over. By the time Kennedy's second term would be over in 1968, Gore might have a realistic chance of being the first modern southern president. When Johnson attempted as vice-president to continue to control the Democratic caucus and keep his majority leader's office, Gore was the leader of the powerful minority that effectively drove Johnson off. Gore spoke with the unguarded vehemence of someone who would not have to worry about Johnson again. They maintained some of the niceties while LBJ was vice-president. Gore inserted LBJ's speeches in Berlin in the *Congressional Record* and praised their wisdom. Johnson consulted Gore on a speech he was to make in Nashville. He made elaborate protestations that he had not encouraged Buford Ellington to run against Gore in 1964. But Johnson also coldly ensured that Gore, who knew more about the control of nuclear weapons than any man in the Senate, was excluded from the congressional delegation that helped negotiate the test ban treaty in Washington. When Kennedy was assassinated, Gore would have realized that he would never have the chance to be president.[31]

Despite Gore's support of Great Society legislation, he infuriated LBJ by his opposition to the tax cut, his opposition to the nomination of Henry Fowler as Secretary of the Treasury, and his repeated criticism of the high interest rates and

---

[30] Harry McPherson, Oral History 1 28, Adrian Fisher, Oral History 1 18, Johnson Library.

[31] Robert Caro, *Master of the Senate: The Years of Lyndon Johnson* (New York: Knopf, 2002), 670, 674-5, 680, 858-9, 1035-39. Gore to Lyndon Johnson, 12 January 1960, Box 44, LBJ Congressional File, Johnson Library. Gordon Petty, interview with the author, April 2004.

tight money in the later Johnson years.[32] But it was foreign policy that was to see a lasting and bitter breach between the two southern New Dealers. Like most southerners, liberal or conservative, Johnson and Gore were liberal internationalists. They were committed to preparedness and support for Britain during the run-up to World War II, supporters of the Roosevelt-Hull foreign policy, supporters of containment, the Truman Doctrine, and the Marshall Plan. They were staunch anti-communists and opponents of Republican isolationism. But they differed bitterly on Vietnam.

John Culver, then a representative from Iowa, remembered being summoned to the White House with other members of the House Foreign Affairs Committee and the Senate Foreign Relations committee, and the two Appropriations committees:

> It was during the build up, the request for more funding to carry this out and there was this very elaborate full briefing and all the foreign policy members of this group participated and were asked back and even Mac Bundy [National Security Adviser], and the budget director and so forth. Everyone was served a couple of strong scotches and quite relaxed and by the time everyone sat down for the briefing and Johnson sat in the front of course, and the members would go up in turn and get their particular briefing, their presentation of the briefing and I had this feeling that he was sitting in a director's chair, because he sat up there with his drink and would not hesitate to interrupt the briefer and say to Bob, "Bob tell me about this" and to Dean "be sure to mention this." And of course it was awkward because he kept interrupting but every time, in fairness, every time that he asked them to make a point or to comment in one way or another, it strengthened the political presentation and clearly he was making points that he thought would appeal and resonate well with the congressmen and senators there. When the briefings were formally finished, he stood up in front of the group and said he would take any questions that anybody asked. He was pretty relaxed at that time and I remember a number of questions. But the question I remember was that posed by Al Cederberg, who was the ranking Republican on the House Appropriations Committee and a long-time house member from Michigan. And he raised his hand and he said, "Mr. President," he said, "I agree with you about this war thing!" And that was exactly what he said, "I agree about this war thing, but what I don't understand is how we give them all this money and they don't do what we want them to." Johnson said . . . "Cederberg, let me tell you something," he said, "my home county in Texas is Blanco County in Texas, and a number of years ago the boys came into my office and said Lyndon we gotta get ourselves a sheriff, who should we get? And I said, boys you should go out and get yourself a good-looking man and make sure he doesn't drink or smoke or think the girls are pretty and he's honest and bring him in here to me. And after a few months they came in and sure enough they had a boy that checked out with every particular. Good, big, strong, handsome man, so I reached in my drawer and there's a big shiny badge and it said 'Sheriff, Blanco County, Texas.' I took it and put it right on his

---

[32] Jack Valenti to Johnson, 5 March 1966, Mike Manatos to Johnson, 5 April 1967, Box 207, White House Central File, Johnson Library.

chest and he was the proudest man in Blanco County. And in the first six months, Cederberg, he was the best Sheriff Blanco County in Texas probably ever had, but the seventh month he started to smoke and the eighth month he started to drink too much, the ninth month he thought everybody's wife was his girlfriend and about the tenth month, every time you paid a fine in Blanco County Texas he thought it was supposed to go in his bank account. So about the eleventh or twelfth month we had to fire him and get ourselves a new sheriff. Now I ask you, Cederberg, if Lyndon Johnson can't even keep a sheriff in Blanco County, Texas, how do you think I can keep a government in Vietnam?" So everybody had a great laugh at that and of course upon reflection, the tragedy was, he didn't follow the moral and the wisdom of his own story.[33]

Johnson committed himself to the war in Vietnam as a means of demonstrating America's resolve in the Cold War, as a way of stopping the dominos falling in South East Asia, and because he thought that defeat in South East Asia would unleash the great reactionary beast in the United States, just as the loss of China, as he saw it, unleashed McCarthyism. But Johnson, as Lloyd Gardner has compellingly argued, also saw Vietnam through the eyes of a southern New Dealer. Like Texas in the 1930s it was ripe for infrastructure development. His billion-dollar development plan, laid out in his Johns Hopkins speech of 1965, would enable the region to be transformed in the same way as the New Deal had changed the South. For the Tennessee Valley, read the Mekong Delta. Johnson liked to believe that other Asian leaders shared his vision, and for a time he believed that Ho Chi Minh would find the bait of that development plan irresistible. LBJ never quite understood why Ho did not react like Lister Hill or John Sparkman or himself to the promise of cheap electrical power. Robert Komer, director of pacification in Vietnam, recalled that LBJ drove him up the wall about rural electrification. Johnson persuaded the old head of the TVA, David Lilienthal, to take charge of special development programs in Vietnam.[34]

Lilienthal had been Gore's mentor. But Gore was unpersuaded by the possibilities of American success in Vietnam. His own visit there in 1959 had led him to doubt American ability to compensate for a corrupt and authoritarian regime. He listened to dissenters like David Halberstam, whom he had nurtured when he was a cub reporter on the *Tennessean*, and to Chester Bowles and John Kenneth Galbraith who had worked with him on price controls in World War II. He pleaded with Kennedy in 1963 to plan for a quick withdrawal. He became a leading opponent of the war on the Senate Foreign Relations Committee. The war compounded Gore's distrust of Lyndon Johnson.[35]

---

[33] John Culver, Interview with the author, 8 December 2003.

[34] Lloyd Gardner, *Pay Any Price: Lyndon Johnson and the War for Vietnam* (Chicago: I. R. Dee, 1995), passim.

[35] Background Material on Indochina for possible use in speech by Senator Gore, Research-Foreign Policy-Indochina 1954, Gore Senate Papers. Gale McGhee's Senate Summary, Gore letter to the editor, 10 January 1960, B 64, Gore Senate Papers, Hodges, "Gore", ch. 1. Appointment Index-Albert Gore 1 August 1963, off record, Kennedy Library. Albert Gore to

He never wavered in his belief that his course of action on Vietnam was right. "If I have ever," he told Gene Sloan in November 1969, "been right about anything in my entire life, then I was right in opposing our involvement in the Vietnam War. I cannot claim a perfect record because I permitted myself to be misled into voting for the Tonkin Gulf resolution. I am confident that I was right in opposing escalation of the war. Indeed, except for the role that I and others played in this regard, we may well have been in war with Red China today."[36]

It was not just Gore's stance on Vietnam that made him vulnerable in Tennessee. Racial and cultural change in southern politics also threatened him. Characteristically in 1965 Lyndon Johnson made two contradictory predictions about the Voting Rights Act. At times he fatalistically assumed that he was handing over the South to the Republican Party for the next fifty years, driving whites into the GOP camp. At other times, notably when Larry O'Brien briefed him on the 1964 elections, he excitedly saw the black vote in the South as the "key" to a future liberal Democratic Party in the South.[37]

Albert Gore's final race in 1970 suggested that Johnson's more gloomy prognosis was correct. Gore went into the 1970 election with a divided state party and almost nothing of a personal organizational base and widespread perception that he had paid insufficient attention to his constituents. One pollster reported that "he is frequently criticized on the basis of being out of touch with the state, a 'politician' who appears on the scene a few months before election time to take popular stands on controversial issues—and once elected is seldom seen or heard from by his constituents." Said one voter "He's a politician . . . plays it like a politician. Until six months before the election we never hear from him, then you start getting mail, films and so on."[38]

In any case, Republicans in Tennessee had been increasingly successful. Moving out from their traditional eastern Tennessee mountain base, they had capitalized on middle- and upper-class white support to win the presidential vote in every election since 1952, except 1964. And in 1964 Dan Kuykendall, a Goldwater

---

David Halberstam, 6 May 1964, Pauline Gore to Halberstam, 22 November 1963, Gore Senate Papers. John Kenneth Galbraith, *A life in our times: memoirs* (London: Deutsch, 1981), 144. John Kenneth Galbraith, *Name-dropping* (London: Aurum, 1999). Badger, *Race and War*, 24-27.

[36] Gore to Gene H. Sloan, 20 November 1969, Gore Papers.

[37] Mark Stern, *Calculating Visions: Kennedy, Johnson and Civil Rights* (New Brunswick, NJ: Rutgers University Press, 1992), 212-214.

[38] Cambridge Opinion Studies, Inc. Report, p. 16, 39, Box 12, Papers of William E. Brock, Special Collections, University of Tennessee Library, Knoxville. Gore vigorously refuted this contention. He was in Tennessee at some point in 43 weeks in 1967, the same in 1968, every weekend in 1969 (he made 75 trips to the state that year) and even more in 1970. Gore, *Let the Glory Out*, 213-214. Washington Report, June 1968, December 1969, C44 Gore Senate Papers. But Gore allies did not dispute the existence of the complaints. Robinson interview, Seigenthaler interview. Nevertheless, as one of the supporters of his opponent, William E. Brock, complained in December 1969, whereas Gore was in Memphis every weekend, there would be eight weeks between's Brock's visits. "If I'm going to sell the product, I've got to give the customers a glimpse of the material." Frank B. Liddle, Jr. to Ken Rietz, 18 December 1969, Box 31, Brock Papers.

public relations man from Memphis, had polled 46.4 percent against Gore. Democratic white support in western Tennessee had already started to crumble. In 1964 only 35 percent of lower-income whites supported Gore in Memphis. The same year Howard Baker, Jr. polled over 47 percent against Ross Bass for the Senate and then won comfortably in 1966. Baker was on his way to building up the strongest political base of the first generation of southern Republicans senators. In 1968 white Democrats in middle and eastern Tennessee switched to George Wallace. His 34 percent of the vote enabled Nixon to win that election.[39]

In 1969 wealthy congressman, William E. Brock, of the Chattanooga candy manufacturing family, made plans to unseat Gore. As early as June 1969 Brock had hired the political consultants who had mapped out a strategy for fund-raising and media (to offset the fact that only 20 percent of voters knew who Brock was). They identified the war as the major issue for Tennesseans, but their polls showed that three major areas provoked "active response or extreme vulnerability":

> A The continuing deterioration of public regard for the law, as symbolized by the violent campus incidents and the weakness of school administrations in coping with them:
> B The national trend toward increased welfare support and priority for Negroes, many of whom appear unwilling to help themselves:
> C The expanding influence of the Federal government in general and the Supreme Court, in particular, in the day to day affairs and activities of the state and local community.

The tactics for the Brock campaign in exploiting this vulnerability were clear:

> In a general election campaign a contrast must first be drawn between political philosophies, as shown in the voting records. Brock is a Nixon conservative. Gore is a Kennedy liberal. There is little doubt that the deciding political force in Tennessee is the Wallace voter. Indications are that the Wallace people would support Brock and actively vote for him against Gore. They should not be courted but great pains should be taken to see that they are not offended.[40]

Brock made it clear that he sought the backlash vote. Nixon's Supreme Court nominations and the regional loyalty they played to were ideal issues. Confronting the Haynesworth nomination, Gore was left in no doubt as to what was at stake. Wrote one Oak Ridge constituent:

> If you have one inch of soul left unsold, if you have one micron of self-respect left, if somewhere in the darkest corner of the coal bin of your psyche you have

[39] Bartley and Graham, *Southern Politics and the Second Reconstruction*, 104-106, 123, 153. Earl and Merle Black, *The Rise of Southern Republicans* (Cambridge, MA: Harvard University Press, 2002), 94-96.
[40] Cambridge Opinion Studies, 6, Box 12, Brock Papers. Poll and Strategy, 16, Box 14, Brock Papers.

remaining to you one shining golden thread of nobility, of fairness, of justice, then you will vote for the confirmation of Judge Haynesworth.

When Gore failed to heed that advice, he was informed of his failings starkly:

> Your vote against Judge Haynesworth marks you as a gutless coward who has sold his soul to the corrupt union bosses and the black militants. It's little comfort to know that you'll get your 'reward' some day.

> I just want you to know that I'm going to do everything in my power to see that you're rewarded NEXT YEAR. I'm going to work tirelessly for Bill Brock starting NOW and I'm going to give what money I can to his campaign. And remember, there are thousands more Tennesseans like me.

> We want to rid this nation's government and the Union-owned Senate of our long-haired, vacuous, arrogant, anti-American disgraceful Senator.

> You make me sick,—p.s.: And don't waste my hard-earned tax dollars, which you so love to redistribute to the lazy, by having your staff send me one of your innocuous form letters.

Similarly Gore's stand on Vietnam seemed to encapsulate a whole world view that was distrusted in Tennessee. The mayor of Memphis, Henry Loeb, so battered by the garbage workers' strike and the King assassination, summed that view up:

> The basic immorality in this country today is not backing our fighting men in Vietnam, and in not winning the war, and I mean winning it. From that immorality, we go to rationalization on smut and pornography, turning away from prayer, etc.[41]

The drive to capture white middle- and lower-income voters who had voted for Wallace in 1968 was at the core of Nixon's Southern Strategy to wrest control of the region from the Democrats. William Timmons at the White House believed that the Brock-Gore race should "become a testing ground of Nixon-Kennedy strength as well as Brock-Gore." Timmons, now a deputy assistant to the President, had been Brock's administrative assistant. The White House was intimately involved in the Brock campaign from the start. Brock's political consultants were Treleavan Associates who had run Nixon's media campaign in 1968. His campaign manager was Kenneth Reitz from Treleavan. The White House and Reitz agreed that grant announcements, patronage appointments, and presidential visits would be carefully coordinated to aid the Brock campaign. Most famously, in September 1970, Agnew, the darling of the hard hats, came to the state to campaign for Brock. And the issues

---

[41] W. M. Woods, Oak Ridge, to Albert Gore, 25 October 1969, AGSC, A46, Issue Mail, 1969. Mrs. Glenda G. Grigsby, Nashville, to AG, n.d., AGSC, A46, Issue Mail, 1969, "Supreme Court," 9 of 10 Gore Papers. Henry Loeb to William O'Hara, copy to Gore, 5 June 1970, B44 Gore Senate Papers.

for the White House were the classic issues of the Southern Strategy. Tully Plesser summed it up for the strategy's mastermind, Harry Dent: "The campaign would appear to involve a political rejection of Albert Gore on grounds of excessive liberalism, with specific emphasis on his opposition to President Nixon's Vietnam policy, prayer in the schools and Haynesworth/Carswell." Brock afterwards isolated Gore's "position on the Supreme Court nominees and RN's VN [Richard Nixon's Vietnam] policies" as major factors in his victory.[42]

Gore, for his part, agreed with his opponents that the Wallace voters were the key. As his long-time aide, Bill Allen, argued, "In my opinion, though, the race issue is the biggest one in the campaign . . . that's why he's concentrating everything on economics—that good old bread and butter issue." Gore hammered away at all Brock's votes against programs that benefited Tennessee and stressed, in turn, what he had done for lower-income voters. He took the message to factory gates, stockyards and courthouse squares. As with all his campaigns, it was highly personal, chaotic, with volunteer staff, no advance men and little money. Brock's campaign was organized by contrast with military precision, with carefully staged events and a meticulous timetable which made sure that the candidate had time between 4 and 6 p.m. to freshen up and was always to be in bed by 11 p.m., so as always to look his best on television.[43]

Gore's bid to reclaim the Wallace voters appeared to succeed, according to Brock's pollsters. But in the final ten days of the campaign, the Brock campaign moved to offset the economic appeal with the media blitz that they had budgeted for eighteen months previously. As Ken Reitz told David Broder,

> We had 18 per cent undecided in our polls—mostly Wallaceites who were anti-Gore but not pro-Brock or pro-Republican. . . . Now we're really going after the undecided with the four big issues we've saved for the last ten days—prayer, busing, gun control, and the judges.

On each issue the television and press advertisements hammered away at the message that Gore was at odds with the people of Tennessee. Gore's press secretary Gene Graham bitterly observed, "Make it read from left to right, John T. Scopes, race, race and race." Brock's carefully crafted television advertisements focused on busing; on supporting the President on the war; on controlling government spending to curb inflation; on combating crime by appointing judges who would put criminals in jail and a Supreme Court that would not tie the hands of the police; on opposition to gun control; on stronger drug laws and enforcement, and the expulsion of violent

---

[42] William E Timmons to President, 8 August 1970, President's Office Files, Richard M. Nixon Presidential Materials Project, National Archives. Jim Allison to Harry Dent, 9 October 1969, John Stuckey to Bill Brock, n.d. Box 31, Brock Papers. Tully Plesser to Harry Dent, 2 October 1970, White House Special Files, Staff Member and Office Files, Harry S. Dent, 1969-70, Politics, Nixon Presidential Materials Project. White House Special Files: Staff Member and Office Files: John D. Erlichman, Alphabetical Subject Files 1963-73, Box 23 1970, Post-election analysis, Nixon Presidential Materials Project.

[43] Kenneth Reitz to Staff, 24 November 1969, Box 31, Brock Papers. Richard Harris, "How the People Feel," *New Yorker*, 10 July 1971.

student protesters. The slots were thirty or sixty seconds and showed Brock talking to ordinary Tennesseans: a parent, a veteran, a pensioner, a farmer, hunters, constituents who had been helped, disaffected Democrats, the wife of a POW, a textile worker, a young man. The message was that Brock listened and took local issues seriously unlike Gore. The repeated mantra was, "Bill Brock believes in the things we believe in."[44]

As a Knoxville evangelist explained why he could not vote for Gore: "the senator seems to think that Tennessee is located somewhere between Connecticut and Massachusetts." Or in Spiro Agnew's formulation, Gore believed "that Tennessee is located somewhere between the *New York Times* and the Greenwich Village Voice."[45]

In the battle for the Wallace votes, Gore made headway in Middle Tennessee but not sufficient to offset the wholesale defection of Wallace voters in the West. Whereas in Nashville Gore retained the support of nearly 60 percent of the lower-income white voters, in Memphis he only won 27.3 percent. He went down to defeat, 52.1 percent to 47.9 percent.[46]

Gore was the only major prize for Republicans in the Southern Strategy in 1970. Elsewhere New South politicians put together cross-class coalitions of affluent whites and blacks. Gore was unable to do so because of business opposition to his economic policies. Unlike New South gubernatorial candidates such as Jimmy Carter, John C. West, and Reuben Askew, Gore was encumbered by specific stances on Vietnam and the Supreme Court nominations. The successful New South candidates campaigned, as Randy Sanders has shown, as new faces who in a rather fuzzy and indeterminate way were racial moderates. In some states, like South Carolina, crass Republican racist appeals in 1970 alienated affluent whites. Brock's appeal on social and racial issues was more subtle. There was a different trajectory to the white backlash in Tennessee. In Deep South states in 1970, which had been the centers of defiance of racial change in the 1950s, the dramatic increase in black voting and the mobilization of economic leaders to facilitate inevitable desegregation enabled New South politicians to triumph. In states such as Tennessee and North Carolina, which had practiced token compliance in the 1950s, not only was the post-1965 rise in black voting less dramatic and less important, but the trajectory of white backlash was different. Token compliance promised black belt areas like western Tennessee and eastern North Carolina that they would be spared desegregation. By the late 1960s it was clear that they would not be spared. Voters in western Tennessee responded in 1970 by defeating Albert Gore and two years later in eastern North Carolina whites would elect Jesse Helms.[47]

---

[44] Harris, "How the People Feel." Gene Graham, "Gore's Lost Cause," *New South* (Spring (1971): 26-34. White House Special Files: Staff Member and Office Files: John D. Erlichman, Alphabetical Subject Files, 1963-73, Box 23 1970, Post-election analysis, Nixon Presidential Materials Project. A complete set of Brock television commercials is held at the Julian P. Kanter Political Commercial Archive, University of Oklahoma.

[45] *Nashville Banner*, 23 August 1970, 23 September 1970.

[46] Bartley and Graham, *Southern Politics*, 150.

[47] Randy Sanders, *Mighty Peculiar Elections: The New South Gubernatorial Campaigns of 1970 and the Changing Politics of Race* (Gainesville: University of Florida Press, 2002), 1-10, 170-175.

Lyndon Johnson and Albert Gore, inspired by the New Deal, helped create the infrastructure that put the South on the road to economic modernization. They helped destroy racial segregation and empower African Americans politically. They did not, however, succeed in eliminating the vast swathes of poverty that were the "Shadows of the Sunbelt," and their policies drove the majority of white southerners into the arms of the Republican Party. They were political allies but their personal rivalry, even hatred, never abated. After the 1970 election Jimmy Stahlman, editor of the *Nashville Banner*, sent two exultant telegrams. Referring to the defeat of both Gore and the Democratic gubernatorial candidate, John Jay Hooker, whom Stahlman hated even more than he hated Gore, Stahlman telegrammed Richard Nixon at San Clemente the day after the election: "WE GOT 'EM BOTH, ONE WITH EACH BARREL. GLADYS JOINS IN BEST TO YOU AND PAT." The next day he sent a telegram to Lyndon Johnson: "THANK GOD, WE HELPED GET RID OF ONE OF YOUR ARCH ENEMIES. NO ACKNOWLEDGEMENT NECESSARY."[48]

---

[48] James Stahlman telegram to Richard Nixon, 3 November 1970, Stahlman telegram to Lyndon B. Johnson, 4 November 1970, papers of James G. Stahlman, Special Collections, Alexander Heard Library, Vanderbilt University.

FROM SCHOOL IMPROVERS TO SCHOOL SAVERS:
ARLINGTON MODERATES AND THE FIGHT FOR PUBLIC EDUCATION
1945-1959

Paul E. Mertz

For the public schools of the South, the post-World War II years were a time of expansion and improvement. But the schools also faced a double crisis. With the *Brown* v. *Board of Education* decision of 1954 the region entered its great struggle over ending segregation. Related to that struggle was the second part of the crisis: the question of whether public education would continue at all. Segregationist hard-liners, many of whom had never strongly supported public schools, proposed to close them rather than yield to desegregation. As this issue grew across the region, public education's supporters had to rally to its defense. One of the most important arenas for this conflict was Arlington County, Virginia. There, parents and civic leaders who had pushed through dramatic school improvements discovered that they would have to defend their achievements against Virginia's massive resistance to desegregation. Their successful fight would have impact well beyond Arlington and Virginia.[1]

After World War II the need for better schools came into sharp focus in the South for at least three reasons. Promoters of economic progress saw improved schools as indispensable. The needs were obvious. A prewar survey, the National Emergency Council's *Report on Economic Conditions of the South*, pointed out the region's low tax base, low spending per school child, poor physical facilities, underpaid teachers, short school terms, and the early dropping out of many students—all resulting in the nation's highest levels of illiteracy. Moreover, the South carried a heavy burden. With only one-sixth of the nation's school revenues, it struggled to educate one-third of America's children. Partly for motives of economic progress, every southern state increased school spending after World War II, apparently agreeing with Georgia governor Ellis Arnall, who advised "Let's get off tobacco road." Second, schools had to be expanded because the tide of baby boom children threatened to overwhelm existing facilities. Third, new attitudes about racial issues loomed just offstage. Informed conservatives like Jimmy Byrnes of South Carolina understood the judicial trends suggesting that preserving segregation might depend on upgrading black schools to lend some credibility to "separate but equal."[2]

---

[1] Two recent works dealing with school desegregation in Virginia are Matthew D. Lassiter and Andrew B. Lewis (eds.), *The Moderates' Dilemma: Massive Resistance to School Desegregation in Virginia* (Charlottesville: University Press of Virginia, 1998) and Ronald L. Heinemann, *Harry Byrd of Virginia* (Charlottesville: University Press of Virginia, 1996). See also James H. Hershman, Jr., "A Rumbling in the Museum: The Opponents of Virginia's Massive Resistance" (Ph.D. dissertation, University of Virginia, 1978), and Benjamin Muse, *Virginia's Massive Resistance* (Bloomington: Indiana University Press, 1961).

[2] U.S. National Emergency Council, *Report on Economic Conditions of the South* (Washington: Government Printing Office, 1938), 25-28. For increased regional school spending see "School Construction Expenditures since 1949," *Southern School News*, November 1955, 1, and for Virginia specifically, Ibid., "Virginia," 3 September 1954, 13.

The imperatives of school improvement and the defense of segregation collided in the 1950s in rapidly growing Arlington County, Virginia. Between 1940 and 1950 Arlington County's population grew from 57,000 to 135,000. Another 28,000 were added during the fifties. This population was not typical of the rest of Virginia. In 1950 blacks were only about 5 percent of Arlingtonians, compared to about 22 percent for the state.[3] Newcomers from all areas of the country created suburban lifestyles. Half of all employed persons worked for the federal government. In 1955 median adult education was 12.5 years, one of the nation's highest levels, exceeded in Virginia only by neighboring Falls Church. The median income of $5,500 was Virginia's best, more than double the state median of $2,602. The number of school children surged from 8,118 in 1940 to 19,400 in 1953.[4]

By 1946 school deficiencies were increasingly apparent. State law placed county schools under the control of five-member boards that were appointed by special "electoral boards" chosen by circuit judges, who were selected by the legislature. Thus, Arlington's well-entrenched board was "four steps removed from direct action of the voters."[5] The School Superintendent had been in office since 1916. Critics complained that he dominated the board, the teachers, and the Parent-Teacher Associations (PTAs). There had been almost no new school construction since before the war. Buildings were "antiquated" and crowded, with all first and second graders on half-day shifts. Teaching programs were limited, with no kindergartens or provisions for exceptional children. There was no regular hiring procedure or standard salary scale for teachers, and the superintendent's purchasing and accounting methods were described as "insufficient." With good reason a

---

Between 1940 and 1952 Virginia's annual spending per student rose from $64.80 to $184.77 in urban districts and from $35.70 to $109.54 in rural districts. The Arnall quote is from John Gunther, *Inside U.S.A.* (New York and London: Harper and Brothers, 1947), 767, and is consistent with Arnall's views of education and progress in his *The Shore Dimly Seen* (Philadelphia and New York: J.B. Lippencott Company, 1946), 29-38. A contemporary assessment of Byrnes appears in *Washington Post*, 22 May 1954.

[3] U.S. Bureau of the Census, *Sixteenth Census of the United States, 1940*, (Washington: Government Printing Office, 1942), I, *Number of Inhabitants*, p. 1101, and II, *Characteristics of the Population*, part 7, p. 173; U.S. Bureau of the Census, *Seventeenth Census of Population: 1950* (Washington: Government Printing Office, 1952), I, *Number of Inhabitants*, p. 46-12, and II, *Characteristics of the Population*, part 46 (Virginia), pp. 46-31 and 46-74. By 1960 the county's population had increased to 163,401. U.S. Bureau of the Census, *Census of Population, 1960* (Washington: Government Printing Office, 1963), I, part 48, pp. 48-14 and 48-60.

[4] Income figures from [Northern Virginia] *Daily Sun*, 23 August 1955. Numbers of school children from "Statement on School Conditions in Arlington County, May 1953, League of Women Voters Papers (hereinafter LWV Papers), Arlington County Public Library (ACPL). An enrollment of 21,340 was projected for 1953-54. On the dynamic growth of Arlington and Northern Virginia see B. Alden Lillywhite, *et al.*, "The Citizens Fight for Better Schools in Arlington, Virginia," undated typescript [c. 1949], Malcolm Miller Papers, ACPL, 1-3; William H. Hessler, "A Southern County Waits for the School Bell," *The Reporter*, 4 September 1958, 21-24; and Virginia Affairs columnist Benjamin Muse in *Washington Post*, 13 June 1954.

[5] Lillywhite, "Citizens Fight for Better Schools," 4.

Washington newspaper could report in the mid-forties about Arlington's "Hill Billy schools in the shadow of the nation's capitol."[6]

In the 1940s and 1950s reform-minded Arlingtonians participated in numerous civic organizations with overlapping memberships. *Washington Post* columnist Ben Muse described Northern Virginia as an area that "teems with associations, leagues, clubs, [and] committees . . . all of which insist on having a hand in running the show," and furthermore, "the women have to be reckoned with seriously here."[7] Parent-Teacher Associations and the League of Women Voters were active forces. By the mid-fifties reformers nominated county board candidates through the non-partisan Arlingtonians for a Better County (ABC). In 1946 parents frustrated by an unresponsive school board formed the Citizens Committee for School Improvement (CCSI) and petitioned for a school improvement bond election. After a year of pressure the school board scheduled a special election for May 1947. The ballot questions included new elementary and secondary schools, kindergartens, and all-day sessions for first and second graders, all funded by $3,250,000 in bonds. Meanwhile, CCSI members, taking "an extremely long chance," approached the General Assembly, seeking to change the school board selection process in Arlington. With the aid of the county's legislators the move succeeded and special legislation allowed a local referendum on the question. Scheduled with the bond election, this referendum included an option for popular election of the board, an arrangement unprecedented in Virginia.[8]

In the election the bond issue was only partly successful, but the crucial question of electing the school board carried by a large margin. In August 1947 a convention of reformers nominated a slate of five school improvers, who were all elected in November and took office 1 January 1948. The key members were the new chairman, Barnard Joy, an educational specialist with the Agricultural

---

[6] "Statement on School Conditions," LWV Papers; Harley M. Williams to editor, *Northern Virginia Sun,* 22 January 1947, clipping in Citizens Committee for School Improvement Papers (hereinafter CCSI papers), ACPL; undated *Washington Post* clipping [summer 1949], Elizabeth Campbell Papers, ACPL (hereinafter Elizabeth Campbell Papers). The "hillbilly schools" reference is quoted in Ivan A. Booker to Roger Dakin, January 28, 1954, Elizabeth Campbell Papers.

[7] *Washington Post*, 13 June 1954.

[8] Such organizations as ABC, CCSI, and the PTAs were important outlets for people who sought to influence public affairs, especially if they were federal employees whose partisan campaigning was prohibited by the Hatch Act. For the background of the CCSI and the ABC see Lillywhite, "Citizens Fight for Better Schools," 5-8; and Franklin Owen Felt, "A Study of a Nonpartisan Political Organization: The Arlingtonians for a Better County (ABC)," (Ph.D. dissertation, Michigan State University, 1961). For a view of the maneuvering by Arlington legislators, see Harrison Mann to editor, *Saturday Evening Post*, 17 May 1950, copy in Elizabeth Campbell Papers. According to Mann, a conservative Democrat in the House of Delegates, the CCSI initially asked only for a school board chosen by the county board (standard practice in Virginia cities), but Arlington legislators added the popular election option to the bill. Because the General Assembly was in a special session, it was supposed to deal only with items specified in the governor's call (in this case teachers' salaries). Getting "local legislation" on the calendar required skillful rule bending and favorable committee placement, which Mann credited to Arlington's delegates and state senator. Mann's letter was not published by the magazine.

Extension Service; Elizabeth Campbell, former dean of Mary Baldwin College of Staunton, Virginia; and Glenn Stahl, a management expert with the U.S. Civil Service Commission. The new board members were well-experienced in a range of organizations, including CCSI, PTA, the League of Women Voters, and non-partisan nominating conventions.[9] Elizabeth Campbell and her husband, Edmund, were remarkable partners, as spouses and civic reformers. Both were in their late forties, had lived in Arlington since the 1930s, and had pushed for better schools since the war years. Edmund was a graduate of Washington & Lee Law School, a prominent attorney and civic activist, a founder of CCSI, and a former county board member.[10]

The new board faced daunting needs. A 1948 assessment foresaw school spending of $7.5 million by 1954 just to provide classrooms for the expected numbers of children. Program improvements and increased salaries would cost still more, so that a "reasonable expansion program" would require $13 million over ten years. But rapid progress was made. In 1948 voters approved bond funding for eight new elementary schools, one new junior high school, and additions to eight other buildings. Included were libraries, laboratories, gymnasiums, and vocational shop facilities. The small junior-senior high school for blacks was upgraded and placed on the state's pre-accreditation list.[11]

In 1949 the board brought in a new superintendent. It began hiring more and better qualified teachers. By 1954 it paid teachers between $3,300 and $5,000, the best salary scale in Virginia and a close second in the Washington metropolitan area. Arlington ranked first in Virginia in annual spending per child ($252 in 1953). Half-

---

[9] Lillywhite, "Citizens Fight for Better Schools," 7-8; "Selecting School Board Candidates in Arlington County, Virginia," and "Report of School Board Nominating Conference and Convention," both 1949, copies in Malcolm Miller Papers; interview of Barnard Joy by Edmund Campbell, 3 December 1983, Oral History Collection, ACPL. The election attracted more than 10,000 voters, the third largest turnout in Arlington's history. The two other new board members were Curtis Tuthill, professor of psychology at George Washington University, and Colin McPherson, an Arlington builder. The only proposal in the $3,250,000 school bond package that passed was $1,776,000 for new elementary school construction.

[10] Biographical folder on Elizabeth Campbell, vertical file, ACPS; Esther Mock, "Ultra-High Frequency: A Profile of Elizabeth Pfohl Campbell," undated typescript, Virginia Collection, ACPL; *Washington Post*, 13 June 1991; clipping from *Winston-Salem Twin City Sentinel*, 19 November 1949, Citizens Committee for School Improvement Papers, ACPL (hereinafter CCSI Papers). Elizabeth Campbell was elected to two terms on the school board, and later served an appointed term. Still later she was a founder and board chairperson of WETA, public television in the District of Columbia. In 1952 Edmund Campbell ran for Congress as an anti-Byrd Democrat. His progressive campaign points are outlined in "Ed Campbell for Congress," flyer [1952], Malcolm Miller Papers, ACPL. By 1956 Edmund Campbell was involved in civil rights litigation, arguing a local test case against a state law requiring segregated seating at public meetings. Interview with Edmund and Elizabeth Campbell, Theda Henle, William Lightsey, and Elizabeth Weihe, Arlington, Virginia, 15 November 1988 (hereinafter Arlington Group Interview); interview of Theda Henle by Edmund Campbell, 9 April 1984, in Oral History Collection, ACPL.

[11] "Statement on School Conditions in Arlington," LWV papers; Lillywhite, "Citizens Fight for Better Schools," 14-15; *Winston-Salem Twin Cities Sentinel,* 19 November 1949, CCSI Papers; *Washington Post* , 9 May 1954; Mock, "Ultra High Frequency." The 1948 bond issue was for $4.25 million.

day sessions were phased out. Curriculum modernization included new courses in social sciences, art, and music. Remedial reading and speech programs were instituted, and health, psychological, and counseling services were added. By 1957 Arlington's Washington & Lee High School was being mentioned in national rankings of secondary schools.[12]

Problems remained, of course. In the mid-fifties critical needs included a new high school, a kindergarten program, and smaller classes. School budgets had to be approved by a conservative county board that might cut the school board's requests. Besides frictions over costs, some critics objected to perceived trends toward "progressive education." As a 1954 League of Women Voters report tactfully put it, "sometimes our educators, in their enthusiasm, have moved ahead of the capacity of the general public to absorb new ideas." The report also pointed to Arlington's "fundamental cleavage . . . between those whose primary interest is keeping taxes down, and [favor] traditional methods, minus the so-called frills . . . and another, probably larger, group who are eager for the best in modern education even if it means higher taxes."[13]

Arlington's school board saw desegregation as compatible with its program. By the time of the *Brown* v. *Board of Education* decision (17 May 1954) the members had quietly discussed the possibility for about a year, and they were ready for compliance. The day after the opinion was announced Chairperson Elizabeth Campbell stated that the Supreme Court was "wise in giving the decision it did." She continued that, although the board would be guided by policies of the State Board of Education, it would appoint an advisory committee to recommend "the best way to meet requirements of the decision and accomplish integration."[14] This may well

---

[12] Barnard Joy to G. Tyler Miller, 24 November 1947, and Joy to Fletcher Kemp, 23 June 1948, Elizabeth Campbell Papers; Lillywhite, "Citizens Fight for Better Schools," 14-15; "Statement on School Conditions" and "Proposed Resume of 'Arlington Schools Today' for Bulletin," spring 1953, LWV Papers; *Winston-Salem Twin City Sentinel*, 19 November 1949; *Northern Virginia Sun,* 22 August 1958; Hessler, "A Southern County Waits for the School Bell," 21; Arlington County School Board, "Facts Concerning Segregation and Integration," November 1954, Record Group 7, Records of the Arlington School Board, ACPL.

[13] An example of budget cutting was the school board's request for $7.3 million for 1953-54 (26 percent more than the previous budget, anticipating a 10 percent enrollment increase), reduced to $6.8 million by the county board. "Statement on School Conditions in Arlington County" and "The Dilemma of Public Schools," May 1954, LWV Papers. By 1953-54 Arlington funded about 75 percent of its school operations from local taxes, received 15.7 percent from the state, and obtained 9.1 percent from federal aid programs. Committee to Study Problems of Integration in the Arlington Schools, 1954-55, minutes of 15 December 1954, RG 7, ACPL (hereinafter Integration Committee Files).

[14] *Washington Post,* 18, 19 May 1954; interview with Edmund and Elizabeth Campbell, Arlington, Virginia, 6 August 1991; notes on conversation with Elizabeth Campbell, Arlington, Virginia, 27 June 1997. In 1954 the Campbells were convinced that the *Brown* decision was both right and necessary. Mrs. Campbell's deference to state policies at the time simply acknowledged the board's obligations under state law. The State Board of Education soon became an impediment for any school board that might want to proceed with desegregation. On 27 May 1954 it directed all local boards to operate as usual for 1954-55, and later renewed those instructions for 1955-56. "Facts Concerning Segregation and Integration," 1954, RG 7, and remarks of Warren Cox in Arlington School Board Minutes, VI

have been the first move toward voluntary compliance by any school board in the South. On 12 June the board approved a 29-member committee of citizens and school staff, including seven blacks. As this group began meeting in the summer of 1954 the board openly referred to it as the "integration committee."[15]

By June 1955 school administrators had outlined a plan, in consultation with the board and the integration committee. Based on existing school attendance zones, it would leave most black children unaffected, but about sixty would be assigned to white elementary schools in September 1956. The next year some black junior high school students and all the high school students (about 122) would transfer to white schools. During the rest of 1955 the plan was kept confidential for board consideration.[16]

Meanwhile, proposals for avoiding integration by closing or privatizing schools arose early and forcefully in Virginia. In one of his first comments after the *Brown* decision, Governor Thomas Stanley suggested amending the state constitution to eliminate section 129, which required the state to maintain a public school system. The idea was immediately endorsed by stalwarts of Senator Harry Byrd's political faction, including numerous legislators. Supporters of public schools took Stanley's remarks as a serious threat. For example, Robert Whitehead, a member of the House of Delegates, asserted that "a powerful element in Virginia and in the General Assembly has always been fundamentally opposed to the public free school system, and has regarded it as socialism to tax the wealthy . . . to pay for the education of poorer people's children." Whitehead thought this opposition had been covert for a generation, content to try to "starve the public schools through inadequate appropriations." But now that element would see Stanley's statement as a new opportunity to "cripple, if not destroy" public education. Senator Ted Dalton, the legislature's most prominent Republican, also charged that Stanley's proposal was a potential first step toward abolishing public schools.[17]

(28 July 1955), RG 7, ACPL. Another uncertainty for local boards was the Supreme Court's delay of more than a year in issuing its implementation decree ("*Brown II*" on 30 May 1955).

[15] *Washington Post,* 13 June 1954; Arlington School Board Minutes, VI, 169 (12 June 1954) RG 7, ACPL; list of committee members,12 June 1954, and minutes of the committee, 23 June 1954, in Integration Committee Files.

[16] "Staff Proposal for Integration," 3 June 1955; minutes of the Integration Committee, 22 June 1955; memo from Stanley V. Smith to T. Edward Rutter, 23 June 1955; and "Preliminary Draft of Suggested Integration Plan for Arlington School Board, 24 June 1955, all in Integration Committee Files; notes on conversation with Elizabeth Campbell, Arlington, Virginia, 27 June 1997. The "Preliminary Draft" of 24 June was substantially the plan approved and announced by the board in January 1956. Copies of the draft plan were numbered and marked "confidential." As of 1954 the total number of school children was 19,350, including 1,165 blacks. "Facts Concerning Segregation and Integration," 1954, RG 7, ACPL.

[17] *Washington Post,* 26, 27, 29 June 1954. Whitehead statement, 26 June 1954, RG 7, ACPL. Stanley's initial comments on the *Brown* decision had been quite restrained. Columnist Ben Muse later wrote that the Governor suggested repeal of section 129 after delegations of Southside legislators "descended" upon him. *Washington Post,* 15 May 1955. It should be noted that plans for closing and privatizing public schools to avoid desegregation had been adopted or were being seriously considered in other states. South Carolina and Georgia had enacted such provisions even before the *Brown* decision. An overview appears in "Table of

Stanley's first official action was to appoint a 32-member Commission on Public Education in August 1954. Charged with recommending post-*Brown* policies to the General Assembly, it consisted entirely of legislators and was heavily loaded with conservatives and segregationists. This group's chair was an ardent segregationist, Senator Garland Gray of Sussex County. One effect of this commission was to forestall local desegregation initiatives; as it deliberated for fourteen months school boards remained uncertain as to state policies they would have to follow.[18]

The Commission's recommendations were developed by its counsel, David John Mays, a well-connected Richmond lawyer. Mays's diary, a rich source on the inner history of the school crisis, reveals a segregationist with a subtle grasp of legal and political realities. Convinced that stonewall resistance was not feasible, Mays drafted a three-part strategy. School boards could assign pupils to schools as they thought best; presumably none would desegregate without court orders. At the same time, no child would be compelled to attend a desegregated school. For those desiring to leave an integrated situation, state tuition grants would defray private school costs. This latter point was crucial and would require an election to call a convention to amend the state constitution. Mays knew this plan might allow some localities to initiate token integration, but he judged that it offered Virginia the best chance to keep segregation almost completely intact. The Commission approved the recommendations unanimously on 11 November 1955. The General Assembly scheduled a special election for 9 January 1956, on calling a convention to consider permitting tuition grants.[19]

School improvers opposed a convention. Taking charge of county-wide anti-convention organizing, William Lightsey, director of the Northern Virginia Council of PTAs, stressed that tuition grants would weaken public schools, for which private

---

Basic Legislation in Eight States on Public School Segregation," *Southern School News,* February 1956, 2. For Georgia see Paul E. Mertz, "'Mind-Changing Time All Over Georgia': HOPE, Inc., and School Desegregation, 1958-61," *Georgia Historical Quarterly* 77 (spring 1993): 41-61.

[18] "Virginia," *Southern School News,* September 1954, 13, includes the list of members. For pressures on Stanley and his appointment of the Commission see Hershman, "Rumbling in the Museum," 44-48, and Heinemann, *Harry Byrd of Virginia,* 330-31.

[19] David John Mays Diary, 11, 29, 30 June, 6, 12 July, 31 August 1955, David John Mays Papers, Virginia Historical Society, Richmond (hereinafter Mays Diary). For the Gray recommendations, see Commonwealth of Virginia. *Public Education: Report of the Commission to the Governor of Virginia,* Senate Document No. 1 (Richmond: Division of Purchase and Printing, 1955) and "12 Recommendations Made by Gray Commission," *Southern School News,* December 1955, 3. Segregation hard-liners disliked recommendations that provided even theoretical flexibility for desegregation. Mays recorded that Gray was so dissatisfied that he could not push his commission in a more radical direction that he even considered resigning from it. But no plan predicated on absolute segregation stood any chance of survival in the federal courts, as Mays well understood. Mays thought Stanley was "inept" and a "fumbler," who had a poor grasp of the strategy. For example, even as late as November 1955, when the recommendations were in final editing, an exasperated Mays had to "tell him all over again" why changing the constitutional mandate for public schools should not be advocated--Mays was certain such a proposal would not only fail, but also cause rejection of the tuition grant recommendation. Mays Diary, 24 June, 12 July, 10 November 1955.

schools would be no substitute. Elizabeth Campbell, speaking in Northern Virginia, Richmond, and Senator Byrd's hometown of Berryville, added a pedagogical perspective: as a scheme to "circumvent the U.S. Supreme Court" the Gray Plan was a bad example for children, who were perceptive enough to see through it. "Is this how we should teach children to be law abiding?" she demanded. But the constitutional convention was approved by a statewide margin of about two to one. The Tenth Congressional district (including Arlington) was the only district with a majority opposed.[20]

After the vote Arlington's school board believed the outlines of state policy were finally clear, though not yet enacted. Focusing on the Gray recommendation for local autonomy in assigning pupils, the board announced its desegregation policy on 14 January 1956. Superintendent Edward Rutter thought the plan would "be accepted by the community, be in accordance with the Supreme Court decree, and also not violate state law." Lawyer and board chairman Warren Cox told his colleagues it fit "very well into the plan contemplated by the Gray Report." Elizabeth Campbell recalled, "We fully expected to implement the integration plan because we felt we were within state law and the governor's policy. But then," she added, "everything changed at the state level."[21]

No doubt the school board would have been disheartened had it known of a meeting in Washington only one day before it announced its plan. Summoned by Senator Harry Byrd, the meeting included Virginia Congressmen Howard Smith, William Tuck, and Watkins Abbitt, state senators Garland Gray, Harry Byrd, Jr., and Charles Fenwick of Arlington, and David Mays. According to Mays, "Big Harry proposed to hold up the recommendations of the [Gray Commission] indefinitely." When Mays and Fenwick defended the Gray Plan as the only practicable course, Byrd countered that "legislation dealing with assignments and tuition grants would be an acceptance of the Sup Ct's decision in the segregation cases."[22] In a crucial

---

[20] *School Improvement* [CCSI newsletter], January 1956, CCSI Papers; "Fact Sheet for Voters," December 1955, CCSI form letter to members, 22 December 1955; press release by Kathryn Stone, 25 November [1955], Elizabeth Campbell Papers; Arlington Group Interview. The statewide vote favored the constitutional convention by 300,243 to 143,636. In the Tenth District 26,164 were opposed and 20,183 were in favor. "Virginia Sets Convention on Tuition Grant Plans for March 5," and "How Virginia Voted (By Congressional Districts)," *Southern School News*, February 1956, 14. Later in the spring the convention met and amended section 141 of the constitution to allow state tuition grants.

[21] *School Improvement*, February 1956; minutes of the Integration Committee, 22 November 1955, Elizabeth Campbell Papers; notes on conversation with Elizabeth Campbell, Arlington, Virginia, 27 June 1997. The board's assumptions about what would be legally permissible were very close to those of Gray Commission counsel David Mays, but of course he would have disapproved the board's desegregation objectives. The *School Improvement* newsletter indicates that the timing of the school board's announcement was influenced partly by a desire to clarify the desegregation situation before the county voted on another large school bond issue later in January.

[22] Mays Diary, 13 January 1956. Byrd and his supporters outlined no alternate program in the meeting, although they did favor cutting off state funds for any district that desegregated, a policy eventually included in the massive resistance package passed in September 1956. Because state aid accounted for a relatively small proportion of Arlington County's school

turn, the Byrd Organization was moving toward a more extreme stance in the spring of 1956, as the Gray Plan was "pushed aside." According to Byrd biographer Ronald Heinemann, new measures were not fully determined until June. Then, in a "clandestine" Washington meeting on 2 July, Byrd, Stanley, and other Organization leaders agreed on a fall legislative agenda that would become "massive resistance."[23]

In retrospect the school board erred in assuming the legislature would follow through with the Gray proposals, but as Edmund Campbell recalled, "I think we took them at their word." Later, after Virginia closed several schools in 1958, Delegate James Webb of Fairfax County charged that massive resisters had consistently misled the people. Recalling that he had predicted in 1955 that after tuition grants were approved the rest of the Gray plan would be discarded, he asserted that the Byrd Organization was leading a "strenuous statewide undercover drive to abolish public schools and remove the state from the field of education."[24]

The board had also failed to anticipate the retaliation of angry legislators who saw Arlington as an Achilles heel of segregation. In March 1956 the General Assembly revoked Arlington County's right to elect its school board. Although incumbent members would not be ousted before their terms ended, henceforth the county board would appoint all new members.[25] The new system led to a shift of school board personnel and perspectives, especially in 1957. By the end of that year three of the five members had been appointed and were regarded as conservatives.[26] Meanwhile Arlington would begin to face court-ordered desegregation.

On 17 May 1956, fourteen parents, backed by the Virginia branch of the National Association for the Advancement of Colored People (NAACP), sued the board. Evidence suggests that so long as the board was pursuing its desegregation plan, the local NAACP had refrained from legal action. But once it was clear the board could not implement its plan, Arlington became one of several new Virginia cases initiated by the state NAACP. On 31 July 1956, U.S. District Judge Albert Bryan ordered Arlington to commence desegregation on 31 January 1957. Although

budget (see note 13 above) the county might have been able to maintain its schools despite a fund cut-off.

[23] "Virginia's Gray Plan Laid Aside; 3 More Suits Are on File," *Southern School News,* June 1956, 13; Heinemann, *Harry Byrd of Virginia,* 336-38. See generally the excellent discussion of Byrd and his Organization in Heinemann's Chapter 17, "Massive Resistance," 325-354.

[24] Interview with Edmund and Elizabeth Campbell, Arlington, Virginia, 6 August 1991; *Northern Virginia Sun,* 20, 25 October 1958. Taking the legislature at its word was not necessarily naiveté. School supporters were well aware that the Gray proposals were only recommendations to the General Assembly. But the plan had been approved unanimously by a commission of 32 influential and mostly segregationist legislators, and on balance, reasonable people might have put some confidence in its full enactment.

[25] "Prince Edward Case Revived As Virginia Slows Legislation," and ""Virginia Lawmakers Overwhelmingly Approve Interposition," *Southern School News,* March 1956, 13-14; Arlington Group Interview.

[26] In the spring of 1955, after serving two terms on the board, Elizabeth Campbell had declined to stand for re-election. Elizabeth Campbell to Marie R. Dresser, April 13, 1955, Elizabeth Campbell Papers. After the board became appointive, new members were installed in late 1956, and in August and December 1957. *Northern Virginia Sun,* 26 August, 27, 28 December 1957. Vacancies had been created by resignations and one death among the holdover elected members.

the board's appeals would consume another year and a half, the eventual outcome was clear.[27]

By far the most dangerous development of 1956 was the legislature's enactment of a battery of "massive resistance" laws in September. To avoid any repetition of Arlington's exercise of local option, a state pupil placement board could assume ultimate control of assigning students to schools. Any school that desegregated (or faced an unappealable deadline) would be taken over by the governor and automatically closed. If the governor could not "reorganize" and reopen schools on a segregated basis, the students could receive state tuition grants to assist them in leaving those public schools. Finally, the governor might (upon petition) return closed schools to local control, but with no state funding. Thus, any school system that complied with a court order would trigger the closing of its schools by state authorities.[28]

In the spring of 1958, with Judge Bryan's deadline reset for September, many feared Arlington's schools would be the first closed by state action. On 1 May Edmund and Elizabeth Campbell hosted a meeting of long-time school supporters. The group included former board chairman Glenn Stahl, PTA director William Lightsey, and League of Women Voters activists Theda Henle and Elizabeth Weihe. Guided by Ed Campbell, the group agreed to form a committee to mobilize the public to keep schools open. This would require seeking the broadest possible support, including people who really preferred separate schools, but valued public education more. Accordingly, the committee would declare neutrality on the desegregation issue. Theda Henle recalled this as "the only strategy . . . that could have succeeded. We never once said publicly that we were fighting FOR integrated schools. Our only avowed purpose was to keep schools open."[29]

---

[27] *Northern Virginia Sun,* 17 May 1956. The case was *Thompson* v. *School Board of Arlington County,* 144 F. Supp. 239. Three of the parents in the suit were white integrationists. Other desegregation suits filed in May 1956 were against the school boards of Charlottesville, Newport News, and Norfolk. *Northern Virginia Sun,* 11 May 1956; "Virginia's 'Gray Plan' Laid Aside; 3 More Suits Are On File." *Southern School News,* June 1956, 13. Undoubtedly, the Arlington NAACP was well informed about the school board's desegregation plan. It was public knowledge that an integration committee was working, and one of its members was a former officer of the local NAACP. School board officers recognized the forbearance of the NAACP. Chairman Warren Cox told one critic that he thought "the Negro leaders in Arlington have been most reasonable" despite delay in initiating the desegregation plan. Warren Cox to Jack Rathbone, 16 November 1955, Elizabeth Campbell Papers. When the board announced its desegregation plan it stated that it believed the plan would forestall expensive litigation. *School Improvement*, February 1956, copy in Elizabeth Campbell Papers. See also Hershman, "Rumbling in the Museum," 110-111 on national NAACP policy of not suing districts that seemed to be moving in good faith.

[28] "Virginia's General Assembly Bars State Funds for Mixed Schools," *Southern School News,* October 1956, 16. See especially Hershman, "Rumbling in the Museum," 171-189, on the ascendancy of massive resisters in late 1956. Events of 1956 must have added urgency to the plans of segregationists. When the year began the only Virginia school district under court order was Prince Edward County, one of the original *Brown* defendants. But by September four major school systems were in court in new cases.

[29] Arlington Group Interview, and additional comments by Theda Henle, 13 January 1997. Hershman, "Rumbling in the Museum, 271, comments that by late 1958 the emerging

Over the summer of 1958 the Arlington Committee for Public Schools, chaired by Glenn Stahl, enrolled 3,400 members. This was the first open schools committee in the South: similar organizations would arise in the late summer and fall in Virginia, Georgia, Arkansas, and Louisiana. In December 1958 Arlington Committee members were key founders of the Virginia Committee for Public Schools (VCPS), which grew to a network of fifteen local committees during the spring of 1959, with William Lightsey as executive director. That same spring Arlington and Virginia Committee school savers fought hard against legislative recommendations that would have fatally weakened the constitutional guarantee of public schools, but which failed narrowly in the General Assembly.[30]

What needs emphasis here, though, is that Arlington school savers made their greatest contribution to public education in the South at large through their early determination to go to court. In August 1958, with school closing imminent, committee leaders prepared for litigation. Speaking on the Georgetown University Radio Forum on 7 September, Ed Campbell, Glenn Stahl, and William Lightsey reiterated the committee's neutrality on integration but stressed the absolute priority of open schools ("infinitely more important," said Lightsey). Forecasting almost certain closure in Arlington, they hoped the governor would promptly return schools to local control. Otherwise, they would support legal action against the massive resistance laws. Speaking later to news reporters, the three spokesmen revealed that papers for a suit had already been prepared. They did not reveal the names of the plaintiffs, Theda and Peter Henle, or their potential attorneys.[31]

The suit was never filed in Arlington, however. As Governor Lindsay Almond closed schools in Warren County (12 September), Judge Bryan deferred Arlington's deadline again, until February, temporarily easing the crisis locally.[32] But additional

---

moderate stance of neutrality combined with an uncompromising pro-public schools position was "not just a clever political ploy, but an expression of genuine feeling emerging from a palpable reality." The Arlington experience supports that assessment. For example, William Lightsey said consistently that although he preferred separate schools, he would never give up public education. Arlington Group Interview, and Interview with William Lightsey, Arlington, Virginia, 24 July 1990. Theda Henle recalled (Arlington Group Interview) that another early and effective recruit was county board member Leone Buccholtz, a conservative segregationist who nevertheless staunchly supported public schools.

[30] Transcript of "Virginia Schools and Private Citizens," Georgetown University Forum radio discussion, 7 September 1958, Elizabeth Campbell Papers. Open Schools organizations in other states included Help Our Public Education (HOPE), Inc., in Georgia, The Women's Emergency Committee to Open Our Schools (Little Rock), and Save Our Schools (SOS) and Citizen's Committee for Public Education (both of New Orleans). All these groups reached the same tactical conclusions—all white membership, neutrality concerning integration, and uncompromising advocacy of public education—as the VCPS. For Georgia see Mertz, "Mind Changing Time All Over Georgia." On the work of the VCPS see Hershman, "Massive Resistance Meets Its Match: The Emergence of a Pro-Public School Majority," Chap. 4 in Lassiter and Lewis, *Moderates' Dilemma*, 104-33.

[31] Virginia Schools and Private Citizens"; *Northern Virginia Sun*, 9 September 1958; Draft "Complaint for Temporary Restraining Order and Preliminary and Permanent Injunction," undated [late summer 1958], copy furnished by Theda Henle.

[32] "Findings of Fact and Conclusions of Law," in *Thompson, v. School Board of Arlington County*, 17 September 1958, copy in Barbara Marx Papers, RG 18, ACPL; *Northern Virginia*

closings came in Charlottesville and Norfolk on 27 September. In the early fall
Edmund Campbell was approached by members of the newly formed Committee for
Public Schools of Norfolk. In that city the closing of six secondary schools had
turned 10,000 white students out of classes. After an unsatisfactory conference with
the governor, the Norfolk group was ready to sue, and Campbell agreed to take their
case.[33]

Campbell and a Norfolk associate argued the case of *James* v. *Almond* before a
panel of three federal judges in Norfolk on 19 November. Their argument was the
same as that in the draft brief for an Arlington suit—that the Fourteenth
Amendment's "equal protection of the law" required the state to provide public
education for all on the same basis, and to close schools in some areas while leaving
them open in others violated that principle. Campbell asserted that locked-out
students were being "severely punished" by the state's anti-integration polices. "The
heart of Massive Resistance," he declared, was "patently unconstitutional . . .
whether we Virginians like it or not."[34]

Years later, William Lightsey recalled Ed Campbell's confidence in the
strength of the anti-school closing argument, which he believed could win in the
U.S. Supreme Court if necessary.[35] That confidence was well-founded. On 19
January 1959, the federal panel found the massive resistance laws unconstitutional.
Selective closing of schools violated students' equal protection rights and, in effect,
the decision left the state with two stark alternatives—provide open schools for all,
or close all schools. Also on 19 January, the state Supreme Court, in *Harrison* v.
Day, held that the school closing laws also violated the state constitution. After these

---

Sun, 18, 19 September 1958. Bryan said the postponement was necessary because schools
were already too far into the fall semester, but it seems more likely he was willing to await
developments in the other Virginia situations where decisions by other federal courts were
almost sure to be made, and in the meantime spare Arlington the disruption of school closing.
It is also evident that federal judges in Virginia were all anxiously awaiting the Supreme
Court's opinion in *Cooper* v. *Aaron,* 358 U.S. 1, concerning closed high schools in Little
Rock. In that decision, on 12 September the Court denounced the state's obstruction of
desegregation and condemned all "evasive schemes" such as transferring public schools to
private control.

[33] Norfolk school closings affected all three white high schools and three white junior high
schools. Forrest White, a pediatrician and leader in the Norfolk Committee recalled that
Almond told them, "You'll get your schools back . . . by order of the federal courts."
Interview with Forrest and Edie White, Norfolk, Virginia, 13 November 1988. Such a
statement by Almond would corroborate second-hand information picked up by David Mays
that "Lindsay said that he realized that 'massive resistance' could not work," and that he
would need to call a special session of the legislature to develop a new approach. Mays Diary,
22 September 1958.

[34] *Northern Virginia Sun,* 20 November 1958. Briefs for the *James* case ("Plaintiffs' Trial
Memorandum," 14 November 1958, and "Plaintiffs' Supplemental Trial Memorandum," 29
November 1958) and the Record of Trial Proceedings, 19 November 1958, are in Archie
Boswell Papers, Old Dominion University, Norfolk. Boswell was the Norfolk lawyer assisting
Campbell. The federal judges were Fourth Circuit Court of Appeals Chief Judge Simon
Sobeloff of Baltimore, Fourth Circuit Judge Clement Haynesworth of South Carolina, and
U.S. District Judge Walter Hoffman of Norfolk.

[35] Interview with William Lightsey.

decisions, closed schools were reopened and desegregated. Meanwhile, in Arlington, with all federal appeals exhausted, four black children entered Stratford Junior High School on 2 February.[36]

The *James* case changed the legal landscape in the South. Even before the decision, Forrest White, of the Norfolk Committee, anticipated that "Virginia is the gateway to the South and Norfolk is the hinge of the gate; public education in the entire South depends on which way the gate swings in the next few weeks."[37] In Alabama the swinging gate was recognized almost immediately. On the very day of the *James* decision, John Patterson was inaugurated as governor. In his election campaign he had advocated Virginia-style school closing laws, a position he reiterated on inauguration day. But he was soon forced to backtrack, admitting that a "reappraisal" of anti-integration defenses was underway.[38] In Georgia there was a slow, steady, realization that the state's draconian school closing laws were untenable—a realization promoted vigorously by the open schools organization, HOPE, Inc.[39] In the Florida legislature in the spring of 1959 there was much talk of strengthening segregation laws, but no school closing measures were passed. Federal courts held Arkansas school closing laws unconstitutional in the summer of 1959. In Louisiana in 1960, an open schools committee sought federal court action to prevent school closing in New Orleans.[40] Not all these actions were directly tied to the *James* decision, but clearly a corner was being turned in the South in 1959 and 1960.

The day after the *Brown* decision was announced, Senator Harry Byrd declared that Virginia faced a "crisis of the first magnitude." As events unfolded in the mid-

---

[36] *James* v. *Almond,* 170 F. Supp. 342. The text of the judges' opinion also appears in *New York Times,* 20 January 1959. *Harrison* v. *Day,* 106 S.E. 2d 636, was initiated by the state to test and confirm the school closing laws. Technically it was a suit to compel Day (state comptroller) to pay tuition grant money to students from closed schools. The great danger of the case was the state's argument that the constitutional requirement for a public school system (section 129) was already inoperative, because it was inseparable from the requirement for segregated education (section 141) which was dead because of the *Brown* decision. The adverse decision of the state's own Supreme Court made it pointless for Virginia to appeal the *James* case to the U.S. Supreme Court. For initial desegregation see "Schools Reopen As Massive Resistance Falls," *Southern School News,* February 1959, 1.

[37] Forrest White to Robert M. Hutchins, 13 November 1958, in Forrest White Papers, Old Dominion University, Norfolk.

[38] "Patterson Inaugurated with Pledge to Continue Separation of State Schools," *Southern School News,* February 1959, 16; *Birmingham News,* 29, 30 January 1959. Patterson could offer no recommendations except to "alter or abandon our public school system and establish a system of private education." Alabama had previously repealed its constitutional guarantees of the right to public education, and it had provided that counties might abolish public schools if necessary for the "preservation of law and order."

[39] Mertz, "Mind Changing Time All Over Georgia."

[40] "Numerous New Segregation Measures Introduced at Legislature's Start," *Southern School News,* May 1959, 14; "Private School Act Signed by Collins, Numerous Other Laws Considered," Ibid., June 1959, 7; "'Mild' School Bills Given Legislative Sanction," Ibid., July 1959, 6; "Federal Tribunal Holds School Closing Laws Unconstitutional," Ibid., July 1959, 8; *Washington Post,* 8 March, 5 April 1959. Information about the New Orleans case (*Williams* v. *Davis*) supplied by M. Hepburn Many, former U.S. Attorney for the Eastern District of Louisiana.

1950s, friends of public education also recognized a crisis, but from a very different perspective. They took action to preserve what they had built up together. Without a common experience, Elizabeth Campbell reflected, "beginning with our fight to get an elected school board . . . we would not have had the same group of people [in 1958]. It was the same group of people, you see. We knew one another, we trusted one another, and that was our strength."[41]

---

[41] *Washington Post*, 18 May 1954; Arlington Group Interview.

THE MISSISSIPPI FREEDOM LABOR UNION

Mark Newman

Begun in April 1965, the Mississippi Freedom Labor Union (MFLU) organized the first labor strike in the Yazoo-Mississippi Delta since a brief cotton pickers' strike twenty years earlier. Within a few weeks of its formation, over 1,200 African Americans in at least six counties had joined the union. By the summer, over 1,000 black Deltans were on strike. Most of the strikers were plantation workers, but they also numbered a few dozen domestic workers and restaurant cooks in Delta towns, along with some hotel maids in McComb, southwest Mississippi. The MFLU's formation reflected an emerging concern in the southern civil rights movement with poverty and economic issues, while the union's failure indicated the intractability of these problems. The story of the MFLU also provides insights regarding divisions within the Mississippi civil rights movement, the difficulties of organizing among impoverished and widely dispersed rural dwellers, and tensions in the relationship between organized labor unions and the civil rights movement.[1]

Formed by alluvial deposits, the Yazoo-Mississippi Delta stretches two hundred miles, almost from Memphis to Vicksburg, and reaches a maximum width of seventy miles. Cleared primarily in the last twenty years of the nineteenth century, the Delta's fertile land made it a prime cotton producing region. Its white-owned plantations depended on the cheap labor of disenfranchised African Americans, who comprised a large majority of the Delta's population but experienced some of the nation's worst levels of poverty, ill health, and education. Such conditions in the eighteen counties that lay within or partially within the Delta presented the civil rights movement with one of its greatest challenges.[2]

Although present in Mississippi since 1918, the National Association for the Advancement of Colored People (NAACP) did not establish a significant presence in the state or any of its Delta towns until the late 1940s and early 1950s. However, the NAACP's pursuit of school desegregation and voter registration brought white economic intimidation and violence in the mid-1950s that stymied the organization.

---

[1] James C. Cobb, *The Most Southern Place on Earth: The Mississippi Delta and the Roots of Southern Poverty* (New York: Oxford University Press, 1992), 201; *National Guardian*, 12 June 1965; "Shaw Mississippi: New Sounds in the Delta," p. 1, n.d., box 11, folder 564, Edwin King Collection, Tougaloo College, Mississippi (King Collection); George Shelton, Jr., "Mississippi Freedom Labor Union State Office," n.d., "Minutes of Statewide Meeting - MFLU- September 4 [1965], George Shelton, "Mississippi Freedom Labor Union: Report," and "Report on Locals and Money Distributed," 7 September 1965, box 113, folder 102, Student Nonviolent Coordinating Committee Papers, Martin Luther King, Jr. Center for Nonviolent Social Change, Atlanta (SNCC Papers); "Mississippi Freedom Labor Union," box 7, folder 22, Delta Ministry Papers, Martin Luther King, Jr. Center for Nonviolent Social Change (DM Papers); "Cotton Workers Strike in Delta," *Student Voice* 6 (30 April 1965): 1, 4; Paul Good, "The Thorntons of Mississippi: Peonage on the Plantation," *Atlantic Monthly* 218 (September 1966): 99.

[2] Cobb, *Most Southern Place on Earth*, viii-ix, 3-5, 82, 98-124, 154-56, 184-205, 254-55, 262-67; Mark Newman, *Divine Agitators: The Delta Ministry and Civil Rights in Mississippi* (Athens: University of Georgia Press, 2004), 9-11.

Building on the work and contacts of the NAACP and other black Mississippi organizations, the Student Nonviolent Coordinating Committee (SNCC) began organizing in the Delta in the early 1960s. SNCC sought to foster and develop local African American leadership, and to help communities develop their own solutions to problems.[3]

SNCC became the dominant group in the Council of Federated Organizations (COFO), an alliance consisting of leading civil rights groups. COFO sponsored the Mississippi Summer Project of 1964 which focused on voter registration, political mobilization, and education through the creation of Freedom Schools. Some Freedom Schools operated the next year, organized by SNCC and members of the Congress of Racial Equality (CORE), a group that shared SNCC's commitment to the Deep South's rural black poor.[4]

In 1965 white SNCC workers Robert Weil and Mary Sue Gellatly ran a Freedom School in Shaw in Bolivar County, thirty-two miles from the Mississippi River. They encouraged local people to discuss their problems, which centered on poverty. African Americans in the Delta had a median annual income of only $456. Mechanization had virtually destroyed the sharecropping system and created a surplus of agricultural labor. While a minority of blacks worked as machine operators, primarily tractor drivers, many African Americans were left to search for a dwindling number of day laboring jobs as cotton pickers or as choppers who weeded the cotton. By 1964, machines picked 68 percent of Delta cotton, and, although far less widely adopted, chemical weedkillers also threatened to displace choppers. Many landowners housed some of their workers rent-free in poorly insulated, cramped plantation shacks that lacked flushing water and toilets. Machine operators and their families, who usually worked as pickers and choppers, generally lived on the plantations but many day laborers, displaced from plantations by mechanization, lived in Delta towns and communities and relied on independent haulers to take them to work.[5]

Plantation employees worked from dawn to dusk, with a minimum ten hour day. African Americans who operated machinery, such as tractors, earned six dollars a day and could expect employment throughout the year, although their working day could last as long as fourteen hours on plantations where tractors had lights. Choppers and pickers worked seasonally. Choppers earned three dollars a day or less, while pickers were paid by the amount they picked. Unemployed between

---

[3] John Dittmer, *Local People: The Struggle for Civil Rights in Mississippi* (Urbana: University of Illinois Press, 1994), 29-32, 41-58, 70-73, 126, 128-38; Clayborne Carson, *In Struggle: SNCC and the Black Awakening of the 1960s* (Cambridge, Mass.: Harvard University Press, 1981), 30, 77-81. On SNCC's role in Mississippi see Charles M. Payne, *I've Got the Light of Freedom: The Organizing Tradition and the Mississippi Freedom Struggle* (Berkeley: University of California Press, 1995).

[4] Dittmer, *Local People*, 118-19, 242-65.

[5] "Shaw Mississippi: New Sounds in the Delta," pp. 1, 6, n.d., box 11, folder 564, King Collection; "Fact Sheet (Background on poor peoples' use of Greenville AFB)," n.d., box 4, folder 6, Amzie Moore Papers, Wisconsin Historical Society, Madison (Moore Papers); *Delta Democrat-Times*, 10 February 1966; Claude Ramsay, "A Report on the Delta Farm Strike," 16 August 1965, p. 2, box 2186, folder 7, Mississippi State AFL-CIO Records, 1947-1986, Georgia State University; *National Observer*, 21 February 1966.

November and April, choppers and pickers depended during this time either on advances from their seasonal employers that kept them in debt and tied to the plantation, or on free federal surplus commodities in counties that participated in that program. Agricultural workers were ineligible for unemployment compensation or social security, and Mississippi denied its meager welfare payments to all but the elderly, disabled, and dependent children who had lost one or both parents. Difficult though their lives were, African Americans in Shaw faced even greater problems in the spring of 1965, when they learned that plantation owners were planning to reduce the wages of cotton choppers to $1.75 a day.[6]

In response to these conditions, forty-five African Americans in Shaw formed the MFLU in April, based on discussions they had held at the Freedom School. These first MFLU members comprised "laborers, tractor drivers, haulers, domestic servants, part-time carpenters, mechanics, handymen, former sharecroppers and renters." MFLU members immediately went on strike at the nearby Seligmann plantation in support of their union's demand for "a $1.25 minimum wage per hour, an eight hour day with time and a half for overtime, sick pay, health and accident insurance and equal employment practices in wages, hiring and working conditions."[7]

While Weil and Gellatly helped with the union's formation, along with Liz Fusco, a white CORE worker, they did not direct or lead it. After some initial assistance communicating the MFLU's message and demands, recruiting in local areas, and soliciting support from northern sympathizers, the COFO staffers turned this work over to union members to undertake for themselves. SNCC reported that "The workers' approach was to let the local people run theor [sic] own union. This meant raise all their funds, do their own organizing and communications work and in short–sink or swim." SNCC adopted this path "because these workers wanted to give the local people a chance to develop and learn to carry on the union after they [SNCC] left."[8] Although COFO contributed to the MFLU's formation, the idea's genesis was shared between COFO and local people. Some of the union's founders had been influenced by friends and relatives outside the South. One founder

---

[6] "Mississippi: A Crisis in Hunger," 6 August 1965, box 1, folder "USDA/NSA Commodity Proposal," Arthur C. Thomas Papers, Martin Luther King, Jr. Center for Nonviolent Social Change; *National Guardian*, 12 June 1965; "Shaw Mississippi: New Sounds in the Delta," pp. 2-3, n.d., box 11, folder 564, King Collection; "Fact Sheet (Background on poor peoples' use of Greenville AFB)," n.d., box 4, folder 6, Moore Papers; *National Observer*, 21 February 1966; Michael Aiken and N. J. Demerath III, "The Politics of Tokenism in Mississippi's Delta," *Trans-Action* 4 (April 1967): 27; "The 1965 Mississippi Plantation Workers Strike," n.d., p. 1, box 1602, folder 132, Southern Office Records, AFL-CIO Civil Rights Department, Georgia State University (Southern Office Records).

[7] "Mississippi Freedom Labor Union," n.d., box 7, folder 22, SNCC Papers; "Shaw Mississippi: New Sounds in the Delta," p. 1 (quotations), n.d., box 11, folder 564, King Collection; Elizabeth Sutherland, "Mississippi Summer of Discontent," *Nation* 201 (11 October 1965), 213.

[8] Mary Sue Gellatly, Eddie Short, and Robert Weil, "Shaw, Mississippi," n.d., Mississippi Freedom Democratic Party Papers, Martin Luther King, Jr., Center for Nonviolent Social Change (MFDP Papers); memorandum "The MFLU" from Margaret Lauren to Northern offices (quotations), n.d., box 113, folder 102, SNCC Papers.

explained that "I have people in the north who belong to the union. When we gets together that's mainly what we talk about—the union. So we began talking about it here."[9]

The MFLU hoped to recruit members from across the Delta and spread the strike. By May, weeds would be coming up in the cotton and plantation owners would need to have hired choppers to protect the crop. In order to have any chance of success, the strike would have to be supported by the vast majority of the potential plantation workforce, including machinery operators and haulers, otherwise planters could simply draw on the vast pool of surplus agricultural labor. But even if the strike succeeded in the short-term, the prospects for long-term success were poor since planters could accelerate mechanization and their use of chemical weedkillers, and provide financial incentives for black machinery operators or recruit operators from outside the region[10]

Aided initially by COFO, MFLU members from Shaw recruited new members from adjoining areas and then further afield. By mid-April 1965, the union claimed to have between 300 and 350 members and had spread to Indianola and Ruleville in neighboring Sunflower County. By the end of the month, the union claimed to have recruited over 1,200 members, with 250 members on strike. The strikers, like the union, mostly comprised choppers and weeders with only a few tractor drivers and haulers. However, the MFLU received a boost at the end of May when twelve tractor drivers at the Andrews Brothers' Plantation at Tribbett, Washington County, joined the MFLU and voted unanimously to strike.[11]

The Delta Ministry, sponsored by the National Council of Churches to assist the Delta's African American poor, had been visiting agricultural workers at Tribbett since December 1964. Delta Ministry member the Reverend Larry Walker, an American Baptist minister originally from Georgia, began taking Isaac Foster, a twenty-two-year-old African American from Sunflower County, with him to Tribbett. Foster, who had grown up on a plantation and had later been fired from Greenville Mill for supporting a protest to end racial discrimination at the plant, understood the difficulties of the workers at Tribbett. He visited the MFLU at Shaw and subsequently explained the union's purpose and aims to the men at the Andrews Brothers' Plantation. Foster helped the tractor drivers form Local 4 of the MFLU and became the chapter's chairman. A. L. Andrews evicted the strikers and their families, who worked as choppers, and replaced them with white workers from Arkansas on the same terms as he had denied the strikers. Local convict labor

---

[9] "Shaw Mississippi: New Sounds in the Delta," p. 6 (quotation), n.d., box 11, folder 564, King Collection; Liz [Fusco] to "Dear George," 21 June 1965, box 86, folder 232, Congress of Racial Equality Records, Martin Luther King, Jr., Center for Nonviolent Social Change.

[10] "Shaw Mississippi: New Sounds in the Delta," pp. 4-5, n.d., box 11, folder 564, King Collection.

[11] "The Mississippi Freedom Labor Union and the Farm Labor Conference at Greenville", *Mississippi Freedom Democratic Party Newsletter* 3 (24 April 1965): 6, box 2, folder 2, Harry J. Bowie Papers, Wisconsin Historical Society; "Cotton Workers Strike in Delta," 1, 4; "Shaw Mississippi: New Sounds in the Delta," p. 5, n.d., box 11, folder 564, King Collection; Newman, *Divine Agitators*, 95. Cotton choppers and pickers accounted for over 90 percent of the MFLU's membership.

dumped the strikers' possessions on the roadside. The Delta Ministry provided the strikers and their families with food and tents as they set up camp on land donated by a black store owner at what became known as Strike City.[12]

The MFLU's strike spread to other plantations and more Delta towns during the summer. The strike also extended beyond plantation workers to include some restaurant cooks and domestic workers in Cleveland, Bolivar County. Seven maids at the Holiday Inn in McComb, located in the southwestern corner of the state, also joined the MFLU and the strike, but they were soon fired and replaced. Most estimates by strike supporters, such as SNCC and the Delta Ministry, pointed to about 1,000 people on strike during the summer. The total number of strikers probably peaked at around 1,300, although their number may have been as much as two or even three thousand according to some media reports. However, more than 30,000 people still worked in the fields, including the vast majority of the Delta's 3,000 tractor drivers.[13]

The fundamental problem faced by the MFLU was its inability to produce a mass walkout that would paralyze the plantations. An MFLU member explained that "some people want to strike but won't be able because they [are] going to have to have something for their children to live on." The MFLU tried to support strikers using financial donations from sympathizers that it solicited through letters to potential donors, and visits by MFLU chairman George Shelton, Jr., and Isaac Foster to northern and western states. However, it never raised more than a fraction of the funds it needed to sustain those who were on strike.[14]

COFO and SNCC's desire to encourage local people to run the union and its fund raising efforts, while understandable from the point of view of trying to develop local leadership, also had some negative repercussions. The union at Shaw had made decisions collectively, but this became impossible for the MFLU as it rapidly expanded. Local chapters of the MFLU often did not coordinate their actions with the Shaw headquarters, and, for their part, Shelton and the state MFLU leadership did not tightly organize the headquarters. Since the MFLU's poorly educated and inexperienced state and local leaders were learning how to organize through trial and error, mistakes were inevitable. The state MFLU's record keeping

---

[12] Aaron German, "Mississippi Freedom Labor Union," box 113, folder 102, SNCC Papers; Newman, *Divine Agitators*, 20, 92, 95-97; "Extent of the Strike and Organization," box 1602, folder 132, Southern Office Records.

[13] "Mississippi Freedom Labor Union," n.d., box 7, folder 22, "Mississippi Freedom Labor Union" pamphlet, box 113, folder 102, "Minutes of Statewide Meeting - MFLU - September 5 [1965]," box 113, folder 102, and "Report on the Cotton-Choppers' Strike in Three Delta Counties in Mississippi," box 169, folder 51, SNCC Papers; Sutherland, "Mississippi Summer of Discontent," 213; *Delta Democrat-Times*, 5 September 1965; *San Francisco Chronicle*, 30 September 1965; "Union Members Talk Strike," [Student] *Voice* 6 (6 June 1965): 1, 4; "A New Alliance Shapes Up in Dixie," *Business Week*, 10 July 1965, 128; "The 1965 Mississippi Plantation Workers Strike," n.d., pp. 1, 3, box 1602, folder 132, Southern Office Records.

[14] "Shaw Mississippi: New Sounds in the Delta," n.d., p. 7 (quotation), box 11, folder 564, King Collection; "Mississippi Freedom Labor Union Financial Report," n.d., box 113, folder 102, SNCC Papers; Claude Ramsay, "A Report on the Delta Farm Strike," 16 August 1965, p. 6, box 2186, folder 7, Mississippi State AFL-CIO Records; *San Francisco Chronicle*, 30 September 1965.

was poor at first. Financial donors sometimes did not receive acknowledgement letters. Some locals raised funds directly rather than asking for them to be directed through the state office, and some individuals solicited funds claiming to be representatives of the MFLU, although their actions had not been authorized by Shelton.[15]

Disputes over the distribution of donated cash and supplies, and local factionalism also hampered the MFLU's organizing efforts. SNCC worker Margaret Lauren reported that people "have not begun working together because of divisions and factions within communities over who gets what food and what money. In some towns people on one end of town won't have anything to do with people in the other part of town."[16]

While some day laborers would not join the strike without the assurance that the immediate needs of themselves and their families would be met by the MFLU, the union also failed to recruit more than a few tractor drivers for strike action. Poorly paid though they were, machine operators still earned twice as much as choppers, and most operators were also employed throughout the year. Furthermore, the strike also led some planters to increase the daily wages of their tractor drivers by a dollar and that of choppers by fifty cents a day, and to improve the plantation housing in which the drivers and their families lived.[17]

Successful civil rights campaigns, such as the recent Selma, Alabama, protest, had often benefited from national outrage at media reported white racist violence. Although some Delta plantation owners used violence and economic intimidation against those already on strike and to deter potential strikers, such action received little coverage in the print media. Television camera crews, like reporters from regional and national newspapers, also did not venture far into the vast Delta, and the scattered nature of the strike made sustained media coverage impractical.[18]

Published by Hodding Carter II and edited by his son Hodding Carter III, the *Delta Democrat-Times*, the Delta's leading newspaper, was renowned for its opposition to racial intolerance. However, the paper favored the more moderate wing of the civil rights movement associated with the NAACP, and condemned the Delta Ministry and SNCC-dominated COFO as dangerous radicals. The paper sided with the NAACP against the Mississippi Freedom Democratic Party (MFDP), formed by COFO in April 1964 to challenge the seating of the state's all-white delegation to the Democratic Party's national convention in Atlantic City. The *Delta Democrat-Times* argued that the Delta Ministry and the MFDP, both of which it had

---

[15] Mary Sue Gellatly, Eddie Short, and Robert Weil, "Shaw, Mississippi," n.d., box 21, folder 23, MFDP Papers; George Shelton, Jr., to "Dear Friends", n.d., box 113, folder 102, SNCC Papers.

[16] Memorandum "The MFLU" from Margaret Lauren to Northern offices, n.d., box 113, folder 102, SNCC Papers.

[17] "Shaw Mississippi: New Sounds in the Delta," n.d., p. 5, box 11, folder 564, King Collection; *Commercial Appeal*, 10 February 1966; "A New Alliance Shapes Up in Dixie," 128.

[18] "Shaw Mississippi: New Sounds in the Delta," pp. 7-8, n.d., box 11, folder 564, King Collection; "Report on the Cotton-Choppers' Strike in Three Delta Counties in Mississippi, n.d., p. 1, box 169, folder 51, SNCC Papers; Good, "Thorntons of Mississippi," 99.

initially supported, had become the preserve of irresponsible militants who were unwilling to achieve progress on civil rights consensually in cooperation with moderate blacks and whites in the state. The Delta Ministry and the MFDP supported the MFLU, which became a target of the paper's editorials.[19]

The *Delta Democrat-Times* accused the MFLU and its supporters of threatening African American plantation workers who refused to join the strike or acted as strikebreakers. The paper reported that Fannie Lou Hamer, a SNCC activist and former Delta plantation worker, had told a meeting near the Andrews Brothers' Plantation that "We've got to stop the nervous nellies and the toms from going to the planters. I don't believe in killing but a good whipping behind the bushes wouldn't hurt them." A reporter for the *New York Times* verified Hamer's words, which the *Delta Democrat-Times* condemned as "distressing" and part of a "needless tactic." The Delta paper argued that workers should not be coerced by the MFLU and should, instead, be free to choose whether to strike or work. Although Hamer did not take a leading role in either the MFLU or the strike, it seems likely, as the *Delta Democrat-Times*, reported that some MFLU strikers utilized threats and intimidation, but so too did some plantation owners and their families.[20]

Unable to find allies among Mississippi's white moderates, the MFLU hoped to get support from national unions, such as those grouped in the American Federation of Labor-Congress of Industrial Organizations (AFL-CIO) which had offered the civil rights movement some degree of support. However, unions offered the MFLU only token backing. By September 1965, the MFLU's state headquarters in Shaw had raised $14,600, mostly from unions in the North and on the West coast, with $8,000 of this amount donated by the United Auto Workers and the remainder mostly from steelworkers and longshoremen. Some MFLU locals also received small sums directly from northern unions.[21]

E. T. Kehrer, director of the AFL-CIO Civil Rights Department office in Atlanta, did not believe that the strike could succeed, but he nevertheless felt a sense of obligation to Mississippi's plantation workers. Kehrer informed *Business Week* that "I shudder to think what would happen to us if we turned our backs and just let all these things go on around us." However, Claude Ramsay, president of the

---

[19] Newman, *Divine Agitators*, 33, 37, 85, 87, 91-92, 93-94, 98, 103; Dittmer, *Local People*, 237, 273-302, 346-48.

[20] *Delta Democrat-Times*, 4 (first quotation), 9, 13 (second and third quotations) June, 2 July 1965; *National Guardian*, 12 June 1965; "Shaw Mississippi: New Sounds in the Delta," pp. 7-8, n.d., box 11, folder 564, King Collection. The *New York Times* quoted Hamer almost in identical fashion: "We got to stop the nervous Nellies and the Toms from going to the Man's place. I don't believe in killing, but a good whipping behind the bushes wouldn't hurt them." *New York Times*, 7 June 1965. According to a report by the Mississippi State Sovereignty Commission, the state's segregationist watchdog, privately Hamer doubted that the strike could succeed, and she urged the MFLU to focus on persuading tractor drivers to join the strike. "Mississippi Freedom Labor Union; Project Head Start," 10, 11, 12, 13 July 1965, box 137, folder 7, Paul B. Johnson Family Papers, University of Southern Mississippi (Johnson Family Papers).

[21] "Mississippi Freedom Labor Union Financial Report," n.d., and "Minutes of Statewide Meeting - MFLU - September 4 [1965]," box 113, folder 102, SNCC Papers; *Delta Democrat-Times*, 5 September 1965.

Mississippi AFL-CIO, criticized the MFLU, thereby ensuring that national unions would not rally behind the fledgling MFLU.[22]

Ramsay had been approached by the Delta Ministry in the summer of 1964 for his advice about organizing the Delta's farm workers. He had rejected the idea arguing that the Delta was too vast and its plantation workers, including the machine operators, too dispersed to be organized for effective mass action. Moreover, a strike, he rightly contended, could not succeed when seasonal day laborers were chasing a declining number of jobs because of mechanization and chemical weedkiller use.[23]

However, Ramsay sympathized with the economic plight of African Americans in the Delta, and he met with the MFLU in July 1965. He advocated, and offered to help the MFLU lobby for, an extension of the federal minimum wage law to include farm labor, and the creation of a federally-funded training program for displaced and seasonal workers. However, the MFLU bristled at the suggestion, arguing that it would not be told what to do. Ramsay, for his part, rejected the MFLU's plea for direct financial support since the MFLU would not affiliate with the AFL-CIO and accept its leadership in negotiations with employers. Convinced also that the MFLU was ill-equipped to ensure that donations were "used in the proper fashion," Ramsay suggested that any funds contributed by sympathetic national unions should be channeled through the Delta Ministry. Determined to be independent in thought and operation, the MFLU rejected the idea.[24]

Mutual antagonism marked relations between Ramsay and the MFLU because of their different approaches to reforming Mississippi. An opponent of segregation and president of the state AFL-CIO since 1959, Ramsay rejected both the segregationist regular Democratic Party in Mississippi and the MFDP, which he regarded as dangerously radical. Like the Carters, he favored consensual change led by moderate blacks and whites in the state. Ramsay regarded the MFLU as a creature of the MFDP in both its creation and behavior. The MFDP, for its part, despised the AFL-CIO for being part of a liberal establishment that had backed away from supporting, and thereby ensured the failure, of the MFDP's bid to be seated at the Democratic Party's national convention in 1964. The MFDP and the MFLU also resented Ramsay's advice to the Delta Ministry that organizing Delta plantation workers was unrealistic. The refusal of the MFLU to affiliate with the AFL-CIO and to accept its leadership marked a psychological break from the dependency on and deference to whites that had long characterized plantation labor. However, it also ended any chance that the AFL-CIO might have provided significant financial support.[25]

---

[22] "A New Alliance Shapes Up in Dixie," 126; Claude Ramsay, "A Report on the Delta Farm Strike", 16 August 1965, pp. 1-6, box 2186, folder 7, Mississippi State AFL-CIO Records.

[23] Claude Ramsay, "A Report on the Delta Farm Strike," 16 August 1965, pp. 1-2, box 2186, folder 7, Mississippi State AFL-CIO Records.

[24] Ibid., 3-4 (quotation on p. 4).

[25] Claude Ramsay, "A Report on the Delta Farm Strike", 16 August 1965, pp. 3-4, box 2186, folder 7, Mississippi State AFL-CIO Records; Steve Riley, "Claude Ramsay - A Life for Mississippi Workers," *Southern Changes* 8 (1986): 19, 21, consulted 15 September 2000 at http:chaucer.library.emory.edu/otbin/we...and&SUBSET=SUBSET&FROM=1&SIZE=100&

Lacking effective organization and a viable support fund, the strike, which had never involved more than a fraction of the Delta's workforce, had begun to fade by August 1965. In need of money, strikers who could, returned to work to harvest the cotton crop, but many found either that employers would not hire them because of their activities or because mechanization and chemicals had replaced the need for their labor. By September, only 268 people were still on strike. The MFLU made an abortive attempt to organize a further strike in the fall.[26]

Isaac Foster issued another strike call in the spring of 1966, but it came to nothing as Delta plantation workers faced a massive rise in unemployment as a consequence of the Federal Food and Fiber Act passed by Congress in late 1965. The act offered landowners payments of 10.5 cents per pound on projected yields from land switched from cotton production. To qualify farmers had to reduce cotton acreage by between 12.5 and 35 percent. As a result, the seasonal work force fell by half in 1966, by which time at least 64 percent of Mississippi's cotton labor force was unemployed.[27]

A federal minimum wage dollar an hour law that came into effect on February 1, 1967, virtually ended demand for day laborers as farmers found it far more cost effective to mechanize and reorganize more efficiently, sometimes at the cost of machine operators as well. A Delta landowner explained: "We knew we couldn't use any more casual labor, because of the minimum wage, and now we're finding out we don't need as much specialized labor either." W. L. Patterson, the mayor of Sunflower, noted that in anticipation of the minimum wage "a lot of people are switching to chemical weed controls as fast as they can." Without the need for their labor, plantation owners no longer gave advances on salaries to see their workers through the winter, and while many owners allowed unneeded workers to remain in plantation shacks, the Delta experienced a net outmigration of 12,000 people in 1967. As historian James C. Cobb concluded, "For some Delta blacks the angry

---

ITEM=59; "Oral History with Mr. Claude Ramsay, president: Mississippi AFL-CIO," interview by Orley B. Caudill, April 28, 30, May 7, 1981, vol. 215, pp. 16-17, 32-34 Mississippi Oral History Program of the University of Southern Mississippi, consulted 22 March 2005, at http://anna.lib.usm.edu/%7Espcol/cdra/oh/ohramsaycb.html; "Report on Edwards Workshop of September 21-24, 1965, Mount Beulah Center, Edwards, Mississippi," box 81, folder 2, Highlander Research and Education Center Records, Wisconsin Historical Society; John Brown, "The Mississippi Democratic Conference Joins the Race for the Future Negro Vote But Gets Off to a Bad Start," *Mississippi Freedom Democratic Party Newsletter* 6 (28 July [1965]): 2-3, box 1602, folder 132, Southern Office Records; Dittmer, *Local People*, 346-48, 351. On Ramsay's life see Alan Draper, *Conflict of Interests: Organized Labor and the Civil Rights Movement in the South, 1954-1968* (Ithaca, N.Y.: ILR Press, 1994), 122-60.

[26] Memorandum "The MFLU" from Margaret Lauren to Northern offices, n.d., and "Minutes of Statewide Meeting - MFLU - September 4," box 113, folder 102, SNCC Papers; *Delta Democrat-Times*, 5 September 1965.

[27] "Jackson Case No. D1387 Mississippi Freedom Labor Union," 12 April 1966, box 138, folder 9, Johnson Family Papers; *New York Times*, 18 November 1965; Ralph Alewine, Jr., "The Changing Characteristics of the Mississippi Delta," in U.S. Department of Labor, Manpower Administration, "Farm Labor Developments," May 1968, mimeo, 37; "Hunger in the Mississippi Delta," n.d., box 4, folder 204, King Collection.

activism of the 1960s simply faded into a life on the edge of subsistence at the edge of a cotton field, while for others it eventually dissolved into the destructive monotony of a northern ghetto."[28]

Had the MFLU been able to organize a widely observed general strike on Delta plantations, it might have achieved some short-term success. But the MFLU failed to act early enough to ensure a widespread strike as the chopping season commenced, and it lacked the experience and financial resources to organize effectively. Divisions within the civil rights movement and its supporters resulted in the MFLU receiving inadequate financial support, but its members' sense of independence and refusal to follow advice from the AFL-CIO contributed to its financial and organizational problems. Even if the MFLU had been more effective, plantation owners would have accelerated the switch to machines and chemical weedkillers, and increased the wages of machine operators as they did in the wake of the strike, the Food and Fiber Act, and the implementation of the minimum wage. Federal agricultural policy undercut the Mississippi civil rights movement's attempt to tackle the Delta's economic problems, while nationally the federal government was to prove unable and increasingly unwilling to support an economic agenda being developed by elements of a fracturing civil rights movement after its triumphs during the first half of the 1960s.

---

[28] Alewine, "Changing Characteristics of the Mississippi Delta," 37-39; Cobb, *Most Southern Place on Earth*, 255-56, 276 (third quotation); Hodding Carter III, "The Negro Exodus From the Delta Continues," *New York Times Magazine*, 10 March 1968, 26 (first quotation), 117; *New York Times*, 7 February 1966 (second quotation).

FROM WILLIAM ALEXANDER PERCY TO WALKER PERCY: PROGRESS OR REGRESS?

Kieran Quinlan

This essay is an experiment, perhaps even a prelude to an experiment, in that it explores a way of seeing things that is not only contrary to received opinion on the matter at hand, but that is also contrary to what I myself have argued in the past. I want to suggest here that we might look at southern planter, poet, and memoirist William Alexander Percy rather differently than has been the custom for decades, and that when we do so, he can appear, in some ways at least, to be more "modern," more our contemporary at the beginning of the twenty-first century, than is his famed younger cousin and nominal "nephew," the novelist and philosophical essayist Walker Percy.[1]

Such an approach goes against the usual view that celebrates the William Alexander Percy-Walker Percy sequence as a progression from an exclusivist and racist patricianism to an inclusivist and respectful desegregationism; from a defeatist, self-enclosed stoicism to a hopeful and universalist Catholicism; and, though less overtly, from an unacknowledged and possibly (if unlikely) latent homosexuality to a more "normal," religiously-sanctioned coupling of opposite sexes. Even most of those not in agreement with Walker Percy on specifics, or who themselves are not especially religious (much less Roman Catholic), tend to acknowledge a basic progress. In some cases even, there is at least the implication of a John the Baptist-Messiah sequence in the two Percys following one another. A recent example of the received view is very clearly stated by John F. Desmond: for him, Walker Percy is "a progressive thinker who searched for ways to unite the best of traditional and contemporary knowledge," while William Alexander Percy's stoicism "commands allegiance to an ethic that is truly outmoded and retrogressive."[2]

It seems to me now, however, that in light of current cultural debate—and also bearing in mind some observations in Jay Tolson's biography of Walker Percy—it is necessary to at least complicate this simple narrative of overall progress and to claim a certain narrowing of philosophical perspective at the same time that there has been an undoubted broadening of social horizons. I have no desire, or ability, of course, to completely overturn the reigning hierarchy and to remake William Alexander Percy into something he was not. I leave aside also the question of how to define "progressive" and "regressive"—after all, who could possibly wish to have the latter term applied to them? And there is the obvious consideration that one person's "progressive" can be another's "regressive." Still, if a post-examination Will Percy remains a man more of the world of 1905 than of 2005, his personal and intellectual uncertainties in some ways strike a more contemporary note than do Walker's more

---

[1] See Kieran Quinlan, *Walker Percy: The Last Catholic Novelist* (Baton Rouge: Louisiana State University Press, 1996), 18-27
[2] John F. Desmond, *Walker Percy's Search for Community* (Athens: University of Georgia Press, 2004), 5.

comforting religious absolutes. It might be noted in passing that a new version of the "This I Believe" series of talks that Edward R. Murrow hosted in the 1950s to give expression to the core values that unite Americans of different classes, genders, and races, and that were so devastatingly mocked by Walker Percy in his 1961 novel *The Moviegoer*, is now airing on American National Public Radio, explicitly referring to itself as an updated version of the original program and presumably expressive of current listeners' interests. In any case, reversing the William Alexander Percy-Walker Percy sequence—even experimentally—should further our understanding of early twentieth-century southern thought.[3]

It must be acknowledged at the outset that while Walker Percy himself frequently criticized the limitations of his uncle's stoic ethic—particularly in regard to race—both in his fiction and in his essays, he has also been a staunch defender of his distinguished relative. Although Walker Percy has claimed against William Alexander Percy that "The Christian is optimistic precisely where the Stoic is pessimistic," he has also summarily dismissed the categories of "liberal" and "conservative" applied to Will Percy as irrelevant, asking if "it [is] a bad thing for a man to care like a father for his servants, spend himself on the poor, the sick, the miserable, the mad who come his way?" Even in regard to Will Percy's reputed homosexuality, Walker Percy has been almost totally silent, though some contend that it acted as a motivating factor in his criticisms of gay culture of the late twentieth century and partly aided his eventual adoption of an authoritarian Catholicism. In all, Walker Percy has generally presented his foster-parent in the noblest of lights, a "fixed point in a confusing world."[4]

But surely this exalted portrayal is hard to reconcile with recent commentary on Will Percy that suggests a more untidy, uncertain, and confused—if still somewhat daunting—patriarch? Put another way, Walker Percy may trump his cousin in terms of artistic achievement, professional philosophical knowledge, and racial sensitivity. After all, Walker very actively supported busing and the establishing of a credit union for blacks in Covington in the 1960s and 70s, and even survived the close personal vetting of African American novelist Albert Murray. In contrast, the disinterestedness and even adequacy of Will Percy's undoubtedly brave deeds in saving blacks during the 1927 Mississippi flood have been called into question. Nevertheless, in terms of sexuality and religious issues, Will Percy seems the more relevant figure today. So, after a brief foray into the racial matter, it is on the latter two topics—sexuality and religion—that I want to dwell in this essay.[5]

We are probably all too familiar with Will Percy's pronouncements on race in the pages of *Lanterns on the Levee: Recollections of a Planter's Son*, his memoir published in 1941: "How is it possible for the white man to communicate with

---

[3] Jay Tolson, *Pilgrim in the Ruins: A Life of Walker Percy* (New York: Simon & Schuster, 1992); Walker Percy, *The Moviegoer* (New York: Alfred A. Knopf, 1961).

[4] Walker Percy, *Signposts in a Strange Land* (New York: Farrar, Straus, and Giroux, 1991), 86; Walker Percy, introduction to William Alexander Percy's *Lanterns on the Levee: Recollections of a Planter's Son* (Baton Rouge: Louisiana State University Press, 1973), xiii; see William Rodney Allen, *Walker Percy: A Southern Wayfarer* (Jackson: University Press of Mississippi, 1986), 12; Walker Percy in *Lanterns*, xi.

[5] Albert Murray, *South to a Very Old Place* (New York: Vintage, 1991).

people of this sort, people whom imagination kills and fantasy makes impotent, who thrive like children and murder ungrudgingly as small boys fight?" Even in the very clarity and lyricism of its articulation, the book seems astonishingly unaware of its own political and social self-interest. Pessimism pervades its pages as it laments the passing of an admirable old order and the advent of an ignorant new one that is being misguided by the political rise of former poor whites in America and by fascists in Europe, while blacks are deceived by false promises and imaginary hopes. "The followers of Jesus and Buddha and Socrates [are] being driven from the face of the earth," Percy concludes poignantly.[6]

Recently, however, McKay Jenkins and others have pointed to certain fissures in this superior-inferior racial relationship, noting that Percy had to turn to stories about how African Americans on his plantation mourned the death of Percy's father in order to express his own repressed sorrow on the occasion. "Blacks for Percy are full of everything that he has been denied," Jenkins observes. Hortense Powdermaker has argued that Percy's criticism of African Americans as living outside time and history is also an expression of his own envy of their positive ability to "turn away from a past that is not only heroic but paralyzing." For all its assumptions of superiority and pristineness, as Jenkins finally comments, "The burnished world of the landed gentry, steeped in the writings of Marcus Aurelius and the Victorians" cannot escape being touched by the local African (American) culture in which it is so deeply embedded. If in the end the overall hierarchical equation remains in place—after all, Percy's most racially important decision involved the overseeing of displaced blacks in the Mississippi Delta after the 1927 floods (where he failed to prevent his father, United States Senator LeRoy Percy, from ensuring that such workers would not be sent out of the area)—its barriers are shown not to have been totally impenetrable.[7]

Will Percy's vulnerability on racial issues leads to a reconsideration of his sexual orientation and mores. He himself certainly saw a connection between the two. In *Lanterns*, he referred to his black driver, Ford Atkins, as "my tie with Pan and the Satyrs and all earth creatures who smile sunshine and ask no questions and understand." But in this controversial matter, Walker Percy rather surprisingly makes his uncle conform to his own desired (if perhaps not quite practiced) standard: in his introduction to the 1973 edition of *Lanterns*, Percy wrote that his Uncle Will would have seen "the so-called sexual revolution" of the 1960s as "alley-cat morality."[8]

Yet how can we reconcile this claim with what we now know about Will Percy's sexuality? Indeed, Will Percy's sexual "outing" in recent years has a kind of parallel in the revelations—once rumors, now apparently confirmed—about Thomas Jefferson that have caused us to rethink that patrician's heritage. Several years ago, when Bertram Wyatt-Brown noted the intensity of Will Percy's male friendships at Sewanee and his association with English writer Norman Douglas at Taormina, a

---

[6] William Alexander Percy, *Lanterns on the Levee*, 305, 313.

[7] McKay Jenkins, *The South in Black and White: Race, Sex, and Literature in the 1940s* (Chapel Hill: University of North Carolina Press, 1999), 88; Powdermaker, quoted in Jenkins, 89; Jenkins, 97.

[8] William Alexander Percy, *Lanterns*, 296; Walker Percy in *Lanterns*, xiv.

resort well known for its "Uranian" clientele, some Percy family members were outraged. The matter received further and far less reverent analysis in John M. Barry's 1997 book, *Rising Tide: The Great Mississippi Flood of 1927 and How It Changed America*. There the emphasis is not only on Will Percy's self-loathing on account of his sexual desires—Barry quotes Percy's own lines from his poem "Sappho in Levkas": "To think nobility like mine could be / Flawed – shattered utterly - . . . //. . . and I, who, most of all the world, / Loved purity and loathed lust, / Became the mark of my own scorning"—but on the seedier side of that lust.[9]

According to Barry, after his father's death Will Percy felt freer to indulge his sexual proclivities, taking "young men, both white and black, on trips to Europe and Tahiti," or buying them cars and paying for them to take flying lessons. "The rumors," Barry notes, "said that blacks had a power over Will." Not only was there such a relationship with Atkins, but when the latter was fired for acting too familiarly, Percy's next chauffeur, a rather flashy dresser whose nickname was "Honey," likely became involved with Percy too. Among his friends, we are told, "Honey" referred to Will Percy as his "whore," while in some places in town Percy felt the need to lie on the floor in the backseat of his large car to avoid being seen by passers-by. The descriptions sashay between the comical and the pathetic, and, however looked at, hardly enhance the man's noble image. Percy is at once exploiter and victim in an age that has not yet come to grips with the Wildean "love that dare not speak its name."[10]

William Armstrong Percy III, a professor of history and cousin of William Alexander Percy, has gone further, criticizing earlier scholars for being so cautious in their assertions about Will Percy's sexuality. According to Armstrong Percy, he was not only gay but actively so. In fact, those who have pursued the matter have been teased with a collection of unavailable files from the Percy inheritors—the late Walker Percy and his two surviving brothers—only to be forbidden their perusal and threatened with legal consequences into the bargain. Even family member William Armstrong Percy failed to obtain them. Instead, he has found the indirect evidence in the poems and in *Lanterns*—the description, for example, of the moonlight on sailors "turning their bodies slender, . . . daubing their cheek-bones . . . [and] the arch of their chests or their buttocks with pallor"—compelling, as well as the testimony of a former Greenville resident who confirmed Percy's relationship with his chauffeur, Ford Atkins, not to mention Armstrong Percy's own parents' disapproval of their "effeminate" cousin. And then, of course, there's the much-noticed *Lanterns* scene in the shower in which Ford Atkins remarks that Will Percy "ain't nothing but a little old fat man." Armstrong Percy acknowledges that Will Percy was worried about his orientation—"Of all the worlds Percy had known in his lifetime . . . the Delta was easily the most hostile to any open expression of homosexual love"—and also felt ashamed that he wasn't quite the male his father desired. But, claims Armstrong Percy, Will was open in his friendship with Norman

---

[9] Bertram Wyatt-Brown, *The House of Percy: Honor, Melancholy, and Imagination in a Southern Family* (New York: Oxford University Press, 1994); John M. Barry, *Rising Tide: The Great Mississippi Flood and How It Changed America* (New York: Simon & Schuster, 1997), 420.

[10] Barry, 420.

Douglas and "was not a man who ran forever from his deepest desires." Will Percy also had many prominent gay friends, including the psychologist Harry Stack Sullivan, who spent a considerable amount of time visiting with him in Greenville. In a footnote, Armstrong Percy acknowledges a letter he received from Walker Percy claiming that in all his years in Uncle Will's house he (Walker) "never heard a single word that would have indicated that Will was gay," and that a more circumspect Shelby Foote assured him in 1993 that Uncle Will "would not have wanted to be outed." Finally, however, Armstrong Percy suggests the possibility of a similar and possibly more acute tension in Walker Percy himself.[11]

Yet it is in terms not of his sexuality but rather of religious issues that William Alexander Percy shows himself at his most modern. Whether this whole pursuit was a kind of willful obfuscation in the face of social and political inequities, I leave to others to judge. How it related to his sexual orientation is also an intriguing question ("As I started to the confessional I knew that there was no use going, no priest could absolve me. . . ."), though it might be noted that the Catholic Church has generally regarded homosexuality as a passing sin rather than a perverse condition, while the Church's elaborate dress and rituals have always had their appeal for those attracted to high camp-style homosexuality. In any case, Will Percy certainly gave far more space to the religious issue in the pages of *Lanterns* than one would normally expect, and he had written earlier in a letter that while he was "interested in contemporary problems—the conflict between capital and labor," and so forth, he "was much more interested in what seems to me the eternal things of human nature—Man and God, man and love, man in the trap of fate." In ordinary circumstances, this interest would attract the requisite attention in the context of any extended study of the loss of religious belief in the early decades of the twentieth century. In the context, however, of Walker Percy's subsequent, and ultimately very public, conversion to the very truths his uncle had rejected, it acquires far more literary and historical significance.[12]

The Percy family line has long contained strains of Episcopalianism, Presbyterianism, and Roman Catholicism among its members, the latter intermittently diluted and strengthened through the generations. William Alexander Percy's father, the United States senator, was nominally an Episcopalian, while his more pious mother was of French Creole Catholic origin. As a young man, Will Percy was, in his own words, "intolerably religious," even to the extent of being "infatuated with the monastic life," and praying and fasting "on the sly." Although such behavior was puzzling to his family, he "just couldn't help it, it was a violent attack, perhaps I've never fully recovered. . . . I wanted so intensely to believe, to believe in God and miracles and the sacraments and the [Catholic] Church and

---

[11] William Alexander Percy, *Lanterns*, 341; William Armstrong Percy III, "William Alexander Percy (1885-1942): His Homosexuality and Why It Matters," in John Howard, ed., *Carryin' On in the Lesbian and Gay South* (New York: New York University Press, 1997), 81, 85; *Lanterns*, 287; William Armstrong Percy, 83, 86, 91-92.

[12] Lewis Baker, *The Percys of Mississippi: Politics and Literature in the New South* (Baton Rouge: Louisiana State University Press, 1983), 154.

everything." At the tender age of nine he informed his astonished mother that he wished to become a priest.[13]

But even at that early age there was uncertainty in Will Percy's mind: "To be at once intellectually honest and religious is a wrack on which I writhed dumbly." In his studies at the University of the South, he encountered the great works of Victorian unbelief by Matthew Arnold and others, along with the resigned hedonism of Edward Fitzgerald's poetic translations. He very dramatically describes a visit to a Catholic church near his college where he realizes that his inherited religion could not "direct my life or my judgment, what most believed I could not believe. . . ." For the rest of his life, Percy was to remain an unbeliever, though many regarded him as a papist and one of his poems survives in the Episcopalian hymnal.[14]

When Will Percy's Catholicism dissolved, he turned to the accepted alternative, one that Thomas Jefferson had also pursued: the teachings of the Roman emperor Marcus Aurelius informed by a purely ethical Christianity. The emperor's aphorisms express doubt about immortality, recommend disinterested public service, patient acceptance of fate, and compassion for the less fortunate, a raft of virtues compatible with a Gospel story shorn of its unacceptable miracles. Yet Uncle Will did not try to make the three Percy cousins (Walker and his brothers) he adopted in 1930 conform to his new belief. Rather, he encouraged them first to try the various religious offerings in Greenville. It was only when they came back "confused, resentful, and distressed" that he expressed his own "honest" opinion on the matter.[15]

In the account offered in *Lanterns*, Percy admits that we understand neither the beauty of the world nor its terrible injustices. Nevertheless, giving "the Master Schemer" the benefit of the doubt, he allows that "the chaos we see" may be just "a hundredth-dimensional plan glimpsed by three-dimensional perceptions." And yet, even here, Percy almost immediately attacks traditional religion for its inherent superstition. In a 1923 poem titled "A Canticle," the speaker noted that all the gods—Astarte, Astoreth, Baal, Zeus, Jehovah—were dead, sharing "a single grave and deep." Now he quotes a saying of his father's in which the latter pities "the thousands who have been sent across [at death], terrified by the lies of priests in all the ages. There's nothing to fear"—a remark that sounds very like historian Diarmaid MacCulloch's conclusion to his magisterial volume on the Reformation that "Both late medieval Christianity and the mainstream Protestantism that sought to replace it were religions of fear, anxiety, and guilt." When Percy recalls from his religious youth "dead phrases—salvation, washed in the blood of the Lamb, He descended into hell, the resurrection of the body, born of the Virgin Mary"—he asks, "Where lies the virtue in attempting to persuade honest young minds to entertain such outworn rubbish?" Will Percy asserts that "Philosophical conceptions—the Trinity, the atonement, the fall, the redemption—cannot save this generation, for they speak a beautiful dead language." Still, Percy finally, and anxiously, stresses the need for some kind of religion "to give anchorage or peace" and to resist the belief in race offered by Hitler, or Stalin's in the State, or even America's in the god

[13] William Alexander Percy, *Lanterns*, 57, 79.

[14] Ibid., 79, 95.

[15] Ibid., 313.

of Mammon. Yet when Percy philosophizes in a more general way, he admits that "All we can know is through the tidings brought us by our five inaccurate senses."[16]

William Alexander Percy's unbelief has already been placed in the broad context of the age of Charles Darwin, Matthew Arnold, and Thomas Hardy, some of the main exemplars of the Victorian crisis of faith, and all of whom began their lives within the traditions of the Church of England and were intimately connected with its ecclesiastical structures. This is probably how it happened for Percy too: their crisis eventually became his crisis, all the more acute because of the intensely Episcopalian world of Sewanee in which he lived. But Percy was also very consciously a Roman Catholic outsider in that world, and so I think it is useful to relate his religious doubts to the Modernist movement within Catholicism of the early part of the twentieth century. This connection becomes all the more important since it is directly relevant to Walker Percy's subsequent religious conversion in 1947. In fact, A. N. Wilson has recently brought the familiar Darwin-Arnold-Hardy contingent and the Catholic Modernists together in the closing pages of *God's Funeral*, his admirably sympathetic study of the history of western unbelief.[17]

The Modernist movement had its origins in the desire of several theologians and lay persons to bring Catholicism into line with modern developments in the physical, cultural, and theological sciences, a desire increasingly condemned by the Vatican from the mid-nineteenth century onwards when Pope Pius IX, a onetime liberal now under siege from the forces of Italian unification, issued a notorious list of modern errors in belief and practice that Catholics were bound to resist. Catholic Modernism was in part a subsequent reaction to such strictures, an attempt to keep Catholics abreast of current intellectual trends in religious and secular scholarship in the confident expectation that the Church would be well able to handle such matters through the sheer force of its historic truths. In any case, while Catholic Modernism's early twentieth century incarnation was so loose as to embrace even the pragmatism of William James, the movement is most often associated with Abbé Alfred Loisy in France, and Father George Tyrell and Baron von Hügel in England. If William Alexander Percy's faith collapsed without his being aware of such names—born in 1885, his crisis of faith seems to have reached its nadir about 1903 when he was a freshman at Sewanee—it is clear that he was moving along the same lines, and indeed it is very likely that he heard of a group or "ism" that was finally condemned in 1907 by the Vatican as "the synthesis of all heresies," priests of the Roman Catholic faith being obliged in subsequent decades to take an oath against "Modernism." With its focus on scriptural exegesis, church history, and theological interpretation, religious Modernism can sometimes appear, unlike the writings of Darwin-Arnold-Hardy, as wholly internal to church politics: a 1904 review of Loisy's *The Gospel and the Church* referred to "the Abbé's troubles with the Roman Curia" as "for most people a marvelous string of academic enigmas." But that criticism misses the huge impact the movement threatened, and sometimes effected,

---

[16] Ibid., 319; William Alexander Percy, *Collected Poems* (New York: Alfred A. Knopf, 1950), 208-209; William Alexander Percy, *Lanterns*, 314; Diarmaid MacCulloch, *The Reformation* (New York: Penguin, 2004), 682; William Alexander Percy, *Lanterns*, 315, 317.

[17] A. N. Wilson, *God's Funeral: A Biography of Faith and Doubt in Western Civilization* (New York: Ballantine,, 1999), 333-354.

in the wider world. Today, at the beginning of the twenty-first century, a renewed and often acrimonious interest in the Catholic Modernist authors is frequently driven by the current ecclesial and political stances of the scholars involved. Thus, von Hügel has been portrayed as a buffoon, Loisy as fussy and French, Tyrell as a volcanic and eccentric Anglo-Irish convert to Catholicism. At all events, a movement that was apparently crushed a hundred years ago has asserted itself once again, though in a rather different cultural climate and with more possibility of success.[18]

As with Will Percy, Loisy too confessed to "mental and moral torture" in trying to imbibe the tenets of Catholic theology as a young seminarian. "For my intelligence could find no satisfaction, and with my whole timid, immature consciousness I trembled before the query that oppressed, in spite of myself, every hour of the day: Is there any reality which corresponds to such doctrines?" Again, Tyrell—Will Percy-like—recommended "a certain temperate agnosticism" which would recognize the "essential incapacity of finite mind to seize the absolute."[19]

The Modernist fringe in Roman Catholicism was at the time either excommunicated or, as with Baron von Hügel, chose cautious reconciliation. The Church strengthened its defenses aided by mandated adherence to the intricate and mind-consuming philosophy of Thomas Aquinas and the Scholastics, so that in time, and with its exotic medievalism, it came to appeal to many writers unhappy with the fragmented and secularized modern world—among them Evelyn Waugh, Thomas Merton, Muriel Spark, Allen Tate, Robert Lowell, even actor Alec Guinness, and, of course, Walker Percy. A decade or two after their joining, however, a fresh—and at the time exciting—new modernist movement (though not so called) was underway within Catholicism, partly identified with theologians such as Hans Küng in Switzerland, Karl Rahner in Germany, and Edward Schillebeeckx in the Netherlands, and gloriously—or notoriously—given popular expression in the 1966 *Dutch Catechism*. Since then, even many of those once enthusiastic for reform— most notably these days the new pope, Benedict XVI—have withdrawn once again behind the anti-modernist ramparts to shore up ancient traditions and interpretations, condemning evolution (at least as understood by the majority of scientists) and even poor Harry Potter along the way; meanwhile, dissidents have scattered to the four winds, blown about by the tempests of eccentric belief and unbelief.

Walker Percy very definitely chose to take his stance behind the ramparts, fulminating graciously and ungraciously against those Catholics who had decided to think otherwise. Given Will Percy's track record and the similarity between his religious thoughts and those of the first Modernists, adding a more liberated

---

[18] "Abbé Loisy's Book," *New York Times*, 7 May 1904, *BR* 313. In fact, the Modernist controversy of the early twentieth century is dramatized in an Irish novel of the period, *Father Ralph* (1913), by former priest Gerald O'Donovan (see the discussion in James H. Murphy, *Catholic Fiction and Social Reality in Ireland, 1873-1922* (Westport, Ct.: Greenwood Press, 1997). For negative views of the Modernists, see Marvin O'Connell, *Critics on Trial: An Introduction to the Modernist Crisis* (Washington, D.C.: Catholic University of America Press, 1994), and Malachi Martin, *The Jesuits* (New York: Simon & Schuster, 1987).

[19] Quoted in Lawrence Gamache, "Defining Modernism: A Religious and Literary Correlation," *Studies in the Literary Imagination*, 25:2 (Fall 1992), 71, 70, 75.

understanding of his own sexuality, and maybe cutting him some slack for his genetically-inherited melancholia, it is hard not to think that he would have stood on the other side of the fence: "We survive or we are annihilated, and all our anguish cannot undo our fate one way or the other." As some contemporary philosophers of evolution tell us, a full understanding of our place in the universe may be forever beyond our mental capacities, a thought not very different from some of Will Percy's observations. Stoicism too, far from being "outmoded and retrogressive" appears to be enjoying—if that's possible—a comeback: "Our Stoic authors," claims Nancy Sherman in relation to the military abuses in Iraq, require "cultivating humanity through empathetic identification and respect" for our enemies. And if Christianity as a whole is judged to have unpersuasive foundations, and if even many of its members are little more than the modern Gnostics that Harold Bloom has described, then there is need for an alternative belief system and Stoicism becomes no more outmoded than any other offering.[20]

Like Will Percy, then, we "moderns"—I use the term presumptively—not privileged with any otherworldly insight or guaranteed knowledge, subject to the successes and errors of the thinking and governing communities of the age, adrift in an unpredictable and dangerous cosmos, will just have to see what lies around the corner. How foolish it was ever to have expected otherwise; how like William Alexander Percy to expect no more. In a limited but not thereby insignificant way, and adapting what Richard Ellmann once said of James Joyce, we are still becoming Will Percy's contemporaries.

---

[20] Nancy Sherman, *Stoic Warriors: The Ancient Philosophy behind the Military Mind* (New York: Oxford University Press, 2005), 179; Harold Bloom, *The American Religion: The Emergence of the Post-Christian Nation* (New York: Simon & Schuster, 1992); for another updated version of Stoicism, see Tad Brennan, *The Stoic Life: Emotions, Duties, and Fate* (New York: Oxford University Press, 2005).

PART III CHALLENGING BOTH AGRIBUSINESS AND WELFARE

A SUGAR CAGE:
POVERTY AND PROTEST IN STEPHANIE BLACK'S *H-2 WORKER*

Nahem Yousaf

> I got some troubles but they won't last
> I'm gonna lay right down here in the grass
> And pretty soon all my troubles will pass
> 'cause I'm in shoo-shoo-shoo, shoo-shoo-shoo
> Shoo-shoo, shoo-shoo, shoo-shoo Sugar Town.
> Nancy Sinatra, "Sugar Town"

> I am a H2 Worka
> Coming from the island of Jamaica
> Cutting cane in a-Florida
> Working so hard in the burning sun
> Wondering if slavery lives on
> I'm working, working, working in your cane fields still
> Working, working, working for your meager dollar bill.
> Mutabaraka, "H2 Worka"

The tension between the presence and absence of a submerged ethnic group in the South as the direct result of their labor is the subject of Stephanie Black's documentary *H-2 Worker*. Four years in the making and released in 1990, Black's first film is a compelling piece of investigative journalism, an exposé of the inside story of a racialized enclave in Palm Beach County, Florida. It recalls a similar scandal in 1942 when U.S. Sugar was prosecuted for conspiracy to enslave African American cane workers in Clewiston, known as "America's sweetest town." In the 1980s, the town that U.S. Sugar owns with its motto "Soil is Her Fortune" became the site of a global rather than a regional system of exploitative wage labor. Stephanie Black set out to show that Jamaican sugar cane workers were being held in peonage; they were indentured laborers, her investigations revealed, sometimes working for as little as $1 an hour even though their presence in the South was regulated by the Department of Labor. Dedicated to the workers with the legend, "The naming of the intolerable is the hope," *H-2 Worker* makes visible an almost captive labor force. These visitors to the South's Number One tourist state see little of their surroundings except the cane fields in which they toil, the barracks in which they live, and the commissary in which they shop.

The position of H-2 workers is anomalous insofar as they play a vital role in the nation's economy but are neither U.S. citizens nor illegal aliens, but legal non-immigrants. The name by which they are known derives from the name of the temporary visa they are issued in order for their labor to be imported. There is a tension between nomenclature and ontology. H-2 Worker is synonymous with the euphemistic "guest" worker and the *bracero*, the name traditionally given to Mexicans on their foreign worker program. The name also signals a loss of role: the men in the film are sons, husbands, and fathers yet they have become merely mail-order workers identified only by their temporary status. They are expected to cut a ton of cane every hour. If not up to speed within the first eight days on the job, they are returned to Jamaica. The mantra that one worker chants, "Hold it, cut it, put it on the pile" sums up their existence for the period of the harvest.

Black's award-winning film was instrumental in bringing the concrete details of the quotidian plight of foreign migrant workers to the attention of the U.S. Congress.[1] It was the first film to focus on Jamaican guest workers, although others have followed.[2] Shot in a fly-on-the-wall manner in necessarily clandestine circumstances, and at considerable risk to those who speak to Black's crew, it reveals a "migrant nation" in a southern locale whose interactions with southerners barely three miles away in Belle Glade are minimal to say the least. This is polemical filmmaking, a strong moral platform for a material analysis that indicts the U.S. government and the sugar industry and explores poverty in two locales: Florida and Jamaica.

Black has repeatedly said that she uses film as "an advocacy tool" and throughout the period in which the documentary was made and shown cane workers were filing action suits against the sugar growers who had exploited them in their poverty. It was precisely the actions taken by workers like those Black filmed in the 1980s that forced changes to the foreign workers' program, under the Immigration Reform and Control Act of 1986 and further reviews in 2000, updating the Thirteenth Amendment to include the kind of peonage explicitly identified and denounced by Black and others as the "new slavery."[3] For example, a class-action lawsuit in 1989 represented some 20,000 Jamaican cane workers and saw them awarded a total of $51million for loss of earnings over previous seasons. Under appeal, the grievances were separated out and while other employers were vindicated in court, U.S. Sugar decided to settle for $5.7million. Although the Vice-President of U.S. Sugar was able to refer to "a historic labor peace" instituted in 1991, *H-2 Worker* is only a single manifestation or distillation of the problems of global agribusiness and its casualties.[4] In the same year, Florida's sugar industry was

---

[1] *H-2 Worker* won the Grand Jury Prize for best documentary and a second for best cinematography at the Sundance Film Festival in 1990 and was chosen as the U.S. representative film in the Semaine de la Critique section of the Cannes Film Festival. It has been screened in New York and London and was shown on British television's Channel 4 as part of the "True Stories" series in February 1991 which was when I first saw the film.

[2] For example, *New Harvest, Old Shame* (PBS Frontline, 1990) a sequel thirty years later to David Lowe and Edward R. Murrow's classic *Harvest of Shame* (1960), both set in the Florida Everglades, draw attention to the abuses of African American and migrant workers. In 1959 Howard Van Smith of the *Miami News* won a Pulitzer Prize for his articles exposing conditions in a migrant worker camp in Florida which was an important spur to Lowe as producer of *Harvest of Shame*.

[3] See for example, Alec Wilkinson, *Big Sugar: Seasons in the Cane Fields of Florida* (New York: Knopf, 1989).

[4] A history of the prosecution is provided in "Cane Cutters Vs. Sugar Growers: A 13-Year Drama," *Palm Beach* Post, 19 May 2002; Robert H. Buker, Senior Vice-President of US Sugar in *US News and World Report* 19 July 1993 in response to that paper's description of

blamed by environmentalists for destroying wetlands in the Glades; more legal costs ensued.[5]

The plight of migrant workers in the South has been a constant source of controversy from tomato and cucumber pickers in North Carolina to the cane cutters whom Stephanie Black films. Historically Jamaicans, Haitians, and Mexican migrants have taken the place of southern blacks in the plantation economy. It is a shift that returns us to the question one of Erskine Caldwell's white characters asks in *Trouble in July* (1940), "who'd do all the work if the niggers was sent away?" Caldwell continues: "The men walked along in silence, wondering to themselves about a country in which there were no Negroes to do the hard work. No one cared to discuss such a far-fetched possibility."[6] The question the 1940 novel poses was answered in 1943 in Florida. In 1942 U.S. Sugar was indicted for conspiracy to enslave African American workers in the Everglades despite Executive Order 8802 of 1941 which set up a committee on employment practices that would investigate racist discrimination in war industries. A year later the switch to Caribbean workers came into effect through what was then called the British West Indies Program. The Program had been instigated as part of the emergency response to World War II and the need to maintain agricultural production in the U.S. Sugar cane workers in Florida were the first targets of the program administered by the Department of Labor. By 1952 the program bringing workers from Jamaica to the cane fields was renamed the H-2 Worker Program.

Black and her team tell a bleak story, a counter to stories about the economic boom of the Sun Belt. But, how important is location and how insistently should one push southern Florida into a "new slavery" topography? While it would be possible to discuss *H-2 Worker* without recourse to the film's southern setting, this feature underpins my reading. Robert Penn Warren's distinction between the South as setting and as theme is important here. Plantation slavery is the theme that foreshadows the viewers' historical understanding of the Jamaican workers' situations, specifically the relationship between labor and commerce and black bodies. Houston A. Baker Jr., for example, has gone so far as to state that "white southern agricultural profits are 'states' rights' at the expense of the black body" and that "states' rights are as mortifying to the body of the 'colored other' as we enter the twenty-first century as they were to black-South bodily interests two hundred years ago."[7] Although his context is former plantation Tuskegee and the prison Parchman Farm as southern plantation models for the U.S. prison system, sugar is a plantation crop and the mortified "colored other" is the black migrant worker in the new trajectory of the plantation analogy.

"The New Slave Trade" on 21 June. Buker responds: "Our workers do not work for 'pennies a day' but for a minimum wage of about $6 an hour; most earn much more."

[5] Rosalind Resnick, "Nothing Sweet About Sugar," *Florida Trend* magazine, 1 March 1991.

[6] Erskine Caldwell, *Trouble in July* (Athens: University of Georgia Press, 1999), 191. See also Douglas Turner Ward's play *Day of Absence* (1965) in which blacks disappear from a southern town leaving the whites unable to conceive of how it will run without them.

[7] Houston. A. Baker, *Turning South Again: Re-Thinking Modernism/Re-Reading Booker T.* (Durham: Duke University Press, 2001), 26.

The plantation characteristics of Caribbean culture extended into the Deep South and the Caribbean has been variously described as "Plantation America" and "a basin of colonialism."[8] The plantation as economic fact and rhetorical device has proliferated in cultural production about the South. The sentimentalized image of the plantation had certainly receded by the time Stephanie Black began researching her film and revisionist examples have multiplied: plantations have become museums, hotels, and condominiums, and they contribute to a reworking of anti-southern imagery away from a "benighted" South to a "Superior South" to borrow Fred Hobson's (ironic) turn of phrase for "a land of oil, aerospace, agribusiness, real estate, and leisure," the last four industries keenly associated with Florida.[9] I have written elsewhere much more positively, of the plantation household revised as a result of new immigrant ventures. In Robert Olen Butler's story "Snow," for example, the plantation's association with slavery is transformed by Chinese and Vietnamese enterprise. A Vietnamese refugee in Louisiana works in a Chinese restaurant—the "Plantation Hunan"—and recognizes that "this plantation house must feel like a refugee. It is full of foreign smells, ginger and Chinese pepper and fried shells for wonton, and there's a motel on one side and a gas station on the other, not like the life the house once knew, though there are very large oak trees surrounding it, trees that must have been here when this was still a plantation."[10] A bucolic sense of place is reanimated as the plantation economy is transformed. However, the plantation arrangements in *H-2 Worker* are recursive insofar as they reiterate the Caribbean and antebellum southern models and because the origin of the workers' experience can be found further back in the historical relationship between sugar and slavery that Richard B. Sheridan charts from 1623 in the British West Indies.[11]

In the 1980s, the manner of harvesting cane had not changed significantly since slavery, but Stephanie Black's 1990 film also captures the precise moment in Florida's agricultural history before the cane cutters were largely supplanted by mechanical harvesters due, in part at least, to the bad publicity that followed films such as Black's.[12] Black contextualizes a plantation mentality as a driving force behind what she discovers. She edits together scenes of Jamaican cane workers in the fields with archival footage from the early 1940s in which the sugar cane harvest is described as the "hereditary urge to go back to the plantation" for southern blacks who supposedly beg time from their city employers every harvest to come back to

---

[8] H. Hoetink, *Caribbean Race Relations: A Study of Two Variants* trans. Eva M. Hooykaas (Oxford: Oxford University Press, 1967), 2; Amon Saba Saakana, *The Colonial Legacy in Caribbean Literature* (London: Karnak House, 1987), 102. See also Rex Nettleford, *Caribbean Cultural Identity* (Los Angeles: Center for Afro-American Studies and UCLA Latin American Center, 1978).

[9] Fred Hobson, "The Savage South," in Patrick Gerster and Nicolas Cords, eds., *Myth and Southern History Vol 2: The New South* (Urbana: University of Illinois Press, 1989), 135.

[10] Robert Olen Butler, "Snow" in *A Good Scent from a Strange Mountain* (London: Minerva, 1993), 126. See Nahem Yousaf and Sharon Monteith, "Making an Impression: New Immigrant Fiction in the Contemporary South," *Modern Languages Forum* 40: 2 (2004): 215.

[11] Richard B. Sheridan, *Sugar and Slavery* (Barbados: Caribbean Universities Press, 1974).

[12] The workers were also captive consumers and after the program ended local businesses had to diversify or go under. See William Yardley, "End of sugar-cane cutters leaves Belle Glade struggling to hold on," *Miami Herald*, 28 September 2003.

the land. In his testimony Samuel Manston, 80 years old when interviewed by Black but a young man when he escaped peonage in 1941, reveals a southern plantation world hidden in the post-war South:

> They wake us about around 2 and 3 o'clock. They had a shack rouser. . . . If you didn't get up when the shack rouser roused you, and went to the dining room he came back with a cane knife and black jack, knocking you out the bed—and if you ran out the door, there was one standing there with a rifle making you get back in line. I found that it was almost the same as a prison but there wasn't nothing I could do but go along with the crew because we were all in the same boat. You couldn't run—there was no way to run, right then.

In threading his testimony in and out of the story of the Jamaican cane workers, Black establishes a powerful relationship between supposedly southern forms of peonage and those sanctioned to take place in the South by the U.S. and Jamaican governments. Testimony—and Black allows voices from all sides of the debate—contributes significantly to the film. Black builds on what Bill Nichols in his study of documentary film calls the "politics of phenomenology."[13] The workers' experiences and what is viscerally engaging for audiences about those experiences is prioritized. This form of empirical realism allows the workers the space to analyze and resist hegemonic narratives created by industries or governments.[14]

The Jamaicans live between two places: the barracks that serves as home and the cane fields. Transported by bus, they are contained within the work routine proscribed by the sugar plantation. They exist in the interstices of southern life; they and the camps they live in are largely invisible and difficult to penetrate. As outsiders, Black and her crew could only enter secretly, and this is made very evident to the viewer.[15] In one scene Black's voice is heard as a police officer takes her name and warns her that should she leave cameras and other equipment in the car, she may return to find them gone. Exactly who it is she should fear is left ambiguous. In another scene, a Jamaican woman selling goods inside the camps explains that she dresses as a man to sneak in because the workers are not allowed to buy away from the company store or from stores specifically opened for them during the sugar season. Black and her team film in the store—a commissary—but are soon told to turn off their cameras. Rules and regulations abound. For example, the men are expressly forbidden from traveling more than thirty miles from the camp or from leaving camp for more than twenty-four hours. There is scant evidence in Black's film, however, that any of them has the leisure or outside connections to take

---

[13] Bill Nichols, *Representing Reality: Issues and Concepts in Documentary* (Bloomington: Indiana University Press, 1991), 224.

[14] This point is made in another context by Anne Shea in "'Don't let them make you feel you did a crime': Immigration Law, Labor Rights and Farmworker Testimony" *Melus*, 22 March 2003.

[15] In interview Black has said, "Every few days we'd rent a new car so the police wouldn't recognize us. I was never arrested but a policeman told me, "You seem like a nice girl but U.S. Sugar owns this town and we got orders to arrest you if we see you one more time," Nancee Oku Bright, "Sweet and Sour," *Guardian*, 6 February 1991.

advantage of either outlet in any case. *H-2 Worker* is also self-conscious in its exploration of the difficulties a documentary filmmaker faces when representing others and the extent to which the camera can enter and reveal the "inside story" of the sugar cage. The relationship between filmmaker and subject is a problematic one that Stephanie Black says interests her little in the ethnographic sense. Nevertheless, the dilemma of involvement is apparent in almost every scene in the camp. Black and her team battled to film even the most transparently obvious scenes: men cutting cane in the fields.

In a new film on a similar topic, *The Guest Worker* (2005), focusing on migrant farm workers in North Carolina, the directors felt the need to create a single protagonist with whom the viewer might empathize—or at the very least sympathize—a named individual, the charismatic veteran picker 66-year-old Calenadario Gonzalez. Co-producer and director Charles Thompson has said in interview:

> Don Cande is an amazingly strong and kind person we fell in love with as we worked with him over a season. We hope the film does him some good and that people learn not only about a program through him, but about a wonderful human being.[16]

Talking with Thompson at the University of North Carolina,[17] I was struck by the filmmakers' beliefs in what are opposite approaches. Black follows a group of men who are cited by their first names only in the end credits and never named on screen. She eschews the need to privilege an exceptional individual who will act as a conduit for the audience and the primary source of empathy.[18]

Instead, Black emphasizes her subjects' "everyman" status. The film makes an entire group of men locked into hard labor both visible and audible: their voices dominate as they tell their own stories, giving the lie to their bosses' protests that "all is fine" in a sugar town surrounded by barbed wire. Such sweet lies are placed in stark contrast to what the camera reveals. In speaking for themselves, cane workers sometimes answer questions posed off camera. At other times, they seem to confide on their own terms. One migrant worker grins sardonically, "This is America, you know" and another confides a staple survival strategy as old as slavery itself: "If you are too clever, they don't want you. You have to play dumb—play fool to catch wise." Still another adds emotionally that "It takes more than guts and heart to do what we are doing." Black shows how the men live, in the most basic of dormitories, the most functional of spaces, and how they philosophize about their conditions. Rather than elevating a single articulate protagonist and translating the wider problems of the sugar industry down through his personal experience, Black reveals

---

[16] For details about the film, see www.theguestworker.com and filmworks@docsouth.com

[17] At the conference Navigating the Globalization of the American South, March 2005.

[18] Similarly, interviewed for the *New Yorker*, Laura Germino of the Coalition of Immokalee Workers refuses to answer in detail on her agency's successful prosecutions for "slaveholding": "Don't make me be the story. The workers are the heroes!" See John Bowe, "Nobodies: Does Slavery Exist in America?" *New Yorker*, 21 and 28 April 2003, 122.

an otherwise hidden community of laborers to be articulate analysts of the cage in which they are trapped.

The scenes Black and her crew decided to include after months of shooting, function cumulatively to show the Jamaican agricultural workers are contract slaves. They endure the kind of forced labor generally defined in the contemporary context as the worker having been lured by the promise of work that will pay fairly and squarely, only to discover that a form of debt bondage is enacted, whereby the worker's continued toil is his only collateral against the financial deductions—often spurious and always unfair—that his employers make. In the 1980s, H-2 migrant workers were charged for their visa and flight to Florida, but shelter, meals, and transportation to and from the fields were the responsibility of employers. However, the wage slips the men produce for the camera show deductions are made each month so that one man is deducted $80 for board and $21 for transport and, because he has been injured, he loses two weeks pay. He finishes the month owing his employer $80. The workers' diet is professedly that which the workers want to eat with cooks from "the islands" in charge of the kitchens but the men Black interviews hate the rice slop and try to cater for themselves in limited space. Whether or not they eat in the canteen, money is deducted for food. The cycle of debt is reminiscent of the experience of southern sharecroppers tied to landlords and the company store.

The situation is overseen by a southern white camp superintendent, who works for the corporation and is paid handsomely for the season, and by Jamaican camp supervisors and timekeepers in the fields. Historically, some of the most hated men on the slave plantation were the slave drivers and in one scene a Jamaican timekeeper explains the systemic poverty that he is complicit in maintaining:

> Each morning we get a piece of paper from the company which shows us how many feet of cane that worker is supposed to cut for the day or the hour. . . . Sometimes they'll say give the man the hours he's worked. Another time they'll come and say cut back on the hours. If a man works 8 hours out in the field and only makes $16 we have to give the man four to four and a half hours, no more, because the company doesn't want to give the men their money to make $41 and a few cents. It's very painful to know that a man is out there all day working and only makes $16 or $18 or $21 and when his day is completed and he goes to his place of rest, he only goes with 3 hours on his ticket. That's cruel, that's part of a bad commitment.

In their modern incarnation a temporarily transplanted black workforce is no longer required to reproduce itself. It is also prevented from establishing a socio-geographical place or identity in the South. Instead, a seemingly never-ending flow of labor is made available to sugar producers only for the period required and the laborers are contained within the "sugar cage" of my title.

This worker-family is gendered male: men young and old, as long as they are fit, are expected to live in uncomfortably close proximity, separated from their families left behind in Jamaica. The migrant's family's suffering is temporary and cannot be compared to the ripping apart of slave families, yet the "structures of feeling" created in the documentary, to borrow Raymond Williams' phrasing, recall that era. The Jamaicans' voices exist only at the "very edge of semantic availability"[19] telling an experience that has been largely ignored because their subaltern status in the capitalist conundrum that is the transnational exportation of labor renders them silent. Stephanie Black emphasizes connections with African American labor history, but she also employs typically Caribbean tropes such as the letter home, a sub-genre in Caribbean poetry. The only time that voice-over is used is when Jamaican voices read the letters that go back and forth between individual workers and their families. These reveal that the wives either believe that the situation is better in America, or they try to close their eyes to the suffering of the men, and that husbands hide their reality, concealing it behind an American rather than a southern myth—the American Dream—or at least the myth of progress. Many of the men are slowly building houses back in Jamaica and, as well as ensuring their families' survival at home, part of what they earn will buy building materials. The implication is that to struggle economically when one is working so hard, even as an H-2 Worker with no citizenship rights, is to fail in America although the struggle may still ensure a modicum of success back home.

The film sets up a series of binary oppositions: between sugar growers and cane cutters; field time keepers and the men; camp supervisors and the men; the U.S. and Jamaica; and the expansive and beautiful Florida landscape and the cramped and brutal conditions in which the migrants exist. Black also uses parallel montage to juxtapose different "talking heads," representative figures placed in contention in racial terms, as well as through the clear distinction between capital and labor. The sugar growers and the members of the sugar lobby are white and the labor is black. Only rarely does this dynamic become more complex through white Congressmen lobbying for the end of the program or when the Jamaican H-2 liaison officer, working out of Washington, spouts homilies, believing the men to be "enlightened" and the system to be unfortunate but fair. And, of course, there is the director herself. Twice the film includes a partial shot of Stephanie Black's hands as she is questioned by the police and the camp supervisor. Her whiteness is made visible, it would seem, as a partial explanation as to why she has been stopped from entering the all-black camp. Generally, Stephanie Black and her editor John Mullen alternate between two worlds to contrast them economically across the color line in the way that, as film theorists have often argued, cross-cutting as narrative form can serve as an ideological analogue of American class and race relations. The cinematic technique of cross-cutting operates to align the workers with the same moral and ethical righteousness that characterized civil rights struggles in the 1950s and 1960s South. The sense of injustice is strong and the men are vocal, despite fear of repercussions.

The men exhibit a dignified resignation: hidden on the edge of Lake Okeechobee, the men's alienation from wider society and their cognizance of the economic default position that is their own nation's participation in the H-2 scheme does not provide a natural platform for activism. One man simply states that "What I was looking for; it never work out that way," and another confides that God is the only force that keeps him going. Most telling is the fourteen-year veteran of migrant agricultural work who says he is giving up. Three hundred and fifty cutters do

---

[19] Raymond Williams, "Structures of Feeling" in *Marxism and Literature* (Oxford: Oxford University Press, 1977), 128-135.

finally stop work because the price for cutting a row of cane has dropped so low that they refuse to continue until the minimum wage specified in their contracts is honored. The viewer has come to understand prior to the onset of the strike that the men had expected to be paid hourly as specified by the program but that they are paid a piece rate. They have withstood this injustice but will withstand it no more. In withholding their labor, the men exhibit the first sign of agency. However, Black conveys that the real source of their immediate poverty lies in their very disposability. In a scene reminiscent of news footage of civil rights struggles of the 1960s, police officers with guns and dogs force the men from the barracks onto the buses that will take them back to the airport. The striking workers are sent home without their belongings and are replaced within a week.[20]

There are, of course, a significant number of watchdogs and regulatory bodies that have endeavored to prevent the suppression of workers' resistance in the state that the U.S. Justice Department has called "ground zero for modern slavery."[21] The Coalition of Imokalee Workers, the Migrant Farmworker Justice Project in Florida, and the Florida Department of Business and Professional Regulation each attempted to monitor or prosecute the program in the 1990s, and Congressman Frank Peterman of St. Petersburg tried to pass a new antislavery bill in 2003, the same year that the *Palm Beach Post* embarked on a nine-month investigation into the lives of migrant workers. The new antislavery movement has been growing and southern scholars and agencies are often found at the forefront.[22] However, far fewer agencies were in place when Stephanie Black filmed this story. The existence of Jamaicans in the plantation economy of the mid to late 1980s exemplifies the long term effects that the then Prime Minister Michael Manley outlines in his contribution to *H-2 Worker*. Manley is measured in his analysis of the power of the International Monetary Fund, Third World Debt, and the ongoing unequal if reciprocal relationship between the U.S. Department of Labor and Jamaican migrant workers. His most telling comment is that the Jamaican has had to become "a migrating person through the generations just to survive." Ironies abound in any transnational model that hides historical, cultural and colonial shifts; such an unequal relationship reduces both nations to economic clichés. This particular brand of home economics can be understood through Peter Hitchcock's idea of the "conscience of space" in which the local intersects with the global at the level of subjection with the Caribbean functioning as a neo-colonial outpost.[23]

---

[20] A further ironic return to civil rights struggles in the South is underlined by recent news reports of Caribbean voter registration drives in South Florida.

[21] John Bowe, "Nobodies: Does Slavery Exist in America?" *New Yorker*, 21 and 28 April 2003, 106-107.

[22] Free the Slaves is the U.S. branch of the London-based Antislavery International founded in 1839 and, I believe, the oldest human rights organization. Free the Slaves was founded by Kevin Bales, a sociologist at Roehampton University in London who grew up in the 1950s South and has returned as a member of the Croft Institute for International Studies at the University of Mississippi.

[23] Peter Hitchcock, *Imaginary States: Studies in Cultural Transnationalism* (Urbana: University of Illinois Press, 2003), 31-32.

Dalton Yancey, apologist for the Florida Sugar Cane League, speaks with pride in Black's 1990 film of the H-2 worker program as a "model" of its kind. His speech could be said to predict its return:

> It's good for the worker and it's good for the industry. It's a program that works. In fact, the program that exists in our industry was a model program used to expand the foreign worker program under the last immigration bill so that other workers could participate in similar programs where they have protection, rights and other benefits that they don't have as illegal immigrants.

In his 2004 State of the Union Address George W. Bush provided something of an echo:

> I propose a new temporary worker program to match willing foreign workers with willing employers when no Americans can be found to fill the job. This reform will be good for our economy because employers will find needed workers in an honest and orderly system. A temporary worker program will help protect our homeland, allowing Border Patrol and law enforcement to focus on true threats to our national security.
>
> I oppose amnesty, because it would encourage further illegal immigration, and unfairly reward those who break our laws. My temporary worker program will preserve the citizenship path for those who respect the law, while bringing millions of hardworking men and women out from the shadows of American life.[24]

The Jamaican workers in Stephanie Black's film are imperial shadows. They may be theorized as "the flotsam and jetsam of latterday imperialism"[25] or romanticized as bluefoot travellers, peripheral figures travelling through the postcolonial night. But the film shows the material effects that the global plantation economy has had on their lives. *H-2 Worker* is not an economic analysis; it is a political film with a hard polemical edge. Nevertheless, the images it privileges provide an insightful illustration of debt and dependency.

Sugar is a spurious staple of little nutritional value in itself; rather it is grown to satisfy Western markets whose addiction to its sweetness has outlasted generations of cane cutters. At the end of the film Black shows the 1988 festival that followed that year's harvest, an all-white sugar fiesta at which locals celebrate the biggest profit so far made: $1.5 billion for 1.48 million tons cut by 45,000 people employed in the Florida Glades. It is a reminder that rather than trading with Jamaica for sugar, the U.S. sugar lobby ensured that the sugar industry would remain heavily subsidized. In the final sequence, parallel montage depicts a black and white labor market divided by segregation: the Glades' harvest festival is attended only by white Floridians. As they eat sugar sweets and candy-floss and play games, the Archies'

---

[24] http://www.whitehouse.gov/news/releases/2004/01/20040102-7.html.
[25] A. Sivanandan, *Communities of Resistance: Writings on Black Struggles for Socialism* (London: Verso, 1990), 189.

popular 1969 hit "Sugar Sugar" plays. The scene is suddenly cut to be juxtaposed with tired black migrants on the airplane bound for Jamaica. As the camera pans around their tired faces, the opening chords of Bob Marley's "Redemption Song" and the lyrics that follow contribute an ironic coda to what is already a cutting critique.

JUNKYARD TALES:
POVERTY AND THE SOUTHERN LANDSCAPE IN JANISSE RAY'S
ECOLOGY OF A CRACKER CHILDHOOD

Sarah Robertson

Harry Crews, in his memoir *A Childhood: The Biography of a Place*, claims that he always knew that he would "someday have to write" about his childhood in the poverty stricken areas of Bacon County, Georgia. He acknowledges that the writing process "would have to be done naked, without the disguising distance of the third person pronoun. Only the use of *I*, lovely and terrifying word, would get me to the place where I needed to go." For Crews, the "convenient and comfortable metaphors of fiction" could not adequately evoke the story he had to tell, a story of people who "Whether on shares or on standing rent ... were still tenant farmers"[1] and people for whom "survival was a day-to-day crisis."[2] In the years since the publication of Crews' text in 1978, numerous autobiographies dealing with white experiences of poverty in the South have emerged. From Dorothy Allison through to Rick Bragg and Barbara Robinette Moss, contemporary southern writing returns repeatedly to autobiographical forms that reveal a place that exists "a million miles from the Mississippi Delta and the Black Belt and the jasmine-scented verandas of what most people . . . know as the Old South."[3]

Janisse Ray's *Ecology of a Cracker Childhood*, which merges autobiography with ecocriticism, joins the ever expanding list of poor white autobiographies emerging out of the region.[4] Her ecological concerns place her text within a tradition of southern autobiography that "explores place to discover family, family to find place, and both to ground a sense of self."[5] However, although Ray seeks to re-attach herself to a way of life that she had "struggled bitterly" to forget, a tension emerges within her narrative between her ecological standpoint and her family memories (31). Ray regards the land as a site in which racial and class distinctions can be erased, proposing in the Afterword that the South, "black and white, urbanite and farmer, workers all" can unite together "in keeping Dixie" (272). Her utopian vision stands in contrast to her attempts throughout the text to place her "people" in history, to make visible the people like her father whose creativity and "genius" would otherwise remain hidden under the mantle of poverty. Placing her father in history necessarily involves an acknowledgment of socio-economic factors, an acknowledgement that undermines Ray's ultimately de-historicized vision of nature.

---

[1] Harry Crews, *A Childhood: The Biography of Place,* 2nd ed. (Athens and London: University of Georgia Press, 1995), 25.

[2] Ibid., 11.

[3] Rick Bragg, *Redbirds: Memories from the South* (London: Harvill Press, 1998), 4. This memoir was published under the title *All Over but the Shoutin'* in the United States in 1997.

[4] Janisse Ray, *Ecology of a Cracker Childhood* (Minneapolis: Milkweed Editions, 1999). Subsequent quotations will be identified parenthetically in the text.

[5] J. Bill Berry, ed., *Home Ground: Southern Autobiography* (Columbia: University of Missouri Press, 1991), 7.

The text remains torn, then, between the need to promote ecological awareness and the desire to raise her family, particularly her father, above the definition of "otherness". Ray's account of her father's junkyard, a place that "was like sticking your head into a wide-angle trash can" (21), certainly falls into the realm of what Kathleen Stewart defines as "those 'trashy' pockets of life across the American cultural landscape" where "collections of used-up things [are] still in use." For Stewart, these "are the kinds of places where the matter has already been settled that this is a place apart—an 'Other America.'"[6] Throughout *Ecology of a Cracker Childhood* Ray draws upon her father's labor in an effort to overcome "otherness."

Ray consistently provides detailed descriptions of her father, Franklin, and his junkyard business. Significantly though, she does not dedicate any one of the fifteen autobiographical sections to her father, unlike, for example, those sections entitled "Mama" or "Beulahland." Arguably, Franklin is uncontainable in the sense that his presence can be detected in each of the chapters. His uncontainability reflects his junkyard which over the years spreads beyond the confines of a "hogwire fence" so that Ray's "Mama gave up trying to keep the junk from around the house and instead mowed around the heaps" (32). In effect, Ray presents her father as an aberration, aberrant not simply in terms of the mental illness that plagued his life but also as an economic aberration.

On the surface, Franklin's move into the junk business seems indebted to the wider capitalist structure. Ray claims that the junkyard began in 1955 as "a chrome glint in my father's eye" (71). The founding of the family business emerges as a result of the economic boom of the post-war years. Changes in labor practices coupled with radical increases in consumption naturally resulted in the generation of waste, or junk. Ray, aware of the economic climate at the time, cites *Auto Facts and Figures*, which stated that in 1955 "Over five million motor vehicles were produced in U.S. plants that year" and that a large percentage of those vehicles "were sold as replacements for vehicles scrapped" (71). Eager to cash in on the economic trend Franklin and his father set up their junkyard, a yard that Franklin, unable to work with others, would eventually own outright. While the Ray family's sustenance depends upon sales from the junk yard, and therefore on a process of exchange that keeps the family within the confines of a capitalist order, the detailed descriptions of her father's skills circumvent capitalist labor practices.

As David Harvey suggests, "capitalism is precisely about the production of a new kind of laboring body," yet Franklin's designs and production methods connect him to a more primitive labor practice.[7] Indeed, one of the major discoveries that Ray makes after leaving the region for a university education is that her father's occupation as a "junk dealer" can be defined in terms of bricolage. As a child, she and her siblings were "ashamed of the junkyard" and she writes that "when we filled out his occupation in forms from school we wrote 'salesman'" (29). Her education, however, provides her with the means to re-conceptualize her father's trade. With hindsight she looks back to the junkyard, stating:

---

[6] Kathleen Stewart, *A Space on the Side of the Road: Cultural Poetics in an "Other" America* (Princeton: Princeton University Press, 1996), 41.

[7] David Harvey, *Spaces of Hope* (Edinburgh: Edinburgh University Press, 2000), 104.

> I know now that my father's occupation has an actual title; he is a *bricoleur*, a term given by French anthropologist Claude Levi-Strauss to folk recyclers, people of creativity, vision, and skill who use castaways for purposes other than those originally intended, sometimes for art. (89)

Throughout the narrative Ray provides the reader with various accounts of her father's bricolage skills. Indeed, she writes:

> Daddy collected hills of aluminum cans out of dumpsters and off roadsides because he intended to roof the house with aluminum shingles one day and went so far as to invent a machine that would slice off the top and bottom and split them down the center to make a curling square. (22-23)

Long before recycling came to prominence Ray's father is involved in a sustainable process, one that accentuates his artistic, or imaginative, capabilities. She claims that "he saw value in things most of us wouldn't glance twice at" (74). Ray's account of her father's skills serves both to challenge and to undermine the wastefulness of privileged classes.

Franklin takes that which has been rendered meaningless or devoid of value by mainstream culture and through a hybridization process, through using "Chevrolet push rods" to make "firing pins" for guns, or using a "Buick piston in a John Deere tractor" he creates new sites of meaning (91). As Judy Attfield claims, "There is life beyond the design phase when the object moves through ... different 'regimes of value' in which objects are enlivened by various types of human transactions in the course of their existence."[8] That enlivening process allows Ray's father to experience a sense of control over his own labor even though the limited objects at hand in the junkyard restrict his creative potential. Levi-Strauss recognizes that the bricoleur's sense of control emerges from the process of seeking a solution, a process that places him "in possession of other possible forms of the same work; and in a confused way, he feels himself to be the creator himself because the latter abandoned them in excluding them from his creation."[9] In terms of Ray's father, his control comes from the fact that he can take an object with one particular use and subvert that use through his own designs, a procedure that serves to hide the original form. As Levi-Strauss writes: "in the continual reconstruction from the same materials, it is always earlier ends which are called upon to play the part of means: the signified changes into the signifying and vice versa."[10] That movement from signifying to signified creates a space in the dominant order; it is a process of reanimation that provides Franklin with an opportunity to create new sites of meaning.

Franklin's position as a bricoleur is further highlighted by his emphasis on use- rather than exchange-value. As Ray disconcertingly shifts from past recollections to imagining her father in the present, she sees him "hunt[ing] the bolts, cotter keys,

---

[8] Judy Attfield, *Wild Things: The Material Culture of Everyday Life* (Oxford: Berg, 2000), 34.
[9] Claude Levi-Strauss, *The Savage Mind* (Chicago: University of Chicago Press, 1966), 24.
[10] Ibid., 21.

wires, shafts, and belts that hold together metal pieces, engineering usefulness" (75). Her vision highlights her earlier assertion that Franklin "is a mechanic in the world's truest sense" because he loves machines "less for their implementation than for their fabrication" (75). Indeed, the junk and the objects he creates from it do not result in huge profits for the Ray family. Ray recalls that "Some weeks nothing sold on the junkyard, and we skipped going to town" (26). Not only does her father make little profit from the junkyard, but Ray's description of his ability to find new materials echoes an older bartering system rather than one dependent upon exchange-value. She writes:

> He was a great salesman, my father, but he was the greatest buyer in all the world. He could get anything he wanted for next to nothing. Psychology was the trick. Buying something, you had to be patient, never overeager to own a piece of merchandise. (72)

Although her account seems to highlight an arguably capitalist skill, she goes on to imagine a conversation between her father and a local man in which Franklin completes the transaction by convincing the man that he has benefited most from the deal. Ray informs the reader that her father "never rubbed a bad deal in someone's face. . . . He let the sellers think they'd bargained and won" (72-73). Ray imagines the transaction in a way that humanizes the exchange.

In effect, throughout the text Ray works to reveal her father as a three dimensional figure, to unveil the qualities that would otherwise remain hidden beneath a redneck stereotype. In presenting her father in such ways, Ray challenges the "aspect-blindness" of the dominant culture. As Malcolm Bull suggests:

> the aspect-blind do not instantly recognize other humans for what they are, but rather see them as objects whose humanity may or may not be decipherable from their appearance and behaviour. Seeing people in this way is . . . akin to seeing them as robots rather than as human beings.[11]

Notions of aspect-blindness become particularly important when discussing poor whites since, in the United States, there exists, "blindness about poverty. The poor are slipping out of the very experience and consciousness of the nation."[12] As Bull suggests, the aspect-blind, who fail to fully recognize the humanity of "others," experience those groups "at a lower level of understanding." For the aspect blind, then, the "other" exists as a "two-dimensional" figure. In the case of poor, southern whites, Ray realizes at a young age that mainstream American society regards her and her family as "slow, dumb redneck hick[s] ... inbred and racist, come from poverty, condemned to poverty" (30). Part of Ray's larger project in *Ecology of a Cracker Childhood* centers around attempts to unveil, and to explore, the hidden dimensions that lie beneath such stereotypes.

---

[11] Malcolm Bull, *Seeing Things Hidden: Apocalypse, Vision and Totality* (London: Verso, 1999), 200.

[12] Michael Harrington, *The Other America: Poverty in the United States* (Baltimore: Penguin Books, 1963), 11.

Indeed, Bull offers a useful account of how one can reveal the veiled aspects of marginalized groups. As he explores post-colonial theories alongside Hegel's master-slave dialectic and Du Bois's notion of double-consciousness, Bull recognizes that if the aspect-blind move towards recognition of the other, then a "dawning of a soul" occurs as the two-dimensional becomes three-dimensional. Such movement necessarily leads to the multiplication of selves as the other takes on new dimensions in the eyes of the aspect-blind and as, potentially, the aspect-blind fragment their own, unified sense of self through the process of seeing themselves in the other. Ray certainly presents the many sides of her father's character as she builds up an image of man who "was an amazing triad of traits" (89). In effect, Ray imbues Franklin with a level of hybridity, or complexity denied to him by those suffering from aspect-blindness (89). Hybridity plays a key role throughout Ray's text, particularly in relation to the junkyard which Ray describes as site of merger.

While the junkyard seems to stand in stark contrast to the natural landscape, Ray often merges the two together. She writes, "In South Georgia everything is flat and wide. Not empty. My people live among the mobile homes, junked cars, pine plantations, clearcuts, and fields. They live among the lost forests" (3). Ray returns repeatedly to the interconnectedness between the land and the people that she highlights in the introduction. This blurring of lines between the man-made and the natural occurs throughout the narrative as we are offered images of a "tin roofed building that smelled both acrid and sweet, a mixture of dry dung, gasoline, hay, and grease" (3-5); of a "good pine, forty feet tall, sturdy and easy to climb if you boosted up from the fender of a '59 Chevy" (12); of blackberries that grow up and around the junk.

The junkyard, as a site of hybridization, works in line with Ray's attempts to rescue those living in poverty in the South from "otherness." What her autobiography does, is to turn stories about an "other," about southern poor whites, into "another" part of an American discourse. Ray works to re-conceptualize that "othered" space, not only through Franklin, but more specifically through her ecological concerns. For Ray, the land itself offers new ways of viewing notions of self. As she asks her southern readers to join together in protecting their land, she attempts to break down the class barriers that separate her people from the rest of southern society. Patrick D. Murphy argues that: "Ecology and ecocriticism indicate that it is time to move towards a relational model of 'anotherness' and the conceptualization of difference in terms of 'I' and 'another,' 'one' and 'another,' and 'I-as-another.'"[13] The discourse of self and another renders "otherness" (or strangeness) redundant, but still allows for the possibility of cultural diversity in the form of another (not the same, yet still recognizable and understandable).

In fact, it is the very idea of cultural diversity that provides the bedrock for ecology. Murphy goes on:

Human diversity can be maintained only by means of cultural conservation being practiced by the marginalized and subordinated groups who defend and

---

[13] Patrick D. Murphy, "Anotherness and inhabitation in recent multicultural American literature," in Richard Kerrridge and Neil Sammells, eds., *Writing the Environment: Ecocriticism and Literature* (London: Zed Books Ltd, 1998), 40.

recover their heritages in order to generate their futures, and thereby resist
being labelled as Other.[14]

Although ecology works to break down the divisions between self and other,
ecological discourse must, as Murphy suggests, nevertheless maintain "human
diversity." Ray's rallying cry in the Afterword to the text, entitled "Promised Land,"
appears to forgo any sense of diversity as she merges all southerners into one,
homogenous unit:

> We Southerners are a people fighting again for our country, defending the last
> remaining stands of real forest. Although we love to frolic, the time has come
> to fight. We must fight. In new rebellion we stand together, black and white,
> urbanite and farmer, workers all, in keeping Dixie. We are a patient people
> who for generations have not been ousted from this land, and we are willing to
> fight for the birthright of our children's children and their children's children,
> to be of place, in all ways, for all time. (272)

Her call for the South to unite, is, of course, problematic. The idea that nature can
erode the racial and class distinctions that have for so long permeated southern
society may lead the reader to dismiss her text as a utopian vision with no historical
or socio-economic grounding. Indeed, in blurring the lines between "urbanite and
farmer," Ray de-historicizes labor, a process that seems to counter her simultaneous
attempts to extol her father's labor.

However, the new self that Ray envisions, one devoid of historical markers,
seems at odds with her own acknowledgment that nature bears the marks of the past.
In reference to the carved initials of her grandfather, found in local woods before the
"pulpwooders" destroyed it, Ray writes:

> *CJ RAY, 1928*, it says. Scars bear testimony to occupation, to event, but not to
> circumstances; to phenomena but not conditions. They are evidence only, not
> details. In which direction was he walking? Were the soles of his boots intact?
> Was the knife fresh-sharpened? What did he witness? I want to know more
> than the fact that my grandfather was in the Altamaha floodplain in 1928. (264)

Her aim, then, is not to eradicate historical markers, rather to imbue them with
greater social significance. Her desire to know more about her family appears, at
times, to stand in contrast to her desire to know more about the landscape. While she
notes the inextricable relationship between poor whites and the environment, her
ecological stance seemingly erodes the historicity of that very land. In "Promised
Land" she repeatedly refers to "our" land, the land that belongs to all southerners.
However, that all inclusive, possessive pronoun overlooks the racial and class
conflicts embedded within that soil.

The contradiction at the centre of Ray's text may result from her dual stance as
one who left the region but also as one who continues to return to that place. Of

---

[14] Ibid., 44.

importance here is Ray's decision to write from an autobiographical rather than a fictional stance. As Laura Marcus suggests:

> autobiography is . . . a major source of concern because of its very instability in terms of the postulated opposites between self and world, literature and history, fact and fiction, subject and object. In an intellectual context in which these are seen as irreconcilably distinct, autobiography will appear either as a dangerous double agent, moving between these oppositions, or as a magical instrument of reconciliation.[15]

Ray's text may be read as a double agent in the sense that she oscillates throughout the text between fact and fiction, between actual memories and imagined scenes. Effectively though, Ray herself acts as a double agent since she is both of the world that she describes, but at the same time, she has moved beyond that world. Her education and experiences outside of the South necessarily impact upon how she remembers the region. In a sense, Ray suffers from a plural identity, an identity as Bull suggests, that "embod[ies] contradictions."[16]

Her dual perspective becomes most pronounced in the section she entitles "Shame." Ray opens the section with Quentin Compson's claim in *Absalom, Absalom!* that: "*I don't hate it. . . . I don't hate it. . . . I don't hate it he thought, panting in the cold air, the iron New England dark; I don't. I don't! I don't hate it! I don't hate it!*" Ray's epigraph stands in contrast with the opening line of the chapter: "A junkyard wasn't a bad place to grow up" (17). While Ray opens the chapter with a marker of her literary education, an education that resulted in her movement away from place, throughout the section itself she works to convince the reader, and arguably herself, that the junkyard was "a playground of endless possibility" (17). However, just as Quentin Compson's frantic denials only serve to undermine his own assertion that he does *not* hate the South, so too do Ray's attempts to glorify poverty in "Shame" merely enhance the difficulties she encounters as she recollects the past.

In the opening pages of the section Ray celebrates the junkyard as site that expanded her own and her siblings' imaginations. She goes on to describe the boxes of food that the family would buy on special deal from the local store, tinned food without labels, claiming that "Surprise is addicting, I think, and I can't tell you how fun it was to come home and unpack boxes of miscellany, a trunkful, not knowing what you might find" (25). In effect, Ray renders that which may be deemed dreadful, not knowing if they are opening "string beans" or "shoe polish" for dinner when "Mama was willing to serve whatever she encountered," into a humorous story from childhood.

By the close of the chapter, however, Ray acknowledges her "shame," her realization as a child that she "was a Southerner, a slow dumb, redneck hick" (30). Part of that shame stems from her developing knowledge. Indeed, Ray acknowledges, in a later section, that by the time she read *Walden* when she was

---

[15] Laura Marcus, "The face of autobiography," in Julia Swindells ed., *The Uses of Autobiography* (London: Taylor and Francis, 1995), 14.

[16] Bull, *Seeing Things Hidden*, 291.

eighteen, she "wanted none of it" (202), none of the "knickknacks and other pretty
things" that her mother collects as a source of distraction from the world around her
(201). Although Thoreau provides Ray with a new vocabulary with which to read
the natural world, such a reading serves to distance her from her family roots. That
sense of distance, or of separation, shapes the entire text as Ray negotiates between
the past and the present, or between being "other" and becoming "another."

Indeed, as she recollects how she felt separated from the mainstream by both
her family's poverty and her father's mental illness and religious beliefs, Ray
acknowledges that "sometimes I felt discontent, not an overwhelming unhappiness,
but an absence of lightness. . . . I would feel as if something dreadful had happened,
and I carried the burden and grief of it" (115). Thinking back Ray realizes that she
felt burdened not simply by the poverty that shaped her family's existence but also
by her father's "mania" (93) that lasted "from 1968 to 1971" (131). Ray sheds that
"burden" through her attachment to nature, an attachment that she defines as her
salvation. In the section entitled "How the Heart Opens" she writes that "one
essential event or presence can save a child" (127). Ray traces her salvation to the
moment that she discovered a pitcher plant in the junkyard.

She attributes that discovery to "the opening of [her] heart" (127). In the plant
she claims that she "was looking for a *manera de ser*, a way of being—no, not for a
way of being but of being able to be" (128). She wanted to find a self that was
defined neither by the "ivory scars" that she gained from playing amongst "piles of
scrap iron and glittering landmines of broken glass" (127) nor by the fear of "losing
[her] father, of him losing himself" (131). She counters that fear through learning: "I
was six, seven, eight, nine during those years, excelling at school, devouring my
lessons, reading as many books in two weeks as the public librarian would let me
bring home" (131). Her literary "devouring" mirrors the pitcher plant that "lures
insects through its lips with a sweet-smelling nectar. The insects can descend but
never climb out again" (128). Just as the insects can never retreat out of the plant,
the words and images that Ray devours remain within her consciousness. Indeed, by
the time she goes to university she has her "heart set on literature. Faulkner and
Styron and Warren, I felt, had saved me; I wanted a life constructed of books" (255).
Her equation of survival with literature leads to a central paradox in the text.

Just like the pitcher plant that adapts "in order to survive" in different soils,
Ray sees her own survival in the same way: "Evolve. Adapt. Survive" (215). The
process of evolution, or adaptation causes Ray some anxiety since as she retreats
from her father's illness through books and nature Ray finds herself retreating from
his wider existence. Throughout the text she celebrates his labor, yet in this section
she acknowledges that his obsession with engineering meant that he "had neither the
time nor the inclination to take us hiking or camping or fishing" (128). For Franklin,
"Nature wasn't ill regarded, it was superfluous. Nature got in the way" (128). Her
education, and her fascination with ecology, begin to sever her ties to her father and
to the junkyard. "How the Heart Opens" partially accounts for Ray's divided sense
of self, for her being torn between the self that grew up surrounded by "ten acres of
failed machines" and the self that seeks nature as a means of solace (23). She exists
in what Raymond Williams terms a "border country," a place "between custom and
education, between work and ideas, between love of place and an experience of

change."[17] Williams discusses the problems for those, like Ray, who "have gone to university from ordinary families" claiming that they "have to discover, through a life, what that experience means."[18] In effect, Ray's autobiographical writings are one route through which she can attempt to unravel that "experience."

Indeed, *Ecology of Cracker Childhood* pivots between Ray's two selves, resulting in her hybridization of the junkyard and of her father's labor. Ray's final call, then, for a united South, forgoes the diversity that shapes the text itself. In effect, Ray's own words undermine her belief that southern categorizations between black and white or between affluence and poverty can be easily overcome. Recalling how she first heard the word environmentalism during her first year at college, Ray claims that "what I learned . . . was the direction my life would go. I also learned that I would never lose the tug of the past on my life" (263). *Ecology of a Cracker Childhood* manifests that "tug," epitomizing Ray's need to find a "*manera de ser*" not in a plant, but in those "ivory scars" that reveal a childhood shaped by poverty.

---

[17] Raymond Williams, *The Country and the City* (St. Albans: Paladin, 1975), 239.
[18] Ibid., 241.

THE SOUTHERN FAMILY FARM AS ENDANGERED SPECIES: POSSIBILITIES FOR SURVIVAL IN BARBARA KINGSOLVER'S *PRODIGAL SUMMER*

Suzanne W. Jones

> In your father's day all the farmers around here were doing fine. Now they have to work night shifts at the Kmart to keep up their mortgages. Why is that? They work just as hard as their parents did, and they're on the same land, so what's wrong?
>
> Barbara Kingsolver, Prodigal Summer

At the same time that some southern studies scholars are positioning the U.S. South in a larger cultural, historic, and economic region that encompasses the Caribbean and Latin America, some southern environmentalist writers, such as long-time essayist and novelist Wendell Berry and activist, turned memoirist Janisse Ray, are finding a pressing need to focus on smaller bioregions and the locatedness of the human subject.[1] These writers believe that agribusiness and consumer ignorance are driving small farmers out of business and that clear cutting timber and farming practices dependant on chemicals are threatening local ecosystems.[2] Best-selling novelist Barbara Kingsolver has joined their ranks. With her most recent novel *Prodigal Summer* (2000), Kingsolver returns to her home region and her academic roots to explore both the crucial ecological issues that most interest the South's environmentalist writers and some of the transnational questions that currently preoccupy literary critics. Setting her novel in southern Appalachia,[3] where she grew up and where she now owns a cabin, she fictionalizes problems that she has since published impassioned essays about[4]: failing family farms, fragmented communities, ecosystems out of balance, and rural-urban, insider-outsider tensions.

---

[1] According to Judith Plant, "Bioregionalism calls for human society to be more closely related to nature (hence 'bio') and to be more conscious of its locale, or regions, or life place (thus 'bioregion'). . . . It is a proposal to ground human cultures within natural systems, to get to know one's place intimately in order to fit human communities to the earth, not distort the earth to our demands" (132). Plant's "Learning to Live with Differences," appears in *Ecofeminism: Women, Culture, Nature*, ed. Karen J. Warren (Bloomington: Indiana University Press, 1997).

[2] Wendell Berry's *The Unsettling of America: Culture and Agriculture* (San Francisco: Sierra Club Books, 1977) is still considered "the definitive contemporary statement of agrarian concerns and priorities," and Janisse Ray's recent memoir, *Ecology of a Cracker Childhood* (Minneapolis: Milkweed Editions, 1999), which won the American Book Award, is required reading in Georgia's public schools and in a number of college environmental studies programs.

[3] The novel is set in the fictional town of Egg Fork, in the vicinity of the Virginia-Kentucky-Tennessee borders.

[4] See Kingsolver's essay collection, *Small Wonder* (New York: HarperCollins, 2002) and her Foreword to *The Essential Agrarian Reader: The Future of Culture, Community, and the*

In *Prodigal Summer* Kingsolver's academic training in evolutionary biology and ecology, her abiding concern for community and family, and her intimate knowledge of a particular place combine to produce no less than a blueprint for saving the small family farm and for restoring ecological balance in a southern Appalachian bioregion that is struggling to survive. Kingsolver, who is at the height of her verbal powers in this novel, employs elaborate Darwinian conceits to link human and natural worlds, both to show how they are connected and how they are similar in needing variety to sustain the health of a complex interdependent ecosystem. Near the end of the novel, Kingsolver places an important Darwinian principle in the mouth of the organic apple grower, Nannie Rawley: "There is nothing so important as having variety. That's how life can still go on when the world changes."[5] And the world of southern Appalachia has changed dramatically. The majestic chestnut trees that once provided a livelihood for some and shelter for many have succumbed to an Asian fungal blight, farming can no longer be relied on to support a family, rural people commute long hours to work in factories or to supplement meager farm income, and their children know little about the ecosystem they inhabit.

Kingsolver thinks of place in much the same way as Arif Dirlik, who has argued that to focus on the groundedness of places through ecology and topography is "not to return to some kind of geographic determinism or bounded notion of place" or to posit an "immutable fixity." For Dirlik, place is the "location," "where the social and the natural meet, where the production of nature by the social is not clearly distinguishable from the production of the social by the natural." He argues that "[a] place suggests groundedness from below, and a flexible and porous boundary around it, without closing out the extralocal, all the way to the global."[6] As Darwin pointed out, difference becomes an important resource for survival. In *Prodigal Summer* Kingsolver employs non-native human and animal species to suggest solutions to local economic and ecological problems in southern Appalachia.

At the same time that Kingsolver reveals how introducing exotic species into the southern landscape can harm the nonhuman ecosystem, she demonstrates that not all exotics are necessarily invasive—biological background for the human social parallel that she sets up. Certainly kudzu, which has no natural enemy in the South, and the Asian fungus that has killed off the American chestnut are damaging invasive species. But some exotic species, such as Asian daylilies, which escaped from flower gardens, now beautify the roadside without taking over the fields and pastures. Other non-native species such as the Chinese chestnut have been imported on purpose by retired agriculture teacher Garnett Walker because their resistance to fungus may prove beneficial in breeding a blight-resistant American chestnut hybrid.

Land, ed. Norman Wirzba (Lexington: University of Kentucky Press, 2003). Kingsolver also published an earlier collection of essays, *High Tide at Tucson* (New York: HarperCollins, 1995).

[5] Barbara Kingsolver, *Prodigal Summer* (New York: HarperCollins, 2000), 390. Subsequent citations will be indicated parenthetically in the text.

[6] Arif Dirlik, "Place-based Imagination: Globalism and the Politics of Place," in *Places and Politics in an Age of Globalization*, ed. Roxann Prazniak and Arif Dirlik (Lanham, MD: Rowman and Littlefield Publishers, Inc., 2001), 22, 18, 22.

Just to give one more prominent example, forest ranger and wildlife ecologist Deanna Wolfe does not judge coyotes, which are migrating to southern Appalachia, "invasive" as most readers might expect, because her research shows that coyotes will help restore the imbalance in the ecosystem caused by the loss of larger predators (wolves and mountain lions) in this habitat.[7] With such examples from the natural world, Kingsolver breaks down simplistic oppositions between natives and non-natives, preparing readers to see the beneficial nature of the human exotic that she introduces in the character of Lusa Maluf Landowski, an urban intellectual with ancestral roots in Poland and Palestine and a family religious heritage of Judaism and Islam.

Rural Appalachia is wary of variety but not totally averse to change. Kingsolver ironically points out that southern Appalachia suffers as much because of the agricultural changes farmers have embraced as because of their resistance to change. Insecticides that the local U.S. Agricultural Extension Service has promoted to protect cash crops such as tobacco are harming other crops, killing the beneficial pollinators so necessary to organic orchard growers like Nannie Rawley. The high cost of chemical herbicides and insecticides has driven many farmers out of business, and more than a few inhabitants of the fictional town Egg Fork have succumbed to cancer. Kingsolver suggests that imbalances in the natural environment caused by human ignorance are creating complex environmental problems that few understand. She uses her main female characters—Nannie, Lusa, and Deanna—to teach these lessons, both to her readers and to the locals, emphasizing the need for an environmental ethic of care to bring balance to the ecosystem and prosperity to local farmers.[8]

The Widener family farm is bordering on extinction. The farm can no longer support the extended family because the drop in governmental price supports has diminished tobacco's profitability. But Cole Widener, the only family member willing to experiment with new crops, has not found a legal crop more profitable than tobacco. His experiment with growing such vegetables as cucumbers and bell peppers for an urban population fails because nearby markets are not large enough to

---

[7] In her acknowledgments (x), Kingsolver cites the source of her coyote research as Mike Finkel, "The Ultimate Survivor" in *Audubon* (May-June 1999): 52-59. For an analysis of coyotes in urban and suburban environments, see Mary Battiata, "Among Us," *Washington Post Magazine* (16 April 2006): 6-11, 17-21.

[8] This environmental ethic of care in *Prodigal Summer* is not gender specific, although to some reviewers it has seemed so, perhaps because of the prominence of these three female protagonists. See for example, Jeff Giles's review in *Newsweek*, 30 October 2000, 82, and Susan Tekulve's review in *Book*, November 2000, 69. But Deanna's father is enlightened, Little Ricky proves a willing listener to his Aunt Lusa's new ideas, and early in his career, Lusa's husband Cole is eager to learn new farming methods. For a comprehensive analysis of the land ethic in *Prodigal Summer*, see Peter S. Wenz, "Leopold's Novel: The Land Ethic in Barbara Kingsolver's *Prodigal Summer*," *Ethics and the Environment* 8.2 (2003): 106-125. He argues that Kingsolver echoes Aldo Leopold's call for "a land ethic [that] changes the role of *Homo sapiens* from conqueror of the land-community to plain member and citizen of it" (106). The quotation is from Leopold's *A Sand County Almanac with Essays on Conservation from Round River* (New York: Ballantine, 1970), 240. See also Plant, "Learning to Live with Differences."

make perishable vegetables maturing at the same time an economically viable alternative. When Cole learns of a potato-chip factory in Knoxville, he hopes that potatoes, which store and ship almost as well as tobacco, might become his cash crop, but the variety that grows best in his soil has too much sugar to make good potato chips. So Cole falls back on tobacco, but he must supplement his farm income by hauling grain for the agricultural conglomerate, Southern States. Wendell Berry would say that Cole's agricultural practices have failed because he has not come up with "good local solutions to local problems."[9] And yet Cole is far from the stereotypical provincial farmer. Hoping to find ways to improve his agricultural practices and thus keep the family farm solvent, he enrolls in a workshop in integrated pest management at the University of Kentucky, which is where he meets Lusa.

Kingsolver shows the importance, indeed the necessity of human variety in an ecosystem when Lusa takes over the farm after Cole's death in a hauling accident. Because Lusa is a "religious mongrel" (438) with a knowledge of Judaism and Islam that the locals do not possess, she knows that the holy days of these religions will converge during her first year of farming and create a demand for goats, necessary for the religious celebrations. Conscious too of the health risks associated with tobacco, she decides not to plant tobacco but to raise goats and sell them to a cousin in New York. To her surprise and that of the Widener family, she succeeds. And at the same time she provides a good solution—though significantly not an entirely local one as Berry advocates—to another local problem, for the county is overrun with the unwanted goats that the children in the 4-H Club have raised for a project.

But this happy ending is neither a final solution to the vicissitudes of small family farms nor a conclusion facilely produced. Following an important rule of agricultural scientists, Kingsolver has Lusa recognize that "good" farming practices will always require flexibility, or the "ability to adapt to local conditions and needs."[10] Lusa is not so naïve as to think that goats can become her sole cash crop; she knows that next year "she might raise no goats at all, depending on the calendar" (438). Instead she contemplates growing grass seed to take advantage of the fact that the U.S. government, in trying to rectify an ecological mistake, has begun to pay people to plant native bluestem grasses in place of the previously championed nonnative fescue, which has destroyed the habitat of native birds, such as the bobwhite. Kingsolver has Lusa think like a bioregionalist, rather than an agri-industrialist, and in so doing highlights current problems in agribusiness practices, which ignore bioregional differences in favor of supposed universal solutions. The novel illustrates how some of the worse so-called "solutions" to agricultural problems, such as the use of broad-spectrum insecticides, have been dispensed by the county Agricultural Extension Service agents with the imprimatur of the U.S. government.

---

[9] Wendell Berry, "Still Standing" (1999) in *Citizenship Papers* (Washington, D.C.: Shoemaker and Hoard, 2003), 159.

[10] Ibid., 159. Berry attributes this rule of thumb to agricultural scientists like Sir Albert Howard and Wes Jackson, whose guiding principle is "harmony between local ways of farming and local ecosystems," as opposed to agri-industrialists who assume universal applicability (159).

As Martyn Bone has pointed out, Kingsolver's agrarianism is not the subsistence farming praised by the *I'll Take my Stand* Agrarians nor is Egg Fork's failing agricultural community emblematic of "the pastoral idea of farmers at one with Nature." Bone argues that the farming advocated in this novel "is not just post-Agrarian or even postsouthern: it is transnational."[11] Certainly Bone is right that this novel takes an important transnational turn with Lusa's immigrant background and Nannie Rawley's Mexican migrant apple pickers. Kingsolver's agrarianism does not come with a capital "A." At the same time, however, although Kingsolver's view of present and past farming practices is more complex and nuanced than that of the Agrarians, it shares some characteristics. As she says in her foreword to Norman Wirzba's *The Essential Agrarian Reader*, "the decision to attend to the health of one's habitat and food chain is a spiritual choice. It's also a political choice, a scientific one, a personal and convivial one. It's not a choice between living in the country or the town; it is about understanding that every one of us, at the level of our cells and respiration, lives in the country and is thus obliged to be mindful of the distance between ourselves and our sustenance."[12] In *Prodigal Summer* Kingsolver certainly advocates growing subsistence crops along side cash crops. Lusa cans and freezes organic fruits and vegetables from her large garden in order to avoid shopping at Kroger, and she patiently explains to her niece Crys why purchasing less flavorful and healthful foods from a supermarket chain is problematic—they come from who-knows-where and are grown under who-knows-what conditions. The community of Egg Fork has not yet become a transnational space, with big box stores that have made the town's architecture placeless and have driven all the local merchants out of business. Indeed the Amish farmers' market is thriving because of their much sought-after homemade baked goods as well as their pesticide-free produce and that of invited organic growers like Nannie Rawley.

But Kingsolver suggests that the Widener family's dependence on Kroger has diminished the quality of their food and changed the nature of their relationship with the land. Crys and her brother are more closely connected to the worlds they see on television than to their own habitat, a point Kingsolver makes when Crys cannot identify the butterflies that captivate her. This single example cannot support the spiritual and ideological weight that Lusa attributes to it. But Kingsolver clearly shows throughout the novel that not understanding the interconnections between the natural and the human world damages the ecosystem, as Nannie's argument with her neighbor Garnett Walker about broad-spectrum insecticides and Deanna's argument with western bounty hunter Eddie Bondo about coyotes demonstrate. In other words, although these farmers are not living a pastoral ideal, Kingsolver thinks they could and should be trying, for the good of themselves and their ecosystem.

Thus Barbara Kingsolver's larger point is as much ecological, as it is agricultural. She uses principles of ecology to question and to illuminate human behavior, and not just the Widener family's actions but Lusa's own. To survive and prosper, this rural farming community, which has become an endangered species, needs more information about the interconnectedness of their world. At the same

---

[11] Martyn Bone, *The Postsouthern Sense of Place in Contemporary Fiction* (Baton Rouge: Louisiana State University Press, 2005), 246, 248.

[12] Kingsolver, Foreword to *The Essential Agrarian Reader,* xvii.

time Lusa, whom the locals view as the "outsider," needs to understand the properties of nonnative species, like herself, in order to live in happy relation to the natives. If the insiders, like Garnett Walker and the extended Widener family have identified Lusa as the Other, because of her non-Christian background, her bookish ways (she openly reads Darwin for pleasure), her urban roots, and her feminist practices (she does not change her name when she marries), she too has stereotyped and distanced herself from them because of their accent, their rural folkways, and their lack of formal education. This stereotypical response on both sides causes problems in Lusa and Cole's marriage.

Philosopher Norman Wirzba's analysis of the urban-rural divide can help illuminate the larger problem. Wirzba suggests that a worldview which has perceived soils, waterways, and forests as "simply resources to feed cultural ambition" has led to "an animosity between the country and the city, each side claiming for itself moral purity or human excellence": "Farming folk have routinely described their way of life as conducive to peace, balance, and simple virtue, and the ways of the city as promoting strife, ambition, and greed. City folk, on the other hand, have considered cities as the entry into sophistication, creativity, and enlightenment, and farms as places of ignorance, provincialism, and limitation."[13] *Prodigal Summer* attempts to deconstruct these simplistic oppositions. Lusa is not simply a "city person" as her husband and his family pigeon-hole her. She is someone who spent her childhood "trapped on lawn but longing for pasture" and "sprouting seeds in pots on a patio" but "dreaming" of the expansive garden she realizes on the Widener farm (35, 375). Deanna Wolfe was raised on a farm in Egg Fork, but in her job as the local forest ranger she practices what she has learned from her degree in wildlife ecology at the University of Tennessee. When Deanna first gets to know newcomer Eddie Bondo, Kingsolver writes that "She was well accustomed to watching Yankee brains grind their gears, attempting to reconcile a hillbilly accent with signs of serious education" (11). Much like Eddie, Lusa brings the same prejudices to Zebulon County.

In order to raise goats successfully, Lusa must critically examine her own practices[14] as an aloof and rather condescending urban outsider, who because she has an advanced degree in biology assumes she knows much more than the locals. Kingsolver gives Lusa what Wendell Berry has called the "provincial . . . half-scared, half-witted urban contempt for 'provinciality,'" a contempt for farmers that Kingsolver herself encountered when she left Kentucky.[15] At the beginning of the novel which opens at the beginning of summer, Lusa fights with Cole about his desire to pull down the fragrant honeysuckle vine crawling up the side of their

---

[13] Wirzba, Introduction to *The Essential Agrarian Reader*, 6.

[14] In "Women in Agriculture: The 'New Entrepreneurs,'" *Australian Feminist Studies*, 18.41 (2003), Margaret Alston argues that in order to make women more visible in agriculture, women must change the language and the way they view themselves, they must question the lack of women in agricultural leadership positions, and they must critically examine their own practices and customs, making sure to value their daughters' desires to be farmers (169-170).

[15] Wendell Berry, "The Prejudice Against Country People" (2001) in *Citizenship Papers*, 110. In her Foreword to *The Essential Agrarian Reader*, Kingsolver says she repeatedly encountered the belief that all farmers are "political troglodytes and devotees of All-Star wrestling" (x).

garage; by the end of the novel and the end of that summer Lusa discovers that he was right to be concerned because the vine has completely devoured the garage. Lusa realizes that honeysuckle, which to her urban sensibility looks lovely and smells heavenly, is in her new rural habitat merely "an invasive exotic, nothing sacred" (440).

Throughout *Prodigal Summer* Kingsolver is at pains to point out that some things in life are known from experience, without the abstract knowledge of scientific theories. Deanna is proud of the fact that her farmer father, who never went to college, knew as much about the natural world as many of her professors. Cole's knowledge of how invasive honeysuckle is in his environment is another example. Lusa acknowledges the error in her own thinking after his death: "*You have to persuade it two steps back everyday,* he'd said, *or it will move in and take you over.* His instincts about this plant had been right, his eye had known things he'd never been trained to speak of. And yet she'd replied carelessly, *Take over what? The world will not end if you let the honeysuckle have the side of your barn.* She crossed her arms against a shiver of anguish and asked him now to forgive a city person's audacity" (360). In the course of the novel, Lusa must face up to the fact that she has romanticized some aspects of rural life, like the honeysuckle, and underestimated others, such as the difficulty of farming and the knowledge of local farmers.

Before Lusa can even begin to call herself a goat farmer, Kingsolver orchestrates the plot so that she must seek the expertise of Garnett Walker, the retired local agriculture teacher and former 4-H Club leader. Garnett is famous for his attempts to cross-breed a new strain of chestnut that will withstand the blight caused by the Asian fungus and infamous for having overseen the 4-H Club project that led to the county-wide goat surplus. By engaging this crusty old loner in her enterprise, Lusa forges links within Egg Fork that have been broken, connecting Garnett with her niece and nephew, Crys and Lowell, who are his grandchildren, although he does not know them. Garnett is estranged from his wayward son, who has divorced the children's mother, Jewel Widener. Such a gradually revealed connection is only one of the many threads that carefully and cleverly knit Lusa's, Garnett's, and Deanna's stories and their three seemingly separate plot lines, each conveyed in a limited third-person point of view.[16] Lusa's successful venture raising goats depends on interdependence in the community and in the family. To help with the day-to-day physical labor, Lusa hires her nephew Little Ricky.

Before Lusa can be accepted as a member of the community and the family, she must overcome their local bias against raising goats and their rural prejudices both against city people and against farm wives operating outside the domestic sphere. Lusa, who had expected to be "a farmer's partner" when she married Cole (42), finds that his family and their neighbors expect otherwise. But Lusa's fiscal success raising goats goes a long way toward elevating her status in the community, no matter her transgressions of the usual gender roles. As time goes on, Lusa establishes herself as an accepted member of the community and the family, proving

---

[16] Garnett's neighbor Nannie Rawley is the only mother-figure Deanna has ever known. Deanna's father has had a long-term affair with Nannie after Deanna's mother's death in childbirth; he would have married Nannie if she had said yes.

herself in ecological terms to be more like the Asian daylilies that bloom throughout Appalachia in July than the Japanese honeysuckle that engulfs the barn—she is non-native, but not invasive. Indeed her arrival, like that of the coyotes in the nearby national forest, begins to right an imbalance in the ecosystem. Lusa pulls the Widener farm out of debt with her successful goat venture, and she promises a loving home to her niece and nephew whose mother is dying of cancer and whose biological aunts do not want the children because they do not behave according to gender-role stereotypes. Crys acts like a boy and Lowell like a girl.

In the final accounting I think Kingsolver succeeds in showing readers that farmers, indeed everyone, need to be more place-conscious. To use Dirlik's terms, Kingsolver shows readers what a "place-based" imagination has to offer. Her ecologically enlightened characters—Deanna, the wildlife ecologist and forest ranger; Nannie, the organic apple grower; and Lusa, the entomologist turned farmer—prosper because they understand both the human and nonhuman ecology of their bioregion.

Kingsolver is less successful in showing how individuals such as Garnett Walker, the Widener sisters, and the western rancher Eddie Bondo can become less "place-bound." Kingsolver resolves the problems Lusa has relating to her sisters-in-law by revealing them to be based more on misconceptions than absolute ideological differences. By having Lusa decide to change her name to Widener, Kingsolver finesses one "place-bound" issue that concerns the family—Lusa's feminism—which she has exhibited by retaining her maiden name. Lusa takes the Widener name when she decides to commit her life to a farm that she knows the locals will always call "the Widener place." Her decision to leave the farm to Crys and Lowell in her will means that the Wideners no longer have to worry that the farm will go out of the family (307).

Physical desire, propelled by pheromones, seems to be Kingsolver's rather too-easy, though biologically explicable, way of bringing ideologically different humans together to debate crucial issues—from Lusa and Cole to Deanna and Eddie. But Kingsolver does not suggest that full understanding, much less an ideological change, necessarily follows dialogue, even if sex is involved. Lusa and Cole argue daily during their short marriage, and Eddie never buys Deanna's argument that coyotes breed more prolifically the more they are killed, although he does respect her enough to stop hunting coyotes in southern Appalachia. Indeed their relationship ends after he reads her master's. thesis about coyotes. Kingsolver does seem to suggest that physical attraction works best in the ideological conversion of youth. Seventeen-year-old Little Ricky is an easy convert to Lusa's innovative farming practices and an eager listener to her lessons about the world's religions because he is smitten with his beautiful, young aunt.

The pairing of Nannie and Garnett is the most unbelievable in the novel. Garnett mellows because of his growing dependence on his spunky seventy-something neighbor, but her Unitarian beliefs, feminist ideals, and organic-farming practices incense him. Garnett, a religious fundamentalist, believes humans have dominion over the earth and so thinks nothing of the consequences of using herbicides to keep his property weed-free and broad-spectrum insecticides to protect his hybrid chestnut seedlings. Garnett is a perfect example of Dirlik's "place-bound" individual: "disguising and suppressing inequalities and oppressions that are internal to place."[17] He blames internal dissension on outside agitators (feminists, Unitarians), and in the face of biological facts, clings to fanciful, often faith-based, points of view. Certain he is right, Garnett does not think about how his choices affect others. As a result, throughout the novel he is at odds with Nannie over the needs of her organic orchard (to be free of the insecticides and herbicides he uses in close proximity to her land), and he withholds from her the shingles that he has discovered in his barn, which he does not need, but which are the very discontinued design that she could use to patch her roof. Despite the heated ideological sparring that goes on between them, Kingsolver wants readers to believe that Nannie's neighborly care for Garnett's health and her frequent appearance in shorts in her orchard combine to spark his physical attraction and a manly desire to protect her. In having Garnett finally decide to give Nannie the shingles, Kingsolver does not go so far as to suggest that their budding friendship will alter their ideological differences about evolution, feminism, or the use of malathion, only that Garnett is becoming less self-centered—a primary step, to be sure, in perceiving one's world ecologically.

Kingsolver's greatest success in this novel is in helping readers to see the human and nonhuman interdependencies in an ecosystem. Kingsolver has said that "this is the most challenging book" she's "ever given" her readers, one whose complexity she believes some reviewers have missed by focusing too much on the humans and not enough on the flora and fauna.[18] Kingsolver understands the tendency of any species to be self-centered and attempts to reach those readers, like Garnett, who persist in anthropocentric thinking. Nannie makes an ironic point by telling Garnett, "I do believe humankind holds a special place in the world. It's the same place held by a mockingbird, in his opinion, and a salamander in whatever he has that resembles a mind of his own. Every creature alive believes this: The center of everything is *me"* (215). The similarity between humans and animals that Kingsolver calls attention to here is repeated in multiple ways throughout the novel.

Prodigal Summer is a metaphor-laden book because Kingsolver is out to change the way readers perceive themselves and their relationship to the natural world. Paul Ricoeur has argued that "a metaphor may be seen as a model for changing our way of looking at things, of perceiving the world. The word 'insight,' very often applied to the *cognitive* import of metaphor, conveys in a very appropriate manner this move from sense to reference."[19] As if to help readers understand the value of metaphor, Kingsolver sets up a situation in which Lusa makes light of the Appalachian people's saying that the "mountains breathe": "she had some respect for the poetry of country people's language, if not for the veracity of their perceptions" (31). After living in the shadow of the mountain and experiencing the air currents, Lusa realizes that their personification is apt: "the inhalations of Zebulon Mountain touched her face all morning, and finally she understood. She learned to tell time with her skin, as morning turned to afternoon and the mountain's

---

[17] Dirlik, "Place-based Imagination," 31.

[18] "*Prodigal Summer* Questions and Answers," http://www.kingsolver.com/faq/answers.asp.

[19] Paul Ricoeur, "The Metaphorical Process as Cognition, Imagination, and Feeling" in *On Metaphor,* ed. Sheldon Sacks (Chicago: University of Chicago Press, 1979), 150. I would like to thank Richard Godden for suggesting that I read Ricoeur.

breath began to bear gently on the back of her neck. By early evening it was insistent as a lover's sigh, sweetened by the damp woods, cooling her nape and shoulders whenever she paused her work in the kitchen to lift her sweat-damp curls off her neck. She had come to think of Zebulon as another man in her life, larger and steadier than any other companion she had known" (33). In this example, Lusa, the scientist, learns Ricoeur's lesson about metaphor: "poetic language is no less about reality than any other use of language but refers to it by the complex strategy which implies, as an essential component, a suspension and seemingly an abolition of the ordinary reference attached to descriptive language. . . . in another respect, it constitutes the primordial reference to the extent that it suggests, reveals, unconceals—or whatever you say—the deep structures of reality to which we are related as mortals who are born into this world and who *dwell* in it for a while."[20]

The "deep structure" Kingsolver wants to reveal is the complex ecosystem in which humans live, but about which they know far too little. In an attempt to disrupt an anthropocentric world view, Kingsolver personifies animals and animalizes people. For example, the coyote pups are "children born empty-headed like human infants," and they live in a "family" (200). The novel concludes with a chapter from a coyote's perspective in which readers experience the acrid odor of crop-dusted farms and the sweet pleasure of Nannie's organic orchard. When the coyote thinks of prey, she does not fixate on Lusa's goats, as Eddie Bondo and some readers might expect, but much smaller animals, squirrels and mice. Similarly, Kingsolver reveals the animalism of humans, both through her metaphors (Eddie marks his "territory" when he urinates off Deanna's porch; Cole's beard is like a "nectar guide" for Lusa's kiss, 26, 38) and the revelation of little known biological facts (women cycle with the moon when exposed to its light, and like female animals they emit a scent when they are fertile). As Lusa points out, smell is a "whole world of love we don't discuss" (237).Through Kingsolver's use of metaphor, she suggests that the natural world could give humans "insight" into their own behavior, and she reminds readers that humans are but one species among many in the world they dwell in. At the same time that Kingsolver gives some animals voices, she does not anthropomorphize animals or romanticize their behavior. For weeks a snake coexists with Deanna and the baby birds she nurtures, preying on the pesky mice in her cabin, only to eat the baby birds at summer's end. At the same time that Kingsolver gives humans animal instincts, she does not strip them of their capacity to reason. The recently widowed Lusa does not have sex with Cole's nephew Little Ricky, despite her powerful attraction to him: "'We're not blood kin,' he argued. 'But we're family,'" said (416).

Much of the pleasure of this text, which increases on second and third readings, comes from developing an attention to detail and from observing how intricately Kingsolver has connected these details, not just metaphorically but structurally

---

[20] Ibid., 151. In suggesting that a metaphor can yield insight about reality, I do not mean to suggest that Kingsolver thinks metaphoric and scientific discourses are the same or are apprehended in the same way. In explaining metaphoric apprehension, which involves making similar what is different, Ricoeur reminds us of the "semantic impertinence or incongruence" that is inherent: "In order that a metaphor obtains, one must continue to identify the previous incompatibility through the new compatibility" (146). Such impertinence and incongruence is evident in several failed communications in the novel.

through her braided narratives. Learning to observe and understand interconnections is an important ecological lesson that readers absorb through the novel's form by doing—by actively making unheralded connections—rather than by passively listening to the characters' Rachel-Carson inspired orations about keystone predators, evolution, and broad-spectrum insecticides.[21] Granted these overt lessons emerge organically because Kingsolver's main characters are teachers, but many of the same "lessons" in this novel of lessons about ecology are taught indirectly.

Readers gradually become aware of the human and nonhuman connections among the novel's three seemingly separate but intertwined narratives at the same time that the characters make them aware of interconnections in the southern Appalachian bioregion. In the human world, these connections range from the serendipitous to the poignant. The stained green brocade arm chair on Deanna's porch was one of a matched pair once in the Widener family's living room; its mate, still in the Widener farmhouse but moved to the bedroom, has become Lusa's favorite reading chair. Garnett's grandfather felled the huge hollowed out chestnut that serves as Deanna's home away from home in the woods. The old woman who gives Lusa such sage advice at Cole's funeral is Nannie Rawley. Lusa longs for a friend who shares her views, and readers come to see what Lusa does not know by novel's end, but what these connections highlight—that among the locals, whom Lusa has stereotyped as environmentally ignorant, are two women who share her knowledge of and passion for ecology, Deanna and Nannie. As regards the non-human world, for example, by novel's end readers have pieced together information from the three separate narratives to learn that pesky cockleburs abound not because God has made "one mistake in Creation" (213) as Garnett suggests, but because the Carolina parakeets that once ate them are now extinct. However, Kingsolver shows that an ecological imbalance may be corrected. Coyotes are taking the place of the extinct red wolves; Magnolia warblers have returned to the Zebulon National Forest now that their habitat has been protected from clear cutting; bobwhites are also coming back, perhaps as Deanna suggests because of the passages the coyotes are opening in the tight clumps of fescue; and Nannie Rawley's organic orchard is "the best producing orchard in five counties" (420). In *Prodigal Summer* Kingsolver demonstrates that both the survival of the Widener farm and the well-being of the southern Appalachian ecosystem depend on understanding the complex interconnections between human and nonhuman worlds, between natives and newcomers, between the local and the global.

---

[21] This is not to say that these lessons, often delightful, are not enlightening to readers. Many of my students have said that they have a better understanding of ecology because of this novel.

SOUTHERN CONSERVATIVES: RACE AND POVERTY, 1980-2006

By Dan T. Carter

For much of the nation's history, white Americans have shared certain racial—to be blunt, racist—assumptions about the relationship between skin color and poverty. But in the case of white southerners, such racist assumptions have been even more important. Many of these assumptions were so ingrained they were rarely discussed or analyzed: they were simply accepted as part of the natural order, like the sun rising in the east and setting in the west. Black people were not simply mentally deficient and child-like in their emotions; they were inherently prone to indolence and sloth. Much of the literature describing ante-bellum slave owners is devoted to describing the ways in which these assumptions shaped their effort to control the black men and women under their authority.

These assumptions hardly changed in the post-bellum period. The South Carolina planter-poet, William Grayson—author of "The Hireling and the Slave"—had summed up the white southerners perceptions of free labor in one of his lesser known poems, a dire description of emancipation in the Caribbean written in the mid-1850s:

> The Bright Antilles, with each closing year,
> See harvests fail, and fortunes disappear;
> The cane no more its golden treasure yields;
> Unsightly weeds deform the fertile fields;
> The negro freedman, thrifty while a slave,
> Loosed from restraint becomes a drone or knave;
> Each effort to improve his nature foils,
> Begs, steals, or sleeps and starves, but never toils;
> For savage sloth mistakes the freedom won,
> And ends the mere barbarian he begun.[1]

In the minds of slaveowners, poetic prophecy became reality with the end of slavery. As a frustrated Louisiana sugar planter argued after one year of free labor, the "nature of the negro" made him totally indifferent to the usual inducements of labor. "All he desires is to eat, drink and sleep and perform the least possible amount of labor."[2] In *American Dreams in Mississippi: Consumers, Poverty, and Culture*, historian Ted Ownby shows how deeply embedded remained these assumptions through the end of the nineteenth and into the twentieth century. Whites were particularly appalled at the entry of the freedmen and women into the marketplace of

---

[1] William Grayson, *The Hireling and the Slave, Chicora and Other Poems* (Charleston: S.C. McCarter & Co., 1856), 34.

[2] A. Franklin Pugh to Sergeant Gardner, 6 September 1864, Pugh Family Papers, University of Texas Archives, Austin, Texas. Pugh's plantation was in an area of Louisiana that had come under federal control in late 1862. By the time he wrote this letter, he had been working with free labor approximately 18 months.

consumption. The "common COMPLAINT," states Ownby, "was that African Americans were such free spenders that they were better off without cash." Thus, from emancipation onward well into the mid-twentieth century, white Mississippians—and most white southerners—agreed with the notion that African Americans—given the opportunity—would "literally spend themselves into starvation."[3] The solution? Keep them on the edge of existence and they would be forced to be responsible in their work habits.

At the end of the 1920s, the United States lacked any national welfare program or policies and only minimally funded state programs of direct relief, old-age pensions, widow's pensions and worker's compensation. However limited elsewhere, such programs were almost non-existent in the South. And even though there were many factors involved in the penurious nature of public relief in the South, race was unquestionably the most important one.

The Great Depression upended old assumptions and created the foundations of the limited American welfare state as we know it today, but the majority of Southern political leaders—particularly from the black belt—sought to limit the impact of New Deal programs on the South. Historians have described the dozens of ways that federal programs contained "exemptions" and "exceptions": regional wage differentials, the discriminatory dispersal of relief payments, the tilt of the Agricultural Adjustment Administration toward landowners and the structuring of Social Security and unemployment compensation in such a way as to make certain that most poor domestic and agricultural workers—preponderantly black—were left uncovered. And even the most liberal of southern congressman voted with their conservative colleagues from the region to remove a proposed provision of the old-age assistance program that would have required the states to furnish public assistance at a "reasonable subsistence compatible with decency and health."[4]

Of course, part of this opposition was simply a reflection of the interests of planters and industrial interests that ferociously defended the low-wage economy of the South, but much of it was also interwoven with traditional racial assumptions. "I don't like this welfare business," a North Carolina landlord told a relief worker in 1934. "I can't do a thing with my niggers. They aren't beholden to me any more. They know you all won't let them perish."[5]

Anyone who is remotely familiar with the history of Lyndon Johnson's War on Poverty and the adoption of Great Society programs in the mid-1960s is aware of the

---

[3] Ted Ownby, *American Dreams in Mississippi: Consumers, Poverty, and Culture* (Chapel Hill: University of North Carolina Press, 1999), 62. Many of the same assumptions applied to shiftless "poor whites," but the attitude toward this group was more often one of bemusement rather than anger and frustration.

[4] Jill Quadagno, *The Color of Welfare: How Racism Undermined the War on Poverty* (New York: Oxford University Press, 1995), 20-22. See also the works by Edward Berkowitz, *America's Welfare State: From Roosevelt to Reagan* (Baltimore: Johns Hopkins University Press, 1991), 13 ff; James Patterson, *America's Struggle Against Poverty* (Cambridge: Harvard University Press, 1986), 72-73; and Edward G. Carmines and James A. Stimson, *Issue Evolution: Race and the Transformation of American Politics* (Princeton: Princeton University Press, 1991), 24.

[5] Quoted in George Brown Tindall, *The Emergence of the New South, 1913-1945* (Baton Rouge: Louisiana State University Press, 1967), 478.

connections many white Americans, North and South, made between blackness, poverty, and government welfare policies.

In 2001, I rediscovered those intellectual connections when I agreed to serve as an expert witness for the United States Justice Department in a voting rights case involving the election system for County Commissioners in Charleston, South Carolina. The Justice Department under President Bill Clinton had sued Charleston County on the grounds that the at-large system of electing County Commissioners made it almost impossible for blacks to elect individuals representing them even though they made up thirty-five per cent of the population. This was true because, by the 1990s, approximately ninety per cent of Charleston County whites voted Republican thus guaranteeing Republican dominance in an at-large system.

I understood the broad outlines of the shift from Democratic to Republican that had taken place among southern whites beginning with Barry Goldwater's 1964 campaign, continuing through the Presidency of Richard Nixon. I had studied and written about the Southern Strategy, a political plan best articulated in the late 1960s by Kevin Phillips, the Republican Party's main expert on ethnic and racial voting patterns. Nixon had received a third of the black vote in 1960, but only fifteen per cent in 1968. And Phillips bluntly urged the President to ignore blacks. "The GOP can build a winning coalition without Negro votes," argued Phillips. "Indeed," he said, "Negro-Democratic mutual identification" was a critical factor in the growth of the Republican Party in the South. With the Democratic Party becoming the "Negro party through most of the South," the Republicans would become the majority party in the region and attract disenchanted white working class voters in the North as well. After reading Phillips' recommendations Nixon wrote a memo to his staff. "Use Phillips strategy," he ordered, "don't go for Jews & Blacks."[6]

What I did not recall was the crudeness with which Republicans had used race in the late 1960s and 1970s to strengthen that identification. In reading through the South Carolina newspapers of the era, I discovered dozens of political advertisements that amounted to a media seminar laying down the themes that would dominate the party's positions for the next three decades.

When South Carolina's white Democrats began timidly to seek the support of black voters in 1968, the Republican Party released a series of newspaper and television advertisements accusing the "Democrat Party" of being controlled by the "Black bloc vote," specifically the National Association for the Advancement of Colored People and the Southern Christian Leadership Conference. In political advertisements that ran in every major state and local campaign from 1968 to 1972, South Carolina's Republican Party warned that a victory by the Democrats—usually identified as "controlled by the black bloc vote"—would lead to an escalation in crime in the streets and the destruction of the state's public schools through

---

[6] Dan T. Carter, *From George Wallace to Newt Gingrich: Race in the Conservative Counterrevolution, 1963-1994* (Baton Rouge: Louisiana State University Press, 1996), 45; Kenneth O'Reilly, *Nixon's Piano: Presidents and Racial Politics from Washington to Clinton* (New York: The Free Press, 1995), 285-86.

integration. But it was the linkage of blackness, increasing welfare costs and higher taxes that was most consistent in these advertisements.[7]

With the election of Ronald Reagan in 1980, conservatives were well on their long march to political hegemony in American society, convincing most Americans that—to quote Reagan—the national government was part of the problem, not the solution, to the problem of poverty in America. Since southern Republican conservatives played a critical role in shaping that conservative revolution, it seemed logical to examine their distinctive regional contribution in this process.

In exploring the role of these conservatives, I began by examining the debate and discussions surrounding two congressional measures enacted during the 1990s that directly affected poverty in America. The first was the 1996 welfare legislation that ended more than sixty years of law that had made welfare a legal right in America, a measure named with Orwellian ingenuity the "Personal Responsibility and Work Opportunity Act of 1996." Since the issues were often interwoven, I also read the debates surrounding Democratic efforts to increase the minimum wage that same year.[8]

While I reviewed the speeches and statements of members of Congress, I took special note of the record and public statements of five southern Republicans who were key players in the Republican conservative revolution: Richard Armey, Phil Gramm, Bill Archer and Tom Delay of Texas, Trent Lott of Mississippi and Georgia's Newt Gingrich. All of these individuals had held key positions in the Republican House and Senate leadership with the exception of Archer and Gramm. Archer's position as chair of the House Ways and Means Committee—which wrote the original welfare "reform" legislation—gave him inordinate influence. Gramm's ability to shape policy, like Tom Delay's, stemmed from his influential conservative views within the party and his ability to raise large amounts of money for other conservative Republican candidates running for office. My assumption from the outset was that, as white southern heirs to a party founded on the solid foundations of racial backlash issues, these southerners covertly or overtly would bring a racial dimension to the conservative agenda.

But the story proved to be more complex than I had imagined.

Certainly race has remained a salient issue in any discussion of poverty and politics by conservatives, North and South, over the last twenty-five years, but in quite different ways than those advertisements I described in the late 1960s and early 1970s. With a few notable exceptions, the overt use of racist language in political debates surrounding poverty almost disappeared.

The Republican sweep in 1994 under the banner of the "Contract With America" was the backdrop for the debate over curtailing welfare support in

---

[7] Dan T. Carter, "Expert Witness Report," in US District Court for the State of South Carolina, *United States of America, et al plaintiffs v. Charleston County Council,* (2001) Civil Action No. 2-010155 11.

[8] In 1996, the Congress narrowly approved an increase in the minimum wage from $4.25 to $4.75 and to $5.15 in 1997. When Jimmy Carter left the White House in 1981, the minimum wage was $3.35; or $8.51 in 2005 dollars. The minimum wage has not been changed since 1997 and a majority of Republican House members have expressed support for a plan to repeal the minimum wage in its entirety.

America. For conservatives it was the ideal issue on which to wage the next battle with traditional liberalism and the culmination of a campaign against welfare entitlements for the poor that had begun in earnest in the early 1970s. Since the early twentieth century, American conservatives have emphasized the dangers of dependency, the importance of work and the inherent inefficiencies and costs of government assistance. In fact, many of their arguments reached backwards to the Elizabethan Poor Laws. But the specific arguments and ideas about the causes of poverty—and particularly the relationship between poverty and government policy—underwent a transformation in the 1960s, and 1970s.

As Americans abandoned overt racism and rhetorically embraced the values of a color-blind society, conservatives, including Southern conservatives, accepted with varying degrees of enthusiasm the new order. At the same time, they rejected the arguments of liberals that the historic legacies of slavery, segregation, and two hundred years of overt racial discrimination continued to play a significant role in causing or perpetuating poverty and inequality. For most conservatives, America was born anew in 1964 and 1965; the past had ceased to exist.

Instead of race there was "culture."

One of the first scholars to develop such a cultural explanation for poverty and inequality was the political scientist Edward Banfield. Banfield's first book was *The Moral Basis of a Backward Society*, a study of a southern Italian village, but in his 1974 *The Unheavenly City*, Banfield made clear his arguments applied to American society as well. Poverty, he insisted, was not the consequence of government policy or structural economic factors. In an open and economically abundant society like the United States, poverty was a temporary phenomena **except** for those individuals who embraced a culture of feckless self-gratification that gave no thought to the future. All of the problems of the residual poor—what had come to be called the "underclass"—were due to the "existence of an outlook and style of life which is radically present-oriented and which therefore attaches no value to work, sacrifice, self-improvement or the service to family, friends, or community."[9] Because the root causes of poverty lay in the failings of the impoverished, they could never be addressed by the kind of traditional welfare or liberal programs like those of the Great Society. In fact, argued Banfield, those programs simply reinforced the very cultural deficiencies that kept individuals in their wretched condition.

While Banfield's work was not widely read, it did influence a number of conservative intellectuals and propagandists, including the right-wing polemicist George Gilder. In his best-selling 1981 book, *Wealth and Poverty*, Gilder provided the new and very conservative administration of Ronald Reagan a rationale for attacking federal welfare programs for the poor. In a striking departure from the rhetoric of the previous 50 years, Gilder explicitly embraced the desirability of income inequality. Only the absence of a governmental safety net and the threat of abject poverty would lead the current poor (who were "refusing to work hard," he argued) to abandon their profligate ways and follow the time-tested formula for success. The poor "must not only work, they must work harder than the classes above them." Poverty was a direct consequence of inherent moral weakness,

---

[9] Edward Banfield, *The Unheavenly City Revisited* (Boston: Little Brown, 1974), 235.

exacerbated by a perverse welfare system that rewarded the indolent and discouraged the ambitious.[10]

Charles Murray's *Losing Ground: American Social Policy, 1950-1980*, published four years later, had an even greater impact. Gilder was essentially a right-wing polemical moralist, but Murray's book was filled with charts and tables, one of the first of dozens of carefully crafted social science works that would emerge in the coming years from conservative think tanks. (Murray was a fellow of the newly created Heritage Foundation). Despite the scholarly apparatus, the argument was little different from Gilder's. Murray described a world in which teenage girls had illegitimate babies only to collect welfare payments, young men refused to take responsibility for their bastard children, and the poor deliberately refused to take "entry level" positions because they could always fall back upon the welfare largesse of taxpayers. Since the Great Society, welfare had become a program of rewarding the "least law-abiding," the "least capable," and the "least responsible" among the poor. And the cost, claimed Murray, was staggering to hard-working American taxpayers. The only solution was to scrap the "entire federal welfare and income-support structure for working-aged persons, including AFDC, Medicaid, Food Stamps, Unemployment Insurance, Worker's Compensation, subsidized housing, disability insurance and the rest." Unlike most conservatives, moreover, Murray was willing to return to traditional racial arguments, insisting that liberal ideologues had conspired to conceal the uncomfortable reality that genetically inherent IQ limited the capabilities of racial groups, particularly blacks who were at the bottom of the ladder.[11]

The Republican sweep in 1994 that gave the GOP control of the House and Senate, brought the years of arguments over welfare to a climax. As Congress took up the issue in earnest in late 1995, the arguments for changes in the welfare law were little more than paraphrases of Banfield, Gilder, Murray, and other conservative ideologues, with a dash of statistics furnished by right-wing think tanks like the Heritage Foundation, the Manhattan, American Enterprise, and Cato Institutes.[12]

House majority leader Dick Armey had begun his career at North Texas State as a middle of the road economics professor. His 1977 book, *Price Theory: A Policy Welfare Approach*, was hardly a right-wing manifesto. In it, he described with some subtlety the social costs involved in embracing free-market policies and abandoning social welfare and environmental programs.[13] By the middle of the 1990s, however,

---

[10] George Gilder, *Wealth and Poverty* (New York: Basic Books, 1981), 82-92, 103

[11] Charles Murray, *Losing Ground: American Social Policy, 1950-1980* (New York, Basic Books, 1985), 227-28, 360, 549.

[12] As New York's Alfonse D'Amato told his fellow Senators, welfare "administers a narcotic to . . . [poor people's] spirit. This dependence on welfare undermines their humanity, [and] makes them wards of the State." *Congressional Record, Senate*, July 23, 1996, 104th Congress, S8493.

[13] See particularly Armey's discussion of the congressional decision to refuse to support the production the supersonic transport, a decision that was rightly made, he suggests, because congress decided that the "economic benefits would . . . accrue to a relatively few individuals, whereas the harmful effects would more pervasively affect society at large. Thus, the potential increase in individual welfare was judged to be less than the potential decrease in social

Armey—then House Republican majority leader—was passionately committed to slashing government welfare programs and regulations of every description. Welfare only produced poverty he argued. In the debates over increasing the minimum wage, he cited the law as a typically perverse example of the consequences of any attempt by the federal government to interfere with the classical laws of supply and demand. "Every economics principles textbook in America proved that raising the minimum wage only resulted in the loss of jobs," he told his colleagues in floor debate. With his voice shaking with emotion, he urged his colleagues to reject the demands of "union bosses" and defend the interests of the jobless poor who—absent a minimum wage—could find entry-level work that would set them on the road to prosperity.

What was intriguing, moreover, was his success, and that of many other fellow conservatives, in taking the offensive on the issue of race, using a language of inverted populism to depict liberals as enemies of the poor. The minimum wage was nothing more than a recipe for assaulting the poorest of the poor; particularly the black poor. Liberals would vote against increasing the minimum wage, shouted Armey, if they had an "ounce of decency and consideration for the most beleaguered victims of minimum wage increases, those [black] youngsters caught in inner cities where the jobs are lost. . . ."[14]

As I said, these debates were—for the most part—free from traditional racial rhetoric that had once dominated southern politics.

But then, of course, the opponents of welfare did not have to draw the connections between welfare, taxes, and race. A 1994 CBS/New York Times poll found that eighty per cent of white Americans believed that blacks made up from fifty to ninety per cent of the nation's poor; the same percentage believed that well over half of the recipients of federal welfare were black. In fact, African Americans made up about thirty percent of those Americans living below the poverty line and approximately the same percentage of those receiving means-tested government assistance. The most unpopular of these programs was Aid to Families of Dependent Children (AFDC) which white Americans overwhelmingly associated with black recipients and believed was exploding in cost. Here again, there was a significant gap between public perception and reality. Only thirty-six percent of the program's grant recipients were African American and the cost of the program had actually declined fifteen per cent between 1975 and 1995 because of the fifty percent cut in the level of support payments.[15]

Thus conservatives did not need to make overt references to skin color. Instead, they relied upon a new kind of thinly veiled or coded racism that had been pioneered by such political figures as George Wallace and even Richard Nixon. In her important book, *The Race Card: Campaign Strategy, Implicit Messages and the*

---

welfare. Dick Armey, *Price Theory: A Policy Welfare Approach* (Englewood Cliffs, NJ: Prentice-Hall, Inc., 1977), 9.

[14] *Congressional Record, House of Representatives,* May 1, 1996, H4371. Majority Whip Tom Delay took a slightly different tack: "Emotional appeals about working families trying to get by on $4.25 an hour are hard to resist," he told a reporter. "Fortunately such families do not really exist" (*Congressional Record, House of Representatives,* April 23, 1996, H3705).

[15] Dan T. Carter, *How American Conservatives Reframed Issues of Race and Economics in the 1990s* (Bundoora, Australia: LaTrobe University Campus Graphics, 2005), 13.

Norm of Equality, sociologist Tali Mendelberg has given us a sophisticated analysis of the emergence of a language of race that was most effective when it was implicit and thus deniable.[16]

And nothing more clearly illustrates this relationship than the discussion of illegitimacy and welfare.

Opponents of federal welfare often emphasized different reasons for their opposition; some focused on the rising costs of income and medical support; others based their argument on a visceral opposition to any governmental interference in the "free market." As California's George Radanovich argued, the "minimum wage is an interference with employer-employee contractual relations. Big brothers in the Federal bureaucracy aren't happy unless they can control conduct throughout the workplace."[17]

But one argument recurred again and again: the looming fear of illegitimacy. And few politicians failed to note directly, or indirectly, the fact that more than six out of every ten black children were born out of wedlock.

In fact "non-marital births" have been rising throughout the western world since the 1950s. As Herbert Klein has noted in his recent study of population trends in the United States, Sweden in 1950 had fertility patterns much like the United States. By the mid-1990s, "non-marital" births rose to more than fifty per cent and, he noted, "such Catholic countries as Spain and Portugal had arrived at 16 percent and 22 percent illegitimacy rates, respectively, and France was up to 38 percent by 1996. Thus the belief that this was a temporary or uniquely North American development does not appear to be the case."[18]

Moreover, during the years of heightened racial consciousness on this issue, the disparity by race declined due primarily to the rising rate for white women. Between 1980 and 1995, the nonmarital birth rate for white women rose 94 percent and the rate for black women increased only seven percent. If there was an "epidemic," it was clearly spreading most rapidly in the white community. Nevertheless, the issue remained racialized. In the congressional debates—even among many liberal Democrats—there was an implicit assumption that unwed mothers and their children were inner city blacks.

While most conservative proponents of changes in the law sought to avoid explicit references to race, there were two euphemisms used repeatedly: "inner city" and "underclass" to refer to these individuals. Factuality went completely out the window as estimates of supporting this rapacious underclass of immoral welfare mothers were described as "billions," then "hundreds of billions" and—in one case—"trillions." (Much of this imaginative book-keeping was made possible by right-wing think tanks like the Heritage Foundation that consistently lumped together a whole range of government programs that clearly benefited predominantly middle class, and white, recipients but left the unmistakable impression that these expenditures were for the poor).

---

[16] Tali Mendelberg, *The Race Card: Campaign Strategy, Implicit Messages and the Norm of Equality* (Princeton: Princeton University Press, 2001), 5

[17] *Congressional Record, House of Representatives*, May 1, 1996, H4371.

[18] Herbert S. Klein, *A Population History of the United States* (Cambridge: Cambridge University Press, 2004), chapter 8.

As Pennsylvania's Senator Rick Santorum told his colleagues illegitimacy was the "great social ill . . . , the cancer within that will destroy this civilization." Again and again, conservative senators and representatives returned to vivid accounts of rapacious welfare mothers living a life of luxury at the expense of hardworking taxpayers. Here is what the "liberals" have in store for America, said Congressman David Funderburk of North Carolina as the debate began: "Have a child out of wedlock, don't have a job and don't live with a man who is working. If you do these things the taxpayer will provide you with everything you need. Uncle Sam will give you a check each month, with free medical care, free food . . . , a Federal job and free child care."[19]

The very justification for the measure as laid out by the committee that originally reported the bill was clear on this point. The most important change in the nation's welfare law, said the Republican majority, was to end any entitlement to welfare under the Social Security act. States would be given financial support, but only for the purpose of ending welfare. Recipients would be required to make "verifiable efforts to leave welfare for work and to avoid births outside marriage." In addition, federal funds could be used to encourage sexual abstinence and to "encourage the formation and maintenance of two-parent families." Even as the federal government of the United States abandoned its responsibility for providing a minimal level of welfare, it took upon itself the responsibility for encouraging marriage, reducing divorce, and regulating the sexual behavior of millions of Americans; implicitly, millions of African Americans.[20]

As significant as the arguments of the conservatives was the silence of liberals. There was a response that could have been made. William Julius Wilson's 1987 study, *The Truly Disadvantaged: the Inner City, the Underclass and Public Policy* and Andrew Hacker's 1992 work, *Two Nations: Black and White, Separate, Hostile, Unequal* had sought to shift the argument away from the issue of the "underclass" (which had become a theme of liberals and conservatives), in order to focus on the economic changes of post-1960 urban America that had left behind an entire generation of individuals who lacked access to jobs and skills and thus the ability to take advantage of any opportunities that might become available. Men, particularly black men, had lost access to well-paying or even modestly supportive blue collar jobs as the growth of the suburbs and the isolation of inner cities led to the spatial separation of low-income urban Americans from the jobs that were available. While these forces had a particularly devastating effect upon minority communities, they applied to whites as well. "Underclass" culture, which was too often marked by collapsing family structures and antisocial criminal behavior, was not a manifestation of innate depravity or a sudden moral collapse among the poor. It was a direct response to the structural changes created by the new post-industrial economy.[21]

---

[19] *Congressional Record, House of Representatives,* March 24, 1995, H3793.

[20] Committee on Ways and Means, U.S. House of Representatives, "Summary of Welfare Reforms Made by Public Law 104-93: The Personal Responsibility and Work Opportunity Reconciliation Act and Associated Legislation," November 6, 1996.

[21] William Julius Wilson, *The Truly Disadvantaged* (Chicago: University of Chicago Press, 1987); Andrew Hacker, *Two Nations* (New York: Scribner, 1992).

In a key departure from some earlier liberal prescriptions that emphasized income redistribution, Wilson and Hacker shared the conservative view that welfare without work led to a debilitating culture of dependency. The only solution, in their view, was a broad program of government intervention emphasizing the creation of private and public sector jobs even as the disadvantaged were helped to acquire basic educational and job skills and support for families during the transition from welfare to work.

But American conservatives had been so successful in discrediting the role of government that the liberal opposition recoiled from such a solution. And one by one, they fell back upon the last line of defense: the enactment of such measures would have a harsh impact upon innocent children who were not responsible for the sins of their wayward mothers and irresponsible fathers.

Viewing this debate as a whole, it is difficult to imagine a set of ideas and mental images more consistent with the long history of racism in America.

But it is clear that white southern conservatives have contributed more than a racial subtext to the debate over poverty. Their clout stems directly from the way in which a particularly hard-line form of conservatism has come to characterize the Republican Party in the South which in turn dominates the political landscape of the region and shapes national policy. Put simply, the national GOP is dominated by its southern wing.

Something of that connection can be seen by the fact that George W. Bush captured *every* southern state in his two campaigns for the presidency, and in the 2004 election, Republicans easily replaced all five of the U.S. Senate seats vacated by retiring southern Democrats. By 2006, the GOP controlled clear majorities in southern congressional delegations, in southern statehouses and in state legislatures and local governments.[22] And southern Republicans have used that power base to shape the policies of the national GOP.

That peculiarly southern cast to these issues can be seen in the passage of the 1996 welfare "reform" package. With Bill Clinton's support, it passed by a wide margin: 78 to 21 in the Senate and 327 to 100 in the House. What is instructive, however, is the fact that not a single white Representative from the South— Republican or Democrat—and only one southern senator (who had decided not to seek re-election) voted against the measure.[23] The conservative rhetoric supporting a changed welfare policy may have differed little between North and South, but the politics suggest that there were differences between southern and non-southern conservatives.

One window into that difference can be seen by examining two books published in 1992 and 1993 cited by Newt Gingrich as the most influential works in shaping the new conservative agenda on poverty: Myron Magnet's *The Dream and*

---

[22] Thomas F. Schaller, *Whistling Past Dixie: How Democrats Can Win Without the South* (New York: Simon and Schuster, 2006), 4.

[23] See "Vote Tallies, 1996 Welfare Amendments," http://www.ssa.gov/history/tally1996.html

the Nightmare: The Sixties' Legacy to the Underclass[24] and Marvin Olasky's *The Tragedy of American Compassion.*[25]

Magnet, a fellow at the conservative Manhattan Institute and editor of the Institute's quarterly magazine of urban affairs, made an impassioned attack on liberal ideas and assumptions; an attack that he carried out for the most part by creating—with great indignation—massive straw-men which he then proceeded to dismantle to his satisfaction. But the most intriguing aspects of *The Dream and the Nightmare* were his discussions of human nature. For Magnet, the great crisis in American society lay in the failure of liberals to accept the insights of Thomas Hobbes and Sigmund Freud. Fundamentally, says Magnet quoting Freud: "man is a wolf to man." Humans as they come from the hand of nature were "instinctively aggressive, with an inbuilt inclination to violence" and aggression. At the same time, their nature was to avoid work unless forced to do so. The liberal delusion that these characteristics—aggression, violence, sloth—grew out of the structure of society had created the nightmare of a growing interwoven culture of immorality, poverty and anti-social violence. There were ample opportunities to move from poverty into the middle class in America's dynamic and open free enterprise society, insisted Magnet. The way out of the morass was to create a world in which compassion was banished and, in Magnet's words, the poor were forced to "take responsibility for themselves" rather than be made "dependent on programs and exempted from responsibility."[26]

Magnet's harsh prescriptions with their ruthless conclusions may have influenced Gingrich, but there is no evidence that they struck a particularly responsive chord among southerners.

But Olasky's book did. Born Jewish, then becoming an atheist and member of the United States Communist Party in the late 1960s and early 1970s, Olasky converted to Christianity in 1976. In 1982 he joined the University of Texas faculty as a journalism professor while editing an influential conservative religious magazine, *World.* His book, *The Tragedy of American Compassion,* was published in 1992. Like Myron Magnet, Olasky emphasized the inherent depravity of men and women, but he spoke in the language of John Calvin rather than Hobbes and Freud.[27] Quoting a nineteenth century evangelist, he declared approvingly that the cause of all evil—including poverty—was "the sinfulness of the heart of Man." Olasky

---

[24] Myron Magnet, *The Dream and the Nightmare: The Sixties' Legacy to the Underclass* (San Francisco: Encounter Books, 1993).

[25] Marvin Olasky, *The Tragedy of American Compassion* (Washington, DC: Regnery Publishing, Inc., 1992).

[26] Magnet, *The Dream and the Nightmare*, 237.

[27] Olasky has been financially supported and subsidized by right-wing millionaire Howard Ahmanson Jr., a passionate Bush supporter who has financed a number of ultra-conservative causes against gay marriage, evolution, and "liberal" churches. Ahmanson is in turn a disciple of R.J. Rushdoony, the founder of "Reconstructionism," a brand of Christian fundamentalism that supports the conversion of the United States into a theocracy governed by Old Testament law. Among other views, Rushdoony supports the stoning to death of homosexuals and women who commit adultery, although Ahmanson has declined to support this aspect of Reconstructionism. Max Blumenthal, "Avenging Angel of the Religious Right," Salon.Com, 6 January 2004.

shared Magnet's profoundly nostalgic and unrealistic view of the efficacy of nineteenth century religious charity. And in practical terms, his prescriptions for change differed little from Magnet's insistence that the poor had to develop self-reliance and take care of themselves rather than depending upon others.

But there was one difference; Olasky offered a way out of the wilderness. By restoring religious charity to its proper place at the center of the problem of poverty, compassion could be restored to its true meaning. Ultimately this meant abandoning any governmental responsibility for welfare in America. "We [first] must place in the hands of state officials all decisions about welfare and the financing of it, and then press them to put welfare entirely in the hands of church and community based organizations," insisted Olasky.[28] His views were not simply a reflection of the conservatives' traditional emphasis upon the inefficiency of government bureaucracies; Olasky believed that only religious groups could resurrect the fundamental, and critical, distinction between the deserving and the undeserving poor. Religious groups would serve as the gateway to assistance, practicing the kind of "tough love" expressed by St. Paul in Second Thessalonians 3:10: "He who does not work, neither shall he eat." If this meant, for example, removing children from undeserving mothers and placing them in foster homes or orphanages or placing them out for adoption, so be it. (He spoke approvingly of a Christian program for unwed mothers that succeeded in "persuading" more than half their clients to give up their children for adoption.) Only by enforcing moral as well as work requirements, for assistance could the poor be redeemed from their wretched condition.

Even before it had been distributed to bookstores, Newt Gingrich distributed copies to every Republican member of Congress, urging them to read and absorb Olasky's arguments. Shortly after his 1994 election to the governorship of Texas, George W. Bush met Olasky and soon turned to him as one of his close advisers on domestic issues. Bush claimed that Magnet's book *The Dream and the Nightmare* was the most important book he had ever read, next to the Bible. But I think it is instructive that—though he met Magnet—he never warmed to him, whereas Olasky became one of his principle unofficial advisers and friends. In 2000 when Olasky published a revised version of *The Tragedy of American Compassion* outlining his belief in substituting religious charities for state aid, Bush wrote a glowing preface and gave credit to Olasky for his ideas about "compassionate conservatism."[29]

Olasky's personal odyssey from Judaism to fundamentalist Christianity and from communism to an embrace of unrestricted capitalism is hardly typical of most white southerners, but his message resonated with the powerful and growing fundamentalist religious community in the South. And no-one should doubt the clout of these conservative evangelicals in shaping GOP politics. In 2004, 84 percent of Southern Baptists—the most numerous and powerful of southern religious groups—voted for George W. Bush. Other evangelical white southerners supported the President by similar percentages.[30] A number of recent studies have documented the

---

[28] *New York Times*, 11 January 2000
[29] *Toronto Globe and Mail*, 13 January 2001.
[30] *Atlanta Journal-Constitution*, 18 June 2005.

overwhelming identification of southern religious conservatives with the Republican Party and with the most conservative policies of the GOP.[31]

George Marsden's account of the rise of fundamentalism in American religious culture does not focus upon the South; indeed, he notes, fundamentalism was a "northern" intellectual enterprise. But historian Will Glass shows how fundamentalism lost ground in the rest of the nation and came to dominate the religious culture of the American South.[32] And amidst such arcane theological issues as dispensationalism, premillenialism, and post-millennialism Marsden described an evolving religious world view that came to dominate the thinking of southern fundamentalists in particular and southern evangelicals in general. It was a world view that reinforced precisely the kind of hostility to governmental support for the poor that Olasky outlined in *The Tragedy of American Compassion.*

As Marsden notes, such influential late nineteenth century evangelists as Dwight L. Moody de-emphasized ministry to the physical needs of the poor: "Conversion inevitably led to personal responsibility and moral uplift, qualities which the conventional wisdom said the poor most often lacked." Once "wanderers" came home "and the poor acquired the sense of responsibility found in strong Christian families, poverty would cease." That hostility to what came to be called the "social gospel" became more pronounced in the 1920s as fundamentalists came to identify the movement with a Godless liberalism that was at odds with traditional religious values. By the 1980s, argues Marsden, most evangelists—even those who did not describe themselves as fundamentalists—had come to embrace the economic values of the most conservative elements in American society.[33]

No group has been more influential in this transformation than Southern Baptists after the takeover by fundamentalists in the early 1980s. The Southern Baptist Convention (SBC) has gone on record against racism in the strongest terms, and it has often spoken of the need to aid the poor. But a review of SBC resolutions and the statements of its most influential spokesmen show that the organization has consistently opposed any efforts to assist the poor through governmental assistance. Private, religious based charity, coupled with evangelizing the poor, is seen as the only solution the problem of poverty.[34] The SBC strongly endorsed the Welfare Reform Bill of 1996, for example. And even though it backed a $300 million federal

---

[31] Glenn Feldman's recently edited collection, *Politics and Religion in the White South* (Lexington: University of Kentucky Press, 2005), documents this identification of evangelicals with the GOP, particularly his essay and those of James L. Guth, Charles S. Bullock III and Mark C. Smith, Ted Ownby, Mark J. Rozell and Clyde Wilcox. An equally valuable insight into contemporary southern religious attitudes can be found in "American Piety in the 21st Century," a research survey conducted by the Baylor, Texas, Institute for Studies of Religion and the Department of Sociology, Baylor University. It is available on-line at www.baylor.edu/content/services/document.php/33304.pdf

[32] Marsden, *Fundamentalism and American Culture: The Shaping of Twentieth-Century Evangelicalism, 1870-1925* (New York: Oxford University, 1980); William R. Glass, *Strangers in Zion: Fundamentalists in the South, 1900-1950* (Macon, GA: Mercer University Press, 2001).

[33] Ibid., 37, 228.

[34] This is a theme repeated in the resolutions of the Southern Baptist Convention and in the statements of other southern conservative evangelicals.

appropriation for "premarital training and counseling" as well as other programs to "enhance" stable marriages, the SBC has thrown its support behind measures that would further limit access to welfare for the poor. When the prominent evangelical author Jim Wallis gently chided the SBC for supporting such cutbacks, Richard Land, head of the denomination's "Ethics and Religious Liberty Commission" angrily responded. Land, one of the most influential conservative leaders in the South, attacked Wallis as an

> economic ignoramus who is wedded to socialist-mandated policies that have failed in every country they've been tried in. . . . Jim Wallis just doesn't understand basic economics. What he calls social justice is what is running Western Europe into the ground. . . . We want to use our money to help the poor. They [liberals] want to tax our money to help the poor. He doesn't understand free-market economics produce more wealth for all people. If you want to alleviate poverty, cut taxes.[35]

The evidence strongly suggests that Land's views are shared by other members of his denomination and indeed by the majority of southern conservative evangelicals and fundamentalists. It would be a mistake to suggest religion has replaced racism as the Rosetta stone of white southern conservative attitudes on this and other issues. But there is clearly a strong connection between this world-view and the politics of poverty: in the South and in the nation. And any attempt to understand public policy for the poor in American society will have to take into consideration the powerful role that these southern religious conservatives have played in shaping governmental policies.

---

[35] *Atlanta Journal-Constitution*, 18 June 2005.

CONTRIBUTORS

Marcel Arbeit is Associate Professor in the Department of English and American Studies, Palacky University, Olomouc, Czech Republic. His main fields of research are contemporary southern literature, American and Canadian independent filmmakers and popular culture. His recent publications focus on Harry Crews, Fred Chappell, Lewis Nordan, and the South in film. He is the main editor of the three-volume *Bibliography of American Literature in Translation* (2000). He co-edited *Southern Narrators* (2006), a Czech anthology of contemporary Southern short fiction. He is the current President of the Czech and Slovak Association for American Studies.

Edwin T. Arnold is Professor of English at Appalachian State University in Boone, North Carolina. He is editor of *Conversations with Erskine Caldwell* (1988) and *Erskine Caldwell Reconsidered* (1990) and has written numerous other essays on Caldwell, most recently "Unruly Ghost: Erskine Caldwell at 100" in *Southern Review* (Fall 2003). He is also co-editor of *Perspectives on Cormac McCarthy* (1999), *A Cormac McCarthy Companion: The Border Trilogy* (2001), and the special McCarthy issue of *Profils Américains* (2006). He is presently co-editor of *The Faulkner Journal*.

Tony Badger has been Paul Mellon Professor of American History at Cambridge University since 1992 and Master of Clare College since 2003. Educated at Cambridge and Hull, he taught at Newcastle University for twenty years from 1971. He received an Honorary Doctor of Letters from Hull University in 1999. He has been a member of the Southern Studies Forum since 1988. He is the author of *Prosperity Road: The New Deal, Tobacco, and North Carolina* (1980), *North Carolina and the New Deal* (1981), and *The New Deal: The Depression Years 1933-1940* (1990). He has edited with Brian Ward, *The Making of Martin Luther King and the Civil Rights Movement* (1996), with Walter Edgar and Jan Gretlund, *Southern Landscapes* (1997) and with Byron Shafer, *Contesting Democracy: The Substance and Structure of American Political History* (2001). A collection of his published and unpublished essays on white southern liberal politicians and race relations since 1930 will be published in 2007. He is currently working on a biography of Albert Gore, Sr.

Robert H. Brinkmeyer, Jr. is Professor and Chair of English at the University of Arkansas. He is author of four books on modern southern literature, most recently *Remapping Southern Literature: Contemporary Southern Writers and the West* (2000) and is currently concluding a book tentatively entitled, "The Fourth Ghost: European Totalitarianism and the White Southern Imagination, 1930-1950." He received a Guggenheim Fellowship for work on this book.

Dan T. Carter, former President of the Southern Historical Association, is the Educational Foundation Professor of History at the University of South Carolina. The author and editor of more than a half dozen works of history, Carter has won four history and literary awards, including the Bancroft Prize for *Scottsboro: A Tragedy of the American South* (1970). His account of the post-Civil War South, *When the War Was Over* (1985), was awarded the Jules Landry Prize and the Avery Craven Award. And his 1995 biography of George Wallace, *The Politics of Rage*, received the Sulzby and Robert F. Kennedy Prizes. In 2000, he won a television Emmy for his work on a PBS documentary that explored the impact of Wallace upon American politics. He is currently revising and bringing up to date his 1996 book, *From George Wallace to Newt Gingrich: Race in the Conservative Counterrevolution, 1963-1994.*

Suzanne W. Jones is Professor of English at the University of Richmond, where she coordinated the Women and Gender Studies Program from 1985 to 1994. Her articles on southern fiction have appeared in a variety of journals and collections. She is the author of *Race Mixing: Southern Fiction since the Sixties* (2004) and the editor of two collections of essays, *South to a New Place: Region, Literature, Culture* (edited with Sharon Monteith, 2002) and *Writing the Woman Artist* (1991), and two collections of stories, *Crossing the Color Line: Readings in Black and White* (2000) and *Growing Up in the South* (1991, 2003). Her current research is on the reappearance of the racially mixed figure in the contemporary American imagination.

Anneke Leenhouts is an independent scholar working mostly in southern studies and film, with recent publications on poor white women, westerns, Thomas Dixon's Reconstruction trilogy, and the detective fiction of James Lee Burke. She is the in-house translator for the Intellectual Property department of Akzo Nobel N.V., Arnhem, the Netherlands.

Paul E. Mertz is Professor of History emeritus at the University of Wisconsin— Stevens Point, where he taught from 1969 to 2006. He chaired the History Department from 1992 to 1998. His interests are in recent and Southern United States history. He is the author of *New Deal Policy and Southern Rural Poverty* (1978). For a number of years he has been interested in the civil rights era in the South, and has done extensive research in school desegregation matters. He is currently working on a book concerning the South's public school crisis in the 1950s and early 1960s, with the working title, "Saving the Schools: Southern Moderates and the Fight for Public Education, 1958-1963."

Sharon Monteith is Professor of American Studies and Film Studies at the University of Nottingham. She publishes on American and British fiction and film but most particularly on the U.S. South. Her books include *Advancing Sisterhood? Interracial Friendships in Contemporary Southern Fiction* (2000), *Gender and the Civil Rights Movement*, edited with Peter Ling (1999 and 2004), *South to a New Place: Region, Literature, Culture*, edited with Suzanne W. Jones (2002), and *Pat Barker* (2002). Forthcoming books are *Film Histories* (2006) and *American Culture* *in the 1960s* (2007). Monteith is writing a study of the Civil Rights Movement in the melodramatic imagination.

Mark Newman is a lecturer in History at the University of Edinburgh. He is the author of *Getting Right with God: Southern Baptists and Desegregation, 1945-1995* (2001), winner of the Lillian Smith Award for Nonfiction, *Divine Agitators: The Delta Ministry and Civil Rights in Mississippi* (2004), and *The Civil Rights Movement* (2004).

Kieran Quinlan comes from Ireland and teaches in the English Department at the University of Alabama in Birmingham. His most recent book, *Strange Kin: Ireland and the American South* (2005) received the Jules and Frances Landry Award for a work in southern studies. He is also the author of *John Crowe Ransom's Secular Faith* (1989) and *Walker Percy, the Last Catholic Novelist* (1996/1998). He is currently completing a book manuscript on Seamus Heaney and religion.

Sarah Robertson is Lecturer of Contemporary American Literature at the University of the West of England. Her publications include articles about, and an interview with, the West Virginian writer Jayne Anne Phillips. Current projects involve a monograph on Phillips' work for Rodopi Publishers as well as an examination of labor in poor white autobiographies.

Elizabeth Hayes Turner is Associate Professor of History at the University of North Texas. She received her Ph.D. from Rice University in U.S. Southern history and women's history in 1990. She is the author of *Women, Culture, and Community: Religion and Reform in Galveston, 1880-1920* (1997), co-author of *Galveston and the 1900 Storm* (2000), author of eight articles, and the co-editor of five books, including *Lone Star Pasts: Memory and History in Texas* (forthcoming). Her most recent research in memory focuses on the evolution and transformation of Juneteenth, an African American emancipation celebration. She was Visiting Managing Editor of the *Journal of Southern History* (1997-1998), President of the Southern Association for Women Historians (1997-1998), and Fulbright Lecturer to the University of Genoa (2003).

Nahem Yousaf is Head of English at Nottingham Trent University. His books include *Alex La Guma: Politics and Resistance* (2001), *Apartheid Narratives* (2001); *Hanif Kureishi's The Buddha of Suburbia* (2002), *Chinua Achebe* (2003) and, as co-editor, *Critical Perspectives on Pat Barker* (2005). He is a general editor of a Manchester University Press series on Contemporary North American and Canadian Writers. His current research is on new immigrants in the American South.

Waldemar Zacharasiewicz has been Professor of English and American Studies at the University of Vienna since 1974. He has also been Visiting Professor or Visiting Scholar at eight universities in the United States and in Canada. He is Director of the Center for Canadian Studies and a full member of the Austrian Academy of Sciences. Over the last few decades his research has focused on the literature and culture of the American South, on ethnic and national stereotypes in Anglophone literatures, and on Canadian fiction. He is the author of several monographs, among them *Images of Germany in American Literature* (forthcoming with University of Iowa Press), and studies on the art of fiction in the American South and on the theory of climate in English literature and literary criticism (in German).

ACKNOWLEDGMENTS

The Southern Studies Forum is an international research network of scholars who meet to discuss and debate the U.S. South. The essays in this collection were originally presented and discussed at the ninth international Southern Studies Forum biennial conference. In September 2005 the Roosevelt Study Center in Middelburg, the Netherlands, generously hosted scholars from the United States and Europe for this interdisciplinary conference, which addressed the key themes of poverty and progress in the U.S. South. From the thirty papers presented, fifteen were subsequently selected and revised for inclusion in this volume. They represent the diversity of interdisciplinary approaches that helps to make the Forum intellectually distinctive.

The editors would like to thank Anneke Leenhouts and the late Stuart Kidd for organizing the conference in close cooperation with Kees van Minnen, Director of the Roosevelt Study Center. We appreciate the comments of conference participants as well as colleagues who read and assessed essays. We owe a special thanks to Leontien Joosse at the Roosevelt Study Center for her kind assistance, to Chris Poole and James Murphy at the University of Richmond for their technical expertise, and to Patricia Cloar for the use of her husband Carroll Cloar's painting, "Where the Southern Cross the Yellow Dog."